FROM VIOLENCE TO PEACE

This book contributes to the literature on jurisprudence and theology by arguing for the role of a theoretically robust Christian theology in a legal community dominated by secular and liberal ideology. It is not a doctrinal or empirical analysis, but a theoretical exposition of the way in which modern law has contingently drifted from its theological origins. As a result, the legal system and the ideal of individual and communal relationship it envisages is characterised by antagonism and alienation, or more broadly, violence. The book contends that the way to restore a legal community of peace is to return to a Christian theology which is informed by Trinitarian thinking or the notion of unity in diversity, and reunites faith with reason. Returning reason to its ground in being allows peaceful persuasion by the revelation of God's perfect being through the Trinity and Incarnation, which models and enables the peaceful coexistence of difference through self-sacrificing love.

This in turn produces the law of love—to love your neighbour as yourself. Since love does no wrong to a neighbour, a legal community operating by the law of love can fulfil the obligations of law by going beyond merely what is required by law and love individuals as part of a community.

From Violence to Peace

Theology, Law and Community

Alex Deagon

• HART •
PUBLISHING
OXFORD AND PORTLAND, OREGON
2017

Hart Publishing
An imprint of Bloomsbury Publishing Plc

Hart Publishing Ltd
Kemp House
Chawley Park
Cumnor Hill
Oxford OX2 9PH
UK

Bloomsbury Publishing Plc
50 Bedford Square
London
WC1B 3DP
UK

www.hartpub.co.uk
www.bloomsbury.com

Published in North America (US and Canada) by
Hart Publishing
c/o International Specialized Book Services
920 NE 58th Avenue, Suite 300
Portland, OR 97213-3786
USA

www.isbs.com

First published 2017

British Library Cataloguing-in-Publication Data
A catalogue record for this book is available from the British Library.

ISBN: HB: 978-1-50991-290-2
ePDF: 978-1-50991-289-6
ePub: 978-1-50991-291-9

Library of Congress Cataloging-in-Publication Data

Names: Deagon, Alex, author.

Title: From violence to peace : theology, law and community / Alex Deagon.

Description: Oxford ; Portland, Oregon : Hart Publishing, an imprint of Bloomsbury Publishing Plc, 2017. | Based on author's thesis (doctoral - Griffith Law School, Australia, 2015) issued under title: Using Christian theology and philosophy to construct a jurisprudence of truth. | Includes bibliographical references and index. | Description based on print version record and CIP data provided by publisher; resource not viewed.

Identifiers: LCCN 2017013634 (print) | LCCN 2017019080 (ebook) | ISBN 9781509912919 (Epub) | ISBN 9781509912902 (hardback : alk. paper)

Subjects: LCSH: Christianity and law. | Law (Theology) | Trinity. | Incarnation. | Truth—Religious aspects—Christianity. | Milbank, John—Influence.

Classification: LCC BR115.L28 (ebook) | LCC BR115.L28 D43 2017 (print) | DDC 261.5—dc23

LC record available at https://lccn.loc.gov/2017013634

Typeset by Compuscript Ltd, Shannon
Printed and bound in Great Britain by Lightning Source UK Ltd

PREFACE

The great Christian theologian and church father Saint Augustine of Hippo once identified a fundamental distinction between the violence of the ancient pagans and the peace of the early Christians. In his magnum opus, *The City of God*, Augustine contrasted the ontological presupposition of Roman and Greek culture (the pagan or 'earthly' city)—a focus on an antagonism and chaos which needed to be controlled or suppressed—with the City of God, a Christian theology that took as its starting point a harmonious communion with God. This dynamic tension between peace and violence also exists in law today. The modern legal system is fundamentally concerned with the regulation of individual relationships through various forms of violence in the pursuit of peace. However, just as the ancient Roman peace confronted by Augustine was really just a false peace of violently controlled violence, so the peace arrived at through the modern legal process is not a real peace. Just as Augustine did with ancient society, using the work of contemporary theologian John Milbank, this book identifies the fundamental agonistic tension between peace and violence within modern jurisprudence, opening the possibility for rethinking law in relation to a community of true peace.

'A crisis in human law is the occasion for the discovery of jurisprudence', and it can often be the case that this 'crisis' is the perceived existence or threat of violence, with the way to avert the crisis being through the existence or threat of violence.[1] Indeed, as one examines the canon of modern jurisprudence, such a theme appears to emerge. For example, recently Giorgio Agamben has disturbingly contended that his notion of the concentration camp 'signals the political space of modernity itself'—in other words, the concentration camp is our modern world.[2] In this space where law is permanently suspended, 'its inhabitants were stripped of every political status and wholly reduced to bare life', such that 'the camp was also the most absolute biopolitical space ever to have been realised, in which power confronts nothing but pure life, without any mediation'.[3] Here Agamben sought to extend the notion of Carl Schmitt's state of exception as the 'temporary suspension of the rule of law on the basis of a factual state of danger' to a 'permanent special arrangement, which as such nevertheless remains outside the normal order' through the concept of exclusion in the camp.[4]

[1] S Buchanan, *So Reason Can Rule: Reflections on Law and Politics* (Farrar, Straus and Giroux, 1982) 267.

[2] G Agamben, *Homo Sacer: Sovereign Power and Bare Life* (Stanford University Press, 1998) 177.

[3] ibid, 174.

[4] ibid, 167.

In the twentieth century, Schmitt articulated a view of law and sovereignty based on the ability to 'decid[e] on the exception', where the exception 'can at best be characterised as a case of extreme peril, a danger to the existence of the state'.[5] On the basis of a perceived threat of violence to the state, the sovereign can decide to suspend the operation of law in order to (potentially violently) eliminate the threat.[6] This notion of absolute state sovereignty can be found in the work of seventeenth-century political theorist Thomas Hobbes. According to Hobbes, the end or purpose of the commonwealth, or legal system, is security.[7] Hobbes argues that we 'would not observe the Laws of Nature … without the terror of some power', and through creating the Leviathan as legal sovereign we escape 'from the miserable condition of war, which is a necessary consequence … of the natural passions of men when there is no visible power to keep them in awe and tie them by fear of punishment to the performance of their covenants'—for the Leviathan destroys all those parts of society which threaten the society itself.[8] Based in the presumption of violence, the law aims to prevent or suspend this violence by postulating even greater violence.

These state-focused approaches to legal regulation are violent in terms of coercion and a universal approach which rejects difference. However, alternative liberal approaches such as those of Locke and Rawls, which focus on the individual, are just as violent, though the type of violence is distinct and more subtle.[9] One might even question whether positive regulation designed to protect members of society is really so violent. Consider the innocuous 'speed limit', which is actually intended to prevent violence caused by dangerous driving. The problem is neither the law itself nor the end in mind (this book is no support for the antinomian or the anarchist); the problem is with the assumptions undergirding the law and the enforcement of the law.

A law regulating individuals by telling them not to drive faster than a particular limit and imposing penalties for a failure to comply assumes a framework of competing individuals who selfishly desire to 'get ahead'. It projects an adversarial background and regulates it. The chosen method of regulation is state-sanctioned surveillance (through speed cameras or police observation) and the penalty if detected is deprivation of property (a fine) or deprivation of liberty (incarceration). The goal, perhaps, is realised—less overt violence in the form of dangerous driving. But the means of achieving that goal is fear of punishment through deprivation, and even the goal itself is not always achieved because some people manipulate the system by continuing to speed and attempting to avoid detection.

[5] C Schmitt, *Political Theology: Four Chapters on the Concept of Sovereignty* (University of Chicago Press, 2005) 5–6.

[6] ibid, 9–10.

[7] T Hobbes, *Leviathan* (Longman, 2008) 113.

[8] ibid.

[9] J Locke, *Two Treatises of Government* (Cambridge University Press, 1967); J Rawls, *A Theory of Justice* (Oxford University Press, 1972).

Though the process does not look violent, the violence is insidiously present and egregiously exacerbated. The presumptively selfish, competitive framework remains and the state increases the application of resources (surveillance and severity of penalties) to regulate this violence.

In short, the law operates within a context of violence, aiming to curtail violence through enforcing even greater violence. An alternative approach might use the same law to achieve the same goal, but it would place itself in a framework of harmonious community rather than adversarial individualism, and produce obedience through persuasion rather than coercion. This would lead to a community of peace where people drive in a way which is selfless and mindful of the safety of others, voluntarily persuading and being persuaded that this is the most desirable way to live.

Broadly, then, the ostensibly more 'peaceful' liberal frameworks are couched in terms of the violence of the purely rational self-interested subject, which breeds the violence of antagonism between individuals through condoning competition and self-assertion. The 'positive assertion of private autonomy' is 'deprivation of our participation in being as gift: in this way privation theory attacks as evil not just exterior and visible destruction, but also interior and invisible self-assertion'.[10]

The crisis in human law which is the occasion for jurisprudence could then be viewed in the sense that it seeks to alleviate the threat or existence of external violence, whether fictitious, as in Hobbes's hypothetical state of nature, or actual in the sense of Schmitt's state of exception, and internal violence, which actually causes antagonism and competition between self-interested individuals framed as adversaries. However, the notion of crisis may also be taken in a slightly different sense—that the existence of law and jurisprudence assumes a foundation of violence. This, in fact, is what I see as the salient crisis of law—that law is ontologically based in a foundation of violence, rather than peace—which suggests the need for a new jurisprudential approach.

Any new jurisprudential approach intended to transcend the violence of modern law needs to have a completely 'other' ontological foundation—peace, rather than violence—together with a method of preserving peace which does not rely on coercion. This book argues that Christian theology is the most appropriate approach to achieve these aims. First, the jurisprudence of modern law is fundamentally a secularisation of theological concepts, and this secularisation has resulted in violence. Redeeming law therefore requires a return to theology. Secondly, (to make an unfortunate legal pun) a theological approach has precedent through the work of Augustine, who critiqued the pagan violence of the ancient Romans and contrasted it with the peace offered by Christianity. Thirdly, the 'otherness' required for a new approach naturally lends itself to the transcendence of Christianity, and in particular the Trinitarian relations of love and peace, unity in diversity, which model this new approach. Finally, the revelation of the

[10] J Milbank, *Being Reconciled: Ontology and Pardon* (Routledge, 2003) 27.

Trinity through the Incarnation of Christ preserves peace not through coercion, but through the persuasion provided by the self-sacrificing love of Christ. By enabling and implementing a new law, the Pauline law of love, which is to love neighbour as self, individual and community are reconciled to produce a jurisprudence of peace.

It should be acknowledged that this book has been revised from what was originally an awarded PhD dissertation, though much of the original content remains. I would therefore like to acknowledge and thank the insightful and passionate advice of my principal thesis supervisor, Professor William MacNeil. His review and critique of the thesis, in conjunction with his suggestions for improvement, were instrumental in contributing to the final form and argument of the thesis. I would also like to thank my associate thesis supervisor, Dr Timothy Peters, for stepping in late and guiding me through the final submission process for the thesis, as well as helping me to better structure and argue it. His advice has really been invaluable. I also thank my initial associate supervisor, Associate Professor Fiona Kumari Campbell (as she then was), for her assistance regarding methodological and theological resources, as well as the early structure and expression of the thesis. Others who provided various forms of feedback and helpful suggestions on the thesis prior to submission include Dr Kieran Tranter, Dr Edward Mussawir and Associate Professor Gideon Baker; their assistance is appreciated.

I would particularly like to thank my external thesis examiners, Professor Adam Gearey and Professor Paul Babie, for their positive and insightful feedback. I also wish to thank Professor Nicholas Aroney for his general encouragement and mentorship, generous giving of time, and helpful feedback on early drafts of the book proposal and the thesis manuscript which assisted in securing the book contract with Hart Publishing. I thank Bill Asquith from Hart Publishing for his willingness to pursue publishing this book and his helpful advice during that process.

Finally, I would like to thank my wife Courtney for her constant support and encouragement, and most importantly I thank the Lord Jesus Christ for enabling me to complete this task, and for providing the good news essential for completing it.

TABLE OF CONTENTS

Preface v

Introduction 1
- I. From Violence to Peace 1
- II. The Nature of Violence 2
  - A. Defining Legal Violence 2
  - B. 'Pagan' Violence and the Augustinian Response 3
- III. Envisaging the Peaceful Legal Community 6
  - A. John Milbank and Postmodern Critical Augustinianism 6
  - B. Trinity, Incarnation, Revelation: The Law of Love 7
- IV. The Secular Challenge 9
- V. The Argument of this Book: From Violence to Peace 11

1. Milbank's Milieu: Theorisations of Truth, Faith and Reason 15
- I. Introduction 15
- II. Milbank's Theoretical Context 16
  - A. 'Postmodern' Critical Augustinianism 16
  - B. Radical Orthodoxy 17
  - C. Doctrine of the Trinity 20
- III. Critiquing the Secular Genealogy 21
  - A. Nietzsche and Truth 21
  - B. Foucault, Nietzsche and Power 23
- IV. The Truth of Theology: Producing Peace through Trinitarian Correspondence 26
  - A. Understanding Milbank and Correspondence 26
  - B. Articulating a Genuinely Milbankian Correspondence 28
    - (i) Being and Participation 28
    - (ii) Revelation and Persuasion 31
- V. Rejecting Secular Reason 33
- VI. Promoting Faith and the Reason of Theology 35
  - A. Faith and Reason in Christian Thought 35
    - (i) The Historical Catholic Perspective 35
    - (ii) The Protestant Perspective 37
  - B. The Limits of 'Secular' Reason 38
  - C. An Incarnational Reason 39

2. Secularising Science: The Divorce of Reason and Revelation 43
I. Introduction 43
II. The Theological Genesis and Subsequent Secularisation of Science 44
A. Voluntarism and the Early Scientists 44
(i) Galileo and the Unity of Truth 45
(ii) Kepler and the Precision of God's Decree 46
(iii) Newton and the Sovereign Architect 47
B. Aquinas, Faith and Reason 48
(i) The Initial Misconception 49
(ii) The Laplace Transform(ation): Collapse of the Architect 51
III. (No) Salvation by Faith Alone: How the Reformation Further Divided Faith and Reason 52
A. Reformation: God as Sovereign 52
B. Counter-Reformation: Imperialising Knowledge 55
C. From (Pure) Reason to (Blind) Faith 57
IV. Uniting Faith and Reason to Restore True *Scientia*: The Participation Model 58
A. Illuminating Aquinas 58
B. Seeking a Science of Peace 60

3. Deconstructing Derrida: Law, Spirit, *Logos* 63
I. The Postmodern and the Pagan 63
A. Derrida and the Text 64
B. The Necessity of Postmodernism for Theology 65
II. Different Perspectives: The Metanarratives of Jacques Derrida 67
A. The Atheist Derrida 67
B. The Jewish Derrida 68
(i) Law and Book 68
(ii) Justice, Spirit and Revelation 69
C. The Christian Derrida? 70
(i) A Theological Language 70
(ii) The Three Become One: Derrida's Trinity 72
III. The Pagan Differ(a)nce 73
IV. Moving Perspectives: From Secular Reason to Christian Theology 77
V. A Genuinely 'Postmodern' Theology 78
VI. The Threshold of Ontological Peace: Constructing a Christian Theology of Legal Community 81

4. An Account of Secular(ised) Jurisprudence: Violence from Duns Scotus to Derrida 83
I. Law and Postmodern Critical Augustinianism 83

II. Faith, Reason and a Theological Natural Law........85
A. Thomas Aquinas and the Classical Tradition........85
(i) The Thomist Framework........85
(ii) The Thomist Context: Augustine, Cicero and the Stoics........86
B. Thomism as a Theological Framework: Some Contemporary Interpretations........88
(i) John Finnis: Secularising Thomism?........88
(ii) Re-establishing the Theological Tradition........88
III. 'Creating' the Secular: Duns Scotus, Univocity and Separating Philosophy from Theology........90
A. Voluntarist Theology: The Univocity of Being........90
B. Knowledge by Pure Nature........92
IV. Machiavelli and Hobbes: Secular Legal Ontology and the Emergence of Governing Violence........94
A. Machiavelli, Dominance and Paganism........94
B. Hobbesian Legal Ontology: A Clash of Pure Will and Rule by Force........97
V. The Final Stage: Austin, Hart and the Violence of Secular Positivism........100
VI. Diagnosing Legal Violence: Cover, Benjamin and Derrida........102
A. Law's Cover: *Logos*, *Nomos*, *Agon*........102
B. Critiquing the Mystical Position of Law........103
(i) A Performative Force........103
(ii) Benjamin's Critique of Legal Violence........105
VII. Escaping Legal Violence and the Possibility for Christian Peace........107

5. Violence, Attestation and Revelation: Reading Law and Truth in the Trial of Christ........111
I. The Trial as a Narrative of Law and Truth........111
II. Laws of Sin and Laws of Spirit: Paul, Faith and the *Torah*........115
A. The Law of Death........115
B. The Law of Life........118
(i) Paul For and Against Law........118
(ii) The New Law: Truth, Revelation, Participation........121
III. Christ Crucified: Conviction by the Law of Death........123
A. Law as Rules........123
(i) Old Testament Context and Rules........123
(ii) Roman and Jewish Rules........125
B. Law as Power........127
(i) The Political Sanhedrin........127
(ii) The Truth of Pilate........129
C. Law as Secular and Pagan?........132

IV. The Revelation of Christ: Faith, Mystery, Atonement........................134
A. Christ as Disrupting Secular Formalism........................134
(i) Christ, Faith and Aletheia........................134
(ii) Against Christ: The Violent Drive for Decision........................137
B. Redeeming the Drive for Decision........................138
V. Light in the Darkness: The Law of Love, Faith and Participation........................139
A. A New Law: Mutual Trust as Communal Good........................140
B. The Perpetual Atonement........................142
C. Resurrection: Christ our Peace........................143
VI. Resurrecting the Peaceful Legal Community........................145

6. The Paradox of Law and Truth in Christianity: On Materialism, the Sublime and Reading the Pauline Law of Love........................147
I. Žižek, Materialism and the Christian Legacy........................147
A. A Paradoxical Position........................147
B. Structuring the Christian Material........................148
C. Sites of the Christian Material: Law, Science, Faith........................150
(i) Death and Absence........................150
(ii) Life, Presence, Hope........................152
(iii) The Place of Faith (and Reason)........................153
II. The Sublime Object: Defeating Death........................156
III. The Sublime Truth of Faith: Paradoxical Law, Love and Life through Resurrection........................158
A. Reconciling Reason and Faith through Incarnational Paradox........................158
B. Revealing the Law of Love through Incarnation........................160
C. Empowering the Law of Love: Participation through Faith in the Resurrection........................161
IV. Manifesting the Peaceful Community: Faith and Practice........................162

7. 'Love Your (Legal) Neighbour as Yourself': Producing Peace through a Theological Jurisprudence of Truth........................165
I. 'The End of Reason': The Blind Faith of Secular Reason and Recovering Reason through the Incarnational Paradox........................166
A. The Blindness and Violence of Secular Reason........................166
B. Kant on Pure Reason, or the Need for Faith........................168
C. Faith, Reason, Peace: A Sacred Polity........................170
II. 'Faith in the Truth of Christianity': Correspondence through Revelation and Rhetoric........................171
A. Correspondence as Analogical Participation in Revelation........................171
B. Participation through Faith........................171
C. A Legally Incarnated Truth........................172

III. Revealing an Ontology of Peace: The Nature of Peace and Violence in Christianity ... 173
A. Back to the Future: Augustinian Peace and Pagan Violence ... 173
B. Confronting History and the Present: Peace and Violence in Christianity ... 176
C. Future Glory: The Hope of Communal Peace ... 180
IV. Christian Theology and the Modern Legal Community: Proposing the Law of Love ... 181
A. Christ against Leviathan ... 181
B. The Law of Love as the Person and Work of Christ ... 183
(i) Gift versus Legality ... 183
(ii) Gift as Forgiveness ... 184
C. Coercion and Love ... 185
V. The Law of Love, or Love beyond Law: Releasing the Spirit of the Good Samaritan ... 186
A. Kelsen and the *Grundnorm* ... 186
B. Understanding the Parable ... 188
(i) The Legal Interpretation ... 188
(ii) The Theological Interpretation ... 190
VI. Fulfilling the Christian Vision of a Peaceful Legal Community ... 193

Bibliography ... 195
Index ... 207

Introduction

I. From Violence to Peace

This book argues that modern jurisprudence, and the ideal of individual and communal relationships it envisages, is characterised by antagonism and alienation and based on a presupposition of violence due to its secular foundation. To shift the culture of law from violence to peace, a secular foundation should therefore be replaced by the Christian idea of the 'law of love'—to love your neighbour as yourself. Loving neighbour as self reconciles both individual and community to produce a harmonious legal system. In a legal community dominated by secular and liberal ideology, the role of a theoretically robust Christian theology is vital. Such a theology can expose the way in which modern law has contingently drifted from its theological origins.

The theology of Duns Scotus, based on a misapprehension of Aquinas, argued that God could be conceived by individual reason apart from faith, and that God and the creation are characterised by will rather than being. Removing reason from its ground in faith and being means that this 'secular' reason actually evaporates, so that there is only violent competition between the clashing wills of individuals rather than peaceful persuasion by people being in a community. These theological assumptions were adopted by Hobbes, Austin and the positivists, so that modern law attempts to regulate these individuals through positing and enforcing. This produces a false peace which is actually a suspended violence, and the means of this so-called peace is itself intrinsically violent coercion.

Thus, the way to restore a legal community of peace is to return to a Christian theology which is informed by Trinitarian thinking or the notion of unity in diversity, and reunites faith with reason. Returning reason to its ground in being allows peaceful persuasion by the revelation of God's perfect being through the Trinity and Incarnation, which models and enables the peaceful coexistence of difference through self-sacrificing love. This, in turn, produces the law of love—to love your neighbour as yourself. Since love does no wrong to a neighbour, a legal community operating by the law of love can fulfil the obligations of law by going beyond merely what is required by law and love individuals as part of a community.

II. The Nature of Violence

A. Defining Legal Violence

Put negatively, violence is the denial and disruption of a flourishing 'web of relationships', the pursuit of 'atomistic individualism' and a 'warring absence of harmony'.[1] The pursuit of atomistic individualism can be seen as violent because the intrinsic difference between individuals implies there will be friction between them as they interact. Like the Hobbesian state of nature, people without a uniting communal factor that provides a basis or motivation for relational harmony attempt to pursue their individual interests at the expense of other individuals. Violence which pursues 'civil peace at the expense of foreign war' actually 'destroys the very structures of the society that it was undertaken to preserve'.[2]

So violence can be understood fundamentally as antagonism, the warring absence of harmony between individuals and society which disrupts the mutual human flourishing that comes through the harmony of life-giving relationships. This violence can be manifested variously through warfare, aggression, dominance, power, cruelty, hypocrisy and the pursuit of self-interest. Furthermore, there is a direct connection between ontological peace/violence and political peace/violence; the disruption of ontological harmony requires the exertion of political power to regulate the community.

From a slightly different angle, we can observe this notion of violence as antagonism as the return of the question of reconciling the one and the many, which may also be understood as the particular and the universal, or the individual and the community. The universal fails to take account of the specific situation due to its ambiguous universality, while the more specified or particularised universal (or the 'particular') cannot be applied universally. Hence, the problem of the one and the many conceived as a problem of violence: the universal alienates the particular, and the particular castrates the universal. There is a gap or alienation between the one and the many which produces an antagonistic violence.

This reveals the second aspect of violence as that which alienates subjects from mutually beneficial, charitable relationships. These aspects of violence are present in and even foundational to the modern Western legal system, especially common law legal systems (eg that of the USA, the UK, Australia, New Zealand and so on). This kind of legal system lies at the heart of society, protecting rights, imposing duties and establishing a framework for the conduct of any social, political or economic activity. This includes punishing offenders, compensating the injured and enforcing agreements, and is consequently a type of contractual, codified or 'legalistic' view of law. Such law exists with the aim of achieving justice, promoting

[1] G Jantzen, *Foundations of Violence* (Routledge, 2004) 37–38, 199.

[2] ibid 117.

freedom, upholding the rule of law and protecting security.[3] However, this modernist conception is undesirable, for there is a focus on totalisation, where one is submitted to a general principle which forms one's identity and subsumes difference. This principle is governed by what is viewed as a pure, universal reason, and as such it is indifferent to the individual. For example, the 'rule of law' claims that the law is objective, applies equally to everyone, and is the authority for and subjectivises society—leading to alienation where personal subjectivity is irrelevant.[4]

Furthermore, legal rules tend to establish categories and draw boundaries between people. This has occurred specifically in terms of people's obligations to others—for example, with the duty to rescue, which will be critiqued in the final chapter.[5] Law's usual boundaries distinguish self from others and 'help implement norms which curb responsibility'.[6] Consequently, 'legal rules often falter when conflicts arise within ongoing relationships'.[7] Fundamentally, 'law has tended to deny the mutual dependence of all people'.[8] The modern legal system creates boundaries which distinguish people rather than allowing mutual giving relationships.

From these considerations we can map our general definition of violence as antagonism and alienation onto a specifically jurisprudential space. Legal violence exists in the sense that it establishes categories and draws boundaries between people (alienation) under the assumption of purely rational self-interest and atomistic individuality (antagonism). These boundaries and categories separate and exclude persons from mutually harmonious relationships, disrupting communal flourishing. This is particularly displayed in law's attempt to balance the individual and the community. Focusing on the atomistic individual differentiates and excludes an interdependent web of flourishing human relationships, while focusing on the community as universal posited sovereignty denies differences between individuals. This legal violence may be manifested in the sense of pure violence, but it often also seems to be engaged more subtly within the institutional level of law.

B. 'Pagan' Violence and the Augustinian Response

The foundations of violence can be traced to the ancient Greeks and Romans, or the 'pagans'. The intrinsically pagan nature of violence is found in the fact that for the ancient Greeks and Romans, violence and death is exalted, seen as glorious and beautiful.[9] The city of Rome was 'premised on violence', grew up under Mars,

[3] R Wacks, *Law: A Very Short Introduction* (Oxford University Press, 2008) 1.
[4] J Bloechl, 'Between Law and Love: Paul and Philosophy', paper presented at the Annual Simone Weil Lecture on Human Value, Australian Catholic University (June 2013).
[5] M Minow, *Making All the Difference: Inclusion, Exclusion and American Law* (Cornell University, 1990) 8.
[6] ibid 9.
[7] ibid.
[8] ibid 10.
[9] Jantzen, above n 1, 39.

the God of War, and valorises the willingness to fight and die violently for the empire.[10] The peace of Rome, 'while representing itself as a golden age, was built on violence … its monuments exalt violence'.[11] In this sense, virtue's 'chief characteristic' was viewed to be 'active control or power'.[12] For both Greeks and Romans, violence was the way through which beauty was depicted, and death in battle is 'sweet and honourable'—ultimately glorious, whether for self (the Greeks) or the city (the Romans).[13] Jantzen asks a pertinent question: 'How can dissent be expressed in a world where there is a single superpower insisting on its global hegemony and masking its violence in a rhetoric of peace?'[14]

This is expressed in the specific context of the Roman peace, but Jantzen acknowledges that the treatment of warfare and the rhetorical legitimation of violence in Ancient Greek and Roman times is also applicable to the contemporary West.[15] In other words, as we countenance this claimed violence of law masquerading as peace, the question is equally important to us today: if, indeed, law is violent, how can we articulate an alternative basis for law—one where peace is the foundation rather than violence? The answer is that, just as Augustine dissented from the pagan violence of his day through orthodox Christian theology, so we may dissent today through Christian theology. For John Milbank, it is Augustine in *The City of God* who most properly articulates the meaning of an ontology of peace in Christian theology, in contrast to pagan violence. Augustine argues that the heavenly peace is unique in that it

> is so truly peaceful that it should be regarded as the only peace deserving the name, at least in respect of the rational creation; for this peace is the perfectly ordered and completely harmonious fellowship in the enjoyment of God, and each other in God. When we arrive at that state of peace, there will be no longer a life that ends in death, but a life that is life in sure and sober truth.[16]

The key here is 'perfectly ordered and completely harmonious fellowship' in the enjoyment of God and each other, which leads not to death or violence, but rather to peace and the good. This problem of whether there can be a harmonious human order is central—whether one can assign to their respective tasks and places many different activities, desires and social formations. If this is not possible, then 'only an "effective" peace is possible, a "secular" peace of temporarily suspended violence or regulated competition', or a temporary 'peace' between the wars.[17]

In the City of God, Augustine retraces the story of the pagan virtues, and, as Milbank argues with regard to the secular, these 'virtues' were hopelessly

[10] ibid 251.
[11] ibid 253.
[12] ibid 268.
[13] ibid 291–92.
[14] ibid 299.
[15] ibid 103–04.
[16] Augustine, *Concerning the City of God Against the Pagans* (Penguin, 2008) 878.
[17] J Milbank, *Theology and Social Theory: Beyond Secular Reason* (Blackwell, 1990) 336.

contaminated by a celebration of violence.[18] The earthly city is marked by the 'denial of love for God and others' and the 'enjoyment of arbitrary and violent power' over others.[19] Augustine argues that the 'peace' of the pagans is limited and apparent, where dominion is pursued as an end in itself and the 'peace' is a result of the victory of a dominant force over other forces. It is an 'arbitrary limitation of a preceding state of anarchic conflict'.[20]

Augustine's critique of pagan religion extends to its many gods and the rituals associated with worshipping those gods. The diversity of gods controlling various areas of life implies those areas are in fundamental conflict, and the honour due to the diverse gods is really a function of their self-assertion of power. In this sense, the reason of the greater paganism is concerned with the ability to adapt cunningly to circumstances and so retain the upper hand through moral tricks, and the gods delight in being spectators and promoters of violence, demanding sacrifice.[21] The pagan gods refused to prevent the 'degradation of morality' and 'did not offer moral instruction', and furthermore sanctioned 'obscenities and violence' as a requirement for their proper 'worship'.[22] The pagans 'sought glory and praise from people', which ultimately lead to the desire for domination and power and produced wars and violence.[23] And war is a 'miserable state of existence', to be deplored and lamented as violent.[24] Ultimately, Augustine argues, this depravity led to the 'destruction' of the 'commonwealth'—both as a general principle and in the specific case of the Roman Empire's eventual decline.[25]

Augustine therefore argues that the Romans, the original pagans, had no real virtue because they knew no real peace, either at the level of practice or at the level of mythical or ontological conception. The Roman heroic virtue only comes as a result of war, and the 'peace' is a peace of suspended warfare caused by war—and thus is no real peace at all. Conversely, Christianity construes virtue as that which aims towards and is possible within a fundamental condition of peace, a living together of different people in mutual agreement. This is true peace, as opposed to the spurious Roman or pagan peace of suspended warfare and the secular 'heroic' virtues which are the result of warfare.[26] For Milbank, Christian peace has ontological priority over conflict, for it is what is most real, most secure and most guarantees human life.[27]

18 ibid 289.
19 ibid 392.
20 ibid 393.
21 Milbank, above n 17, 395.
22 Augustine, above n 16, 54.
23 ibid 212–15.
24 ibid 861–62.
25 ibid 72–77.
26 Milbank, *Theology and Social Theory*, above n 17, 332–33.
27 ibid 367.

III. Envisaging the Peaceful Legal Community

A. John Milbank and Postmodern Critical Augustinianism

This ontological priority of peace over violence marks the fundamental contrast between the two ancient cities, and parallels the contrast between the earthly city of the contemporary legal system and the heavenly city of a loving Christian community. In this modern or even postmodern context, Milbank is following Augustine in the sense that Augustine deploys a Christian ontology of peace in a theological critique of pagan violence—hence 'Postmodern Critical Augustinianism'. For Milbank,

> Augustine already put the idea of the peaceful community at the centre of his theology; thought of God, of revelation from God, was for him inseparable from the thought of heaven … the heavenly city meant for Augustine a substantial peace.[28]

Milbank recognises that 'one way to secure peace is to draw boundaries around "the same" and exclude "the other"'.[29] Drawing boundaries and dividing people into various categories is a form of alienating violence as it separates individuals; this is the characteristic process claimed of law. Here there is the dualistic violence of the included versus the excluded, 'an ever-renewed conflict' which is the 'traditional mode of violence'.[30] However, in Christianity there is no exclusion, but only 'that which denies and takes away from Being … the violent' or the negative—evil.[31]

To articulate an alternative Christian foundation for a (legal) community based on true peace rather than violence, Milbank proposes the model of the Trinity, God as three divine persons: Father, Son and Holy Spirit. This is an 'infinite relation' of love and perfect peace, since God as Trinity is both unity and 'himself community'—which can therefore be a 'differential ontology', or a mode of being which allows the harmonious existence of difference in a community.[32] So, put crudely, ontological peace is the affirmation of Being as the harmonious ordering of difference, and ontological violence is the denial of Being with the violent conflict or war of difference. Peace itself therefore is also beyond virtue because peace is the final end and condition in which virtue can flourish, the culmination of Being itself—or, as above, the harmonious ordering of difference. Thus, the new Christian imagination of peace is more elegantly defined as 'the reconciliation

[28] J Milbank, 'Postmodern Critical Augustinianism: A Short *Summa* in Forty-Two Responses to Unasked Questions' in G Ward (ed), *The Postmodern God: A Theological Reader* (Blackwell Publishers, 1997) 269.

[29] ibid.

[30] ibid 270.

[31] ibid 269.

[32] ibid 274.

of virtue with difference'.[33] Christianity can rescue virtue from violent, agonistic difference, for the Christian multiple in the Trinity, the 'infinite flow of excessive charitable (love) difference', is in a much more genuine sense simultaneously unity, and manifests unity.[34] Christian Trinitarian ontology reconciles the one and the many, promoting peace through the unity of individuals in the community.

Reconciling virtue with difference and consequently producing ontological peace initially involves forsaking the Roman or pagan virtues resulting from war. As Augustine argued, these virtues 'sought for the sake of pride and self-glory', apart from the 'life of faith and love of God and others', are to be reckoned as vices rather than as virtues, for they come from below, not from above.[35] The 'ultimate good', peace, consists in the selfless sacrifice and love through the forgiveness of sins modelled and enabled by Christ rather than in the 'perfection of personal virtue'.[36] Milbank considers that this doctrine of the Incarnation allows us to 'imagine a peaceful, totally charitable [loving] God', and 'it suggests that divine goodness is no generalised intention, but always takes a very particular form, that it is inseparable from aesthetic harmony [peace]'.[37] This idea supposes the possibility of a community based on self-giving love and togetherness, a perfectly existing and peaceful unity in diversity—or a community existing according to what the Apostle Paul terms 'the law of love'.

B. Trinity, Incarnation, Revelation: The Law of Love

The love and peace inherent in the Trinitarian relations are *revealed* (truth-as-*aletheia*) through the Incarnation of Christ and *persuade* (faith-as-*pistis*) members of the community to 'love your neighbour as yourself'—the law of love articulated by the Apostle Paul in the New Testament.[38] This fulfils the codified law since 'love does no wrong to a neighbour'.[39] As a first (and very rough) approximation, law can be understood as a principle or set of principles which govern individual relationships within a community. Love, as defined above and modelled by Christ, involves the voluntary sacrifice of oneself for another. So the law of love, to 'love your neighbour as yourself', is the voluntary giving of oneself for another as the principle which governs individual relationships within a community.

The ultimate consummation of this community of differences in perfect peace and love, then, is heaven. The vision of heaven (or for Augustine, the City of God) allows the 'denial of the necessity of violence' and 'exposes the manner in which

[33] Milbank, *Theology and Social Theory*, above n 17, 332–33.
[34] ibid 380–81.
[35] Augustine, above n 16, 891.
[36] ibid 892.
[37] Milbank, *Theology and Social Theory*, above n 17, 273–74.
[38] Romans 13:9.
[39] Romans 13:10.

the assumption of an always-prior violence preserves violence'.[40] Furthermore, it indicates that there is a 'way to act in a violent world which assumes the ontological priority of non-violence', and this way is called forgiveness of sins, brought through the Incarnation and loving sacrifice of Christ.[41] Such action can preserve a peaceful, loving community—the Christian community as an example for and within the legal community.

This is contrasted with the pagan mythos, which is that the legality of the earthly city is based in the suppression of an anarchy that was ontologically prior. This legality (as well as the modern legality) has claimed validity by preventing the dominance of what is an 'essentially imaginary chaos'.[42] Consequently, what came first was not anarchy, but this legal, coercive, and itself anarchic and ultimately violent, assertion. So Christian theology rejects this dominance on the basis of a false anarchy, and instead reorients the foundation of law and the legal system to the ontological peace of Christian theology, the truth or revelation of the law of love expressed through the Trinity and Incarnation.

The law of love, modelled on and enabled by the Incarnation and Crucifixion of Christ, consequently encourages love for one's neighbour in terms of humility and sacrifice. Importantly, this is not forced or coerced (for that would necessitate violence), but rather freely volunteered as an imitation of Christ, for each member of the community participates by faith as their mind is persuaded by the revelation of love and peace in the Trinity. It is in this sense that Augustine argues that the eternal city, or the Christian community, possesses the heavenly peace by faith, and 'lives a life of righteousness based on this faith, having the attainment of that peace in view in every good action it performs in relation to God, and in relation to a neighbour, since the life of a city is inevitably a social life'.[43] For

> just as the individual righteous man lives on the basis of faith which is active in love, so the association, or people, of righteous men lives on the same basis of faith, active in love, the love with which a man loves God as God ought to be loved, and loves his neighbour as himself. But where this justice does not exist … there is no commonwealth.[44]

More specifically, Augustine allows that when a person is persuaded by faith, they will fulfil the law in accordance with the everlasting law (to love your neighbour as yourself) for the good and peace of the society.[45]

Thus, through the paradigm of the law of loving your neighbour as yourself, which is the unity and diversity in the community of the Trinity, a model is provided from Christian theology which allows a harmonious relationship between the individual and the society, one which avoids the violence of antagonism and

[40] Milbank, *Theology and Social Theory*, above n 17, 416.
[41] ibid.
[42] ibid 397–98.
[43] Augustine, above n 16, 878–79.
[44] ibid 890.
[45] ibid 873.

alienation, and provides for a peaceful legal community which privileges one's neighbour as an individual and therefore strengthens the community as a composite of unique individuals.

IV. The Secular Challenge

Another central aspect of constructing a loving and harmonious community is to address the challenge of the secular, particularly manifested in the idea of a 'secular reason' or 'pure' rationality—namely, a reason that is separated from faith. One of Milbank's aims is to rescue reason from the domain of the secular and restore it to its rightful position as fundamentally based in belief or theology.[46] This reason based in belief is universal in the sense that it undergirds all disciplines—theology, philosophy, law, science, economics and so forth. Indeed, Milbank wishes to defend the idea that such a universal logic is 'necessarily theistic', endorsing belief in a transcendent deity in operation with reason.[47] He states that his most important task is to transform the Greek philosophical *logos* through encounter with the theological *logos*, so that thought or reason itself becomes inescapably Christian and, as such, 'beyond secular reason'.[48] Reason may consequently subscribe to belief in a transcendent source.[49]

This is important because if Christianity is persuasive then this persuasion should be inherent to the Christian *logos* itself, not to the mediation of secular reason. Milbank asserts that any positioning of theology by secular reason either idolatrously confines knowledge of God to immanent disciplines, such as cosmology or psychology (idolatrous because it exalts these disciplines above a knowledge of God through faith), or causes appreciation of the divine in terms 'beyond reason', thus serving to confirm the myth of an 'autonomous secular realm of reason'.[50] Moreover, Milbank claims that secular reason, left entirely to its own devices, always destroys itself, since the over-abstraction of reason leads to scepticism and nihilism regarding reason.[51] This is particularly seen through the glorification of pure reason in modernity and the subsequent transformation of reason in certain forms of postmodernism.

It is, then, possible to see the violence present in legal ontology as resulting from the secularisation of reason—especially if we accept Milbank's argument that the

[46] J Milbank, 'The Double Glory, Or Paradox versus Dialectics: On Not Quite Agreeing with Slavoj Žižek' in C Davis (ed), *The Monstrosity of Christ: Paradox or Dialectic?* (MIT Press, 2009) 111.
[47] ibid.
[48] Milbank, *Theology and Social Theory*, above n 17, 147.
[49] ibid 181.
[50] ibid 1. See, eg, A Davison (ed), *Imaginative Apologetics: Theology, Philosophy and the Catholic Tradition* (SCM, 2011).
[51] Milbank, 'Double Glory', above n 46, 216.

secular is not actually an 'autonomous discipline' but borrows 'modes of expression from religion'—in this sense, secular reason is actually constituted either by 'heresy in regard to Christian orthodoxy' or a 'wholesale rejection of Christianity that is more neo-pagan than anti-religious' (one might recall the previous discussion of the violence associated with the pagans contrasted with the peace of Christianity).[52] The governing assumptions of secular theory are bound up with the modification or rejection of orthodox Christian positions, and these are no more rationally justifiable than the Christian positions themselves.

Two consequences follow from these claims. First, a theological critique of secular reason by authentic Christian doctrine is the most appropriate course, bearing in mind the genesis of the concept of the secular. This critique would seek to identify the contingent moments in theological history which led to this development, and propose an alternative interpretation that would reconcile faith with reason and theology with philosophy. Secondly, if the suggestion that the secular is the basis for legal violence were to be taken seriously, at least provisionally, it would open the possibility for considering an alternative foundation for law based in faith united with reason, a jurisprudence which removes the underlying assumptions of the secular (which have dominated jurisprudential discourse since the rise of modernity), rescues pure reason from its violent ends and establishes a community of peace. It is just this kind of jurisprudence which I propose in this book.

So, in the secular foundation for modern law, we actually return to the original pagan violence Augustine addressed—a society of self-interested individuals agonising to overcome chaos. Milbank's Postmodern Critical Augustinianism, specifically applied to jurisprudence, may then be seen as the contemporary equivalent of Augustine's project to found a harmonious community which encompasses difference and diversity through the law of love, rather than the pursuit of individualism violently striving to defeat some sort of always-prior violence. When one then bears in mind Milbank's claims that the secular is actually a type of theology, it is significant that there is a type of theological soteriology implied in law, even in its most 'secularised' iterations:

> Great hope is placed in law, properly understood and administered, as a vehicle for the transformation of society. Most movements for modern reform accept without question law's account of itself as autonomous, universal, and above all, secular—meaning, in the first instance, religiously neutral, but also, more strongly, paradigmatically rational … law's claim to the universal resembles—indeed arguably derives its power from—the universalism that is claimed by … Christianity.[53]

Similarly, every legal system needs a supernatural, transcendent source to give authority to its contents—even if, in lieu of a 'higher source', that is law itself.[54]

[52] Milbank, *Theology and Social Theory*, above n 17, 1.

[53] W Fallers-Sullivan, R Yelle and M Taussig-Rubbo, 'Introduction' in W Fallers-Sullivan, R Yelle and M Taussig-Rubbo (eds), *After Secular Law* (Stanford University Press, 2011) 2–3.

[54] ibid 3.

In other words, if there is no transcendent source attracting people's trust, law becomes the entity which people trust. 'To work effectively law must rely on more than coercive sanctions ... it must attract people's trust and commitment. Quite simply, citizens must ... place their faith in it.'[55] Law encourages belief in its own sanctity in order to encourage obedience. This modern, secular position assumes that there is nothing beyond law to have faith in—an assumption which has led to law's violence. For if there is no real transcendent source, law has no intrinsic reason and can only coerce obedience by manipulation through force.

In addition to what we may call this transcendent or 'universal' question of faith in law, the relationship is also relevant in a more immanent or 'particular' sense—namely, that legal interactions between persons require some level of personal faith, or mutual trust in the community. Jantzen draws the contrast starkly:

> the willingness to nurse hatred and grievances, to refuse to negotiate or compromise, to look to violence and ultimately to control rather than to mutual trust as a solution, and to use the rhetoric of justice as an excuse for violence can lead only to a situation in which everybody loses.[56]

In the final analysis, then, the claim of this book is that where a secularised law seeks to control and coerce an antagonistic conglomerate of self-interested agents (ie the Hobbesian state of nature), a community genuinely based in Christian theology interacts through the law of love and mutual trust modelled, revealed and enabled by the Trinity and Incarnation, producing a peaceful and harmonious existence.

V. The Argument of this Book: From Violence to Peace

This book argues that, through a series of historically contingent philosophical shifts, the secular became naturalised as the undergirding presupposition of modern jurisprudence. This secular law is based on a mythic or theological foundation which seeks to enforce peace by violence, coercively bringing 'peaceful' (pagan) civilisation to savage humanity. The contingency of the secular assumption allows a sustained interrogation of its validity, and in turn opens the space for a reconstruction of jurisprudence based in Christian theology. Rather than a legal community premised upon and regulated by violence, Christian theology promotes a community of peace through the law of love.

Chapter 1 reviews and critiques John Milbank's work in terms of constructing working definitions of truth, faith and reason. It initially notes the place of

[55] R Ahdar, 'The Inevitability of Law and Religion: An Introduction' in R Ahdar (ed), *Law and Religion* (Ashgate, 2000) 5.
[56] Jantzen, above n 1, 111.

Milbank's Postmodern Critical Augustinianism within the context of Radical Orthodoxy, before suggesting that the secular genealogy of truth is about power, and therefore violence. The chapter then moves to critique Milbank's own use of the term 'truth', examining it in terms of correspondence. Milbank's idea of truth is not correspondence in the analytical, empiricist sense, but is instead intrinsically theological, and so is concerned with the revelation of the Trinitarian relations which persuades the mind, producing faith and participation in these relations. The chapter therefore considers the relationship between faith and reason in Milbank's work and in Christian thought more generally, arguing that the secular dichotomisation of faith and reason leads to the end of reason. And since persuasion ends where reason ends, only violent coercion remains. Therefore, reuniting faith with reason recovers reason and allows the possibility for peace by persuasion, rather than an imposed coercion. Thus, truth is God's gracious revelation of himself. This leads to faith or persuasion of the mind, and consequently recovers reason and produces peace, so that truth, faith and reason are in this sense interdependent in Milbank's framework.

Chapter 2 focuses on science in explaining how the contingent division of faith and reason was historically manifested, and how this violently affected faith and theology. This can be seen particularly through the approach of the early modern scientists, who in various ways were revolutionary in their development of science in relation to faith, on the basis of how they understood the nature of God and the relationship between faith and reason. Accordingly, the chapter analyses the underlying theology of these early modern scientists, indicating that they had a view of God as pure will, as a sort of divine architect. This idea has its foundation in a theological misconception of Thomas Aquinas, one that allows the distinction between reason and faith in obtaining knowledge. This distinction in principle was consequently realised, and faith and theology were subsequently evacuated from scientific discourse. However, by re-examining Aquinas and emphasising an authentic Thomist participation in the divine, a foundation is laid for a Christian theology which unites faith and reason.

Chapter 3 picks up the contention that the secularisation of reason ultimately leads to the end of reason, and traces this nihilistic end of reason through Jacques Derrida's concept of deconstruction. The chapter focuses on Derrida because, as Milbank identifies, in Derrida there is the potential to articulate a postmodern theology which avoids the modern or secular problem of separating faith and reason. Although Derrida states that he quite rightly passes as an atheist, his language and legal concepts are infused with theology. Moreover, together with Derrida's notion of deconstruction as justice, an *aporia* or undecidability requiring faith which fulfils the law, he could even be elaborating a form of Christianity. But it is a distorted Christianity which embraces the pagan *agon* of difference and a peace of suspended violence, and ignores the appearance of truth in Christ. Through expositing Derrida and working with his theology, the chapter completes the construction of a Postmodern Critical Augustinianism beyond Milbank that can be deployed in an analysis of modern jurisprudence. Therefore, Derrida's postmodern turn is actually necessary for the return of theology, for the collapse of secular reason provides a space for the return of faith and the theological in Christ.

Chapter 4 applies the proposition that there was a contingent separation of faith from reason, which results in violence, to the ontology of law. The chapter demarcates the secularisation of law through the rejection of Thomist (theological) natural law to its eventual arrival as Hartian (secular) positivism. First, the adoption of the Voluntarist theology of Duns Scotus (God as pure will) in conjunction with the division between faith and reason allowed Thomism to be discarded, and the paganism of Machiavelli and the violence of Hobbesian positivism to rise in its place. This violence was picked up by Austinian positivism before it was displaced into the rules system itself by Hart. An analysis of law through Cover, Derrida and Benjamin, key theorists of law and violence, further illustrate this violence of law detached from faith. However, Benjamin and Cover also allude to the way the foundational concepts of law and consequently the legal system itself may be redeemed and positively reconfigured to have an ontology of peace rather than violence, with 'peaceableness and trust' as two of its subjective preconditions. In other words, this way is the return of a legal community united through underlying notions of faith and the theological.

Chapter 5 continues the process of recalibrating jurisprudence in the shape of a Christian ontology of peace through the revelation of theological truth by reading law and truth in the trial of Christ. In particular, it explores the trial of Christ from the gospel narratives and the writings of the Apostle Paul on law and spirit in the New Testament, suggesting from these that the old, secularised law of the letter (attestation) ultimately leads to violence and death—even the death of Christ himself. Indeed, the very nature of the secularised, rule-based trial implies that it cannot comprehend truth as the revelation of the divine, and so violence will inevitably follow. However, the new law of the Spirit in faith, the law based on truth as *aletheia* or divine revelation, redeems this law of secular attestation and leads to life and peace. This law is another name for the Pauline law of love, the command to love your neighbour as yourself which is the revelation of loving relations in the Trinity through the Incarnation of Christ. Hence, a legal community of peace has its foundation in adopting the law of love, the truth of Christian theology revealed in the Incarnation of Christ.

Chapter 6 argues for the relevance of Christian theology to a secular audience and presses the Incarnation as key to implementing the law of love through engaging directly with Slavoj Žižek, whose extensive interactions with Milbank allow the development of Milbank's thinking in relation to the structure of the Incarnation. The chapter notes the paradox of Žižek's atheism and his view that the Christian legacy ought to be recovered, and observes that his promotion of Christianity is based on its materialism—the dead God leaves behind the manifest church or 'Holy Spirit'—the pursuit of the sublime object. However, the far more material fact is Christ's resurrection, the ultimately sublime defeat of death that we may participate in by faith. For God has not truly left or 'forsaken' us, but has died and risen so that we too may live again with our sins forgiven and the capacity to forgive and exist harmoniously with others, which is just the law of love. This paradox of dying to live is precisely the Incarnational Paradox from which truth emerges and which opens the possibility for a peaceful community to exist in accordance with the law of love.

Chapter 7 returns to Augustine and explores the nature of this peaceful legal community through developing the ideas of truth as revelation and faith as persuasion, applying the book's critique to a specifically legal context. The chapter considers the shortcomings of the codified law through a critical comparison of the neighbour principle in doctrinal negligence with Christ's Parable of the Good Samaritan based on the law of love, and suggests how society can begin to move towards this Christian community of peace.

Ultimately, Milbank contends that the only alternative to a secular approach which sunders faith and reason and produces ontological violence through subjective alienation is the return of a theology which is able to mediate between faith and reason and unite them. This theology arrives in the form of the Incarnational Paradox, where reason is recovered through faith in the truth of the divine being, and this is revealed in Christ as the interface between the finite and the infinite, eternal God and temporal man. In the disclosure of the divine being as love and ontological peace through the incarnation, crucifixion and resurrection of Christ, the law of sin and death is replaced by a new law, the law of love, which can then become the theological truth which redeems law, restores reason to faith and removes the violence of antagonism and alienation.[57]

In short, this book provides a theological model for how to consistently recover a system of law which does not alienate or antagonise. Secular philosophers have attempted this through appropriating the Apostle Paul, and are right to seek their solution in Christian theology, but their mistake is to approach that theology using a secular methodology which dichotomises reason and faith—effectively rendering that theology impotent to resolve the problem.[58] Instead, what is required is to revive an authentically Christian theological jurisprudence in a modern context—that is, to articulate a way in which the system of modern law can be redeemed by theological truth, which is the law of love. At its core, then, this book is concerned with recovering the theological and using it to redeem the secular system of law, so that the individual may exist harmoniously within the community through the truth, faith and reason of Christian theology.

[57] J Milbank, *The Future of Love: Essays in Political Theology* (Cascade Books, 2009) 154.

[58] See, eg, S Žižek, *The Puppet and the Dwarf* (MIT Press, 2003); A Badiou, *St Paul: The Foundation of Universalism* (Stanford University Press, 2003); G Agamben, *The Time That Remains: A Commentary on the Letter to the Romans* (Stanford University Press, 2005).

1

Milbank's Milieu: Theorisations of Truth, Faith and Reason

I. Introduction

This chapter explores the relationship between truth, faith and reason, which is foundational to the book's argument. In particular, it outlines the theology of John Milbank and Radical Orthodoxy as the focal point for articulating this relationship. It is important to properly explain these terms, for Milbank uses them in various ways, and without a careful definition of what is meant in each instance the meaning can become ambiguous. For example, although he endorses a correspondence theory of truth, his notion of 'correspondence' differs significantly from the typical philosophical notion of mirroring facts to reality. Milbank also states that reason ultimately leads to nihilistic violence and uncertainty, and reason leads to certainty and peace—which can seem strange without explicitly distinguishing between secular reason and the reason of faith. So this chapter also aims to clarify what Milbank himself means by these terms. I argue that Milbank endorses a theological correspondence between immanent intellect and the divine, transcendent intellect through revelation; that he rejects secular reason in favour of the reason of faith; and that he sees faith as trust or participation in the divine.

This chapter continues in section II by defining what is meant by the frequently employed terms 'postmodern' and 'nihilism'. It situates Milbank within the broader movement of Radical Orthodoxy, noting the centrality of the doctrine of the Trinity. As part of Milbank's project, section III then turns to consider the relationship between truth and power in the secular genealogies of Nietzsche and Foucault, suggesting that these narratives of history instantiate violence. In section IV, I examine how Milbank ultimately rejects these positions in favour of an ontology of peace based in faith, which implies an idiosyncratic correspondence theory of truth through revelation and participation. Section V subsequently moves to consider Milbank's contentions that secular reason ultimately results in violence, before examining his rejection of secular reason's violence and the promotion of peace through the reason of faith and theology in section VI. Finally, the chapter concludes in section VII by providing definitions of truth, reason and faith in Milbank's theological framework as a foundation for the argument in the rest of the book.

II. Milbank's Theoretical Context

A. 'Postmodern' Critical Augustinianism

Milbank's consideration of postmodernism and its connection with nihilism is of central importance, because the idea of the postmodern follows from the modern separation of faith from reason. Milbank argues that the postmodern results from modern secular reason exhausting itself. So

> the most serious essence of the 'postmodern' is best captured by [the] idea of an inevitable lapse of the 'metaphysical' liberal era of universal laws and abstractions towards the 'positive' era of diverse given facts, reworked myths and rituals and novel or renewed papacies.[1]

In postmodernism there is a rejection of liberal positivist metaphysics, the existence of universal laws, abstractions and brute facts. In other words, postmodernism eschews the idea of abstract, culturally independent categories, such as the liberal notion of the pure individual, and attempts to show that so-called universal or eternal facts about physical or social reality are really the contingent outcomes of constructed narratives.

According to Milbank, postmodernism as involving a historical or genealogical aspect therefore tends to ground its analysis in a mythically violent ontology—the 'pagan' version of an ontology of difference. A narrative is constructed which has violent difference at its core, and to bolster this narrative, difference is elevated to a fundamental mythical ontology or metaphysics. However, rejecting an objective or universal metaphysics and acknowledging that there is now no associated 'absolute truth' (nihilism) does not imply that we are compelled to settle for the result of violence intermingled with fortune.[2] The very fact that the nihilistic understanding is mythical (and therefore contingent) allows scope for critique. In particular, this critique is a theological one, thereby enabling the Christian mythos, which assumes an ontology of peace to be proposed in its place. Given that nihilism is 'a parody both of the Christian view that we are created from nothing and that therefore all that is finite is indeterminate, and equally of the likewise Christian view that ordered beauty is paradoxically in-finite', it follows that there is scope for such a properly theological or Christian articulation—for nihilism as a theological distortion implies that its trajectory can be theologically corrected.[3]

A theological correction is also essential because the postmodern and nihilist end results from a pure, secularised reason. When reason is separated from faith and the other virtues of feeling that Milbank describes (hope, charity and so forth), only uniform being remains. Ontologically, there exists mere reason or

[1] J Milbank, *Theology and Social Theory: Beyond Secular Reason*, 2nd edn (Blackwell, 2006) xiv.
[2] ibid 278–79.
[3] ibid xiv–xv.

rationality; being is uninterrupted and unchanging (univocal), with no variety—there is just a plain of nothingness. When it is recognised that this reason is nothing but an illusion or projection, the immutable void of being, or nothingness (what Milbank calls nihilism), is revealed. So to choose pure or secular reason is actually to ultimately elect non-reason or nihilism.[4] More significantly, Milbank asserts that 'nihilism narrates the nihilistic destiny of science, namely, the necessity for the discipline of truthfinding to admit that there are no truths, and therefore no objective goods'.[5] If this is so, there is only nothingness, a privation of transcendence—no truths and no goods imply a void of violence. This void is violent because it is a realm of pure difference, without the good. As a result, the differences exist as inevitable conflict and strife, always in competition. This is why a nihilistic genealogy requires an ontology of violence.

The fact that this secular framework is contingent and mythological, just another religion, allows a different religion to be proposed in its place—one which rescues truth, reason and the good, establishing a peaceful ontology rather than a violent one. This, Milbank argues, is Christianity; but it is particularly a Postmodern Critical Augustinianism which (like any postmodernism) portrays itself as an absolute historicism through a genealogical account, and possesses an ontology of difference. While pure nihilism possesses a violent ontology of difference,

> Christianity … pursued from the outset a universalism which tried to subsume rather than merely abolish difference: Christians could remain in their many different cities, languages, and cultures, yet still belong to one eternal city ruled by Christ, in whom all 'humanity' was fulfilled.[6]

Following this Augustinian aspect, however, Christianity does not

> imply mere mutual tolerance, far less any resignation to a regulated conflict … while it is open to difference … it also strives to make of all these differential additions a harmony … true community means the freedom of people and groups to be different, not just to be functions of a fixed consensus, yet at the same time it totally refuses *indifference*.[7]

Christianity as deployed in Postmodern Critical Augustinianism acknowledges the necessity of difference. Rather than trying to deny difference or regulate it with violence, at the ontological level Christian theology seeks a universal harmony of difference through incorporating the virtues contained in a faith united with reason, thereby enabling a community of peace at the political level.

B. Radical Orthodoxy

Radical Orthodoxy fashions itself against the modern theology of the twentieth century, which sought to (sometimes unwittingly) ally with the tenets of

[4] ibid xvi–xvii.
[5] ibid 284.
[6] ibid 267–68.
[7] ibid 268.

modernism. The postmodern critique of the Enlightenment project also calls for the demise of secular modernity, and with it modern theology in both its conservative and liberal forms. The result is a confessional theology proclaimed in the public or political sphere, yet not in a Constantinian-theocratic sense; rather, what is at stake is the transformation of this culture.[8] As a 'postmodern' movement, then, Radical Orthodoxy also draws upon the likes of Derrida, Foucault and Nietzsche, and utilises their critical methods of genealogy and deconstruction. It can therefore engage in the vernacular of contemporary critical thought while simultaneously demonstrating the 'paucity of postmodern nihilism' (which is a critique of certain types of postmodernism) and returning to pre-modern sources of knowledge without simply reinscribing pre-modernity.[9]

There are a number of key aspects which characterise Radical Orthodoxy. The first is a critique of modernity and liberalism. Radical Orthodoxy views modernity, with its elevation of reason above faith, as allowing theology to be shaped by culture rather than grounding theology in God's revelation which then shapes culture. Secondly, Radical Orthodoxy is 'post-secular', in the sense that it eliminates the modern distinction between secular and sacred, and the opposition between faith and reason. Thirdly, Radical Orthodoxy rejects pure materialism, which, it argues, leads to nihilism ('the real squandered into nothing'), and instead contends for a participatory ontology which advocates universal connection to the transcendent and immaterial through an incarnational account of revelation.[10] More broadly, then, Radical Orthodoxy eschews a modern theology which 'accepts that philosophy has its own legitimacy, its own autonomy apart from faith', and refuses to 'concede the criteria for responsible public discourse to the neutrality of the secular'.[11] Having influenced much of Radical Orthodoxy, John Milbank too emphasises that culture should be based in a reasonable Christian theology, and by appropriating Augustine, Milbank extends the notion of theology as foundational through articulating a theological narrative of Christian peace in contrast to the secular narrative of violence.

Milbank's crucial point is that the secular is not the neutral position one gets when theology is removed, but rather it is the replacement of a certain view of God and creation with a different view which makes theological claims regarding origins, purpose and transcendence.[12] The problem is these claims are 'bad theology', which properly renders the secular as a 'Christian heresy—an ideological distortion of theology'.[13] Secular modernity then changes the context in which theories of nature and society are articulated, so that there is a 'primordial

[8] JKA Smith, *Introducing Radical Orthodoxy: Mapping a Post-Secular Theology* (Baker, 2004) 33.
[9] ibid 42–43.
[10] ibid 74–75.
[11] ibid 35, 41–42.
[12] S Oliver, 'Introducing Radical Orthodoxy: From Participation to Late Modernity' in J Milbank and S Oliver (eds), *The Radical Orthodoxy Reader* (Routledge, 2009) 3.
[13] ibid 6.

violence' in Creation which must be 'tamed by the exercise of power'.[14] According to the modern view, at the heart of this violence is 'difference'. For example, the Hobbesian Leviathan as the 'modern' foundation for the legal society is premised on violent conflict emerging from a differentiated social body—with the result that this difference must be violently suppressed and eradicated through a central sovereign authority.

In response, Radical Orthodoxy proposes that peace is ontologically prior to violence, for difference exists in society and between God and the creation by divine inscription of the difference 'at the heart of being itself'—the perfect love and peace that exists in the Trinity.[15] This heavenly peace is realised on earth through a 'metaphysics of participation', where creation apprehends and instantiates the eternal peace via transformation of the mind by faith (united with reason) in the divine gift of Being (particularly seen in the Incarnation and Crucifixion of Christ).[16] This is not a gift in the sense of a trade or exchange, but rather a pure 'expression of divine love—of charity', so that we ourselves are constituted constantly by the flow of God's gift and our response to it.[17] This produces 'a "true" body of ecclesial unity-in-diversity, neither atomically individualist nor collectively universalising on an abstract basis ... a new sort of "interpersonal" society'.[18]

Participation in this context means that if we allow Christian theology to become the transcendent foundation of modern society and culture, society and culture will possess in part that which is possessed perfectly by God: namely, love and peace. This participation occurs and is displayed through the Incarnation—the event of Christ where man and God are united in the person of Jesus—which Milbank terms 'Incarnational Paradox'. He deconstructs the word 'paradox' etymologically and describes it as an 'overwhelming' or 'double glory (*para-doxa*)', which is a 'coincidence of opposites'.[19] In Christ, man and God are united, infinite meets finite and temporal meets eternal. The Christ Event is the moment of true theology, and so all philosophy and reason must be framed in terms of this event (while blending its intuitions with metaphysical reasoning and empirical appeal) in order to produce an ontology of peace.[20] In this way, the modern community participates in or apprehends a part of God's very nature.

Milbank therefore suggests a parallel need to undertake a theological critique of philosophy itself in its instantiation of the specifically modern dualism between reason and revelation. It is knowledge by faith and personal trust in the divine through poetic communion of the visible which simultaneously recognises God

[14] ibid 7.

[15] ibid 11.

[16] ibid 17.

[17] S Oliver, 'Introduction' in J Milbank and S Oliver (eds), *The Radical Orthodoxy Reader* (Routledge, 2009) 200–01.

[18] J Milbank, 'The Grandeur of Reason and the Perversity of Rationalism: Radical Orthodoxy's First Decade' in Milbank and Oliver, ibid, 393.

[19] J Milbank, 'The Double Glory, Or Paradox versus Dialectics: On Not Quite Agreeing with Slavoj Žižek' in C Davis (ed), *The Monstrosity of Christ: Paradox or Dialectic?* (MIT Press, 2009) 163.

[20] J Milbank, *Theology and Social Theory: Beyond Secular Reason* (Blackwell, 1990) xxv.

and rescues reason by providing access to the necessary or transcendent infinite invisible.[21] The conception of reason as achieving truth only when it gives creative expression to its recognition of God as visible in the world is far more critically viable. This creative expression of the visibility of God may be 'seen' through the Holy Spirit and the communion of believers, and their interaction with the divine through the poetic. God is no longer categorised and limited by secular human abstraction, but experienced and trusted through metaphor. Milbank consequently argues that the insistence on knowledge only by faith, whereby we allow that the visible (finite) affords some clue to the invisible (infinite), alone prevents nihilism.

It is because of this that Milbank also argues for the recognition and deconstruction of an 'autonomous secular reason', aiming to return reason to its inherent and proper basis in the theology of Incarnational Paradox, and return theology to its inherent reason.[22] Theology fully arrives in the incarnational event, the coming of Jesus Christ as the God-man, which is comprehended not through pure reason, but through a reason combined with faith which can apprehend the unity of the Trinitarian relations. God's Incarnation saves us by opening up a way beyond the material realm into the beyond of the infinite Trinitarian life of God.

C. Doctrine of the Trinity

The notion of the Trinity in Christian theology is central both to Milbank's Postmodern Critical Augustinianism and Radical Orthodoxy more generally, as well as to the argument of this book. This is because the notion of unity in the diversity of the Trinity, a community of love and perfect relationship existing in an ontology of difference, provides a model which may be implemented in order to produce a legal community of peace. The Trinity is a systematic understanding of the Bible's description of the Father as divine being, Jesus the Son as divine being, and the Holy Spirit as divine being, all eternally uncreated, yet individual loving persons living in community. It is not three gods or one person, but three persons in a perfect community of personal being: a Tri-Unity.

This can be ostensibly contrasted with the doctrine of divine simplicity held to by Aquinas. According to Aquinas, God is purely simple in the sense that He is purely constituted by his attributes, including being, so that existence is equated with being—'God is the same as His essence or nature … His essence is His being'.[23] In principle, this causes conceptual difficulties for Aquinas in relation to the idea of the Trinity existing as three persons and one God, for that would appear to undermine simplicity. Aquinas's divine simplicity fails to adequately reconcile the problem of unity and diversity, so Milbank postulates a fully Trinitarian ontology,

[21] ibid 4–5.
[22] ibid 6.
[23] T Aquinas, *Summa Theologica* (William Benton, 1952) vol 1, 16–17.

where the difference of the three members of the Trinity is fully reconciled in their unity of the Godhead.

The peace of Christian Trinitarian theology is found in the fact that the Triune God, existing in a divine loving relation of Father, Son and Holy Spirit, consequently exists in a form where disengaged individual agency is impossible. The will of God is realised through a 'community of love' such that the Trinitarian members ensure the non-arbitrary character of the creation.[24] Hence God is not just a singular, arbitrary will, but a community of love and perfect relationship, and, I propose, the basis for such in the legal community.

III. Critiquing the Secular Genealogy

A. Nietzsche and Truth

The postmodern nature of Milbank's project necessarily draws on the methods of postmodernism, including, in this context, genealogy. To properly situate Milbank therefore requires a brief overview of the secular genealogy he aims to counter with an authentic Christian genealogy. Since Milbank contends that a secular genealogy is related to the connection of truth with power, it is particularly instructive to consider Friedrich Nietzsche and Michel Foucault (as Milbank himself does) as theorists who attempt to historicise a developing relationship of truth and power.[25]

Nietzsche, in *Beyond Good and Evil*, defines truth as 'semantic games', 'rhetorically intensified human relations' which become 'culturally entrenched'; as such, truth 'is an illusion of which one has forgotten that it is an illusion', a 'vacuous metaphor', and truth itself is not discovered, only 'assumptions'.[26] For Nietzsche, truth is the 'will to power' or an instrument of dominance, and inherently questionable as a matter of perspective.[27] Nietzsche notes that the true and the good are not necessary partners—something may be true while being 'evil, harmful, dangerous and violent'.[28] Indeed, he claims that Christianity is embraced only due to the 'fear of truth' and the 'will to the inversion of truth'.[29] We are ignorant in order to enjoy life, and on this 'solid foundation of ignorance true knowledge rises'. The 'will to knowledge' is based on a far more fundamental will—the 'will to ignorance, the uncertain and the untrue as knowledge's refinement'.[30] Ultimately,

[24] C Gunton, *The One, the Three and the Many* (Cambridge University Press, 1992) 120.
[25] Milbank, *Theology and Social Theory*, above n 20, 128.
[26] F Nietzsche, *Beyond Good and Evil* (Vintage, 1966) 80.
[27] ibid 10, 16, 48.
[28] ibid 49.
[29] ibid 71.
[30] ibid 35.

truth is 'nothing more than appearance', and there are 'degrees of apparentness and perspectivism, gradations and shades', with no essential opposition of true and false.[31]

According to Nietzsche in 'On Truth and Lies in a Nonmoral Sense', this will to truth or power comes not from the desire for truth itself, but from a desire for the positive effects and consequences of truth.[32] Truth that is harmful or destructive is hostilely rejected. Thus, the closest Nietzsche comes to defining truth is that:

> [Truth is] a movable host of metaphors, metonymies, and anthropomorphisms: in short, a sum of human relations which have been poetically and rhetorically intensified, transferred and embellished, and which, after long usage, seem to a people fixed, canonical, and binding.[33]

In this sense, then, truth is a function of the will to power—the concept of truth is used as an instrument for dominance, antagonism and alienation.[34] Nietzsche even claims that truth stands in a 'hostile and destructive relationship to the world'—'truth kills' and even kills itself when it 'realises error is its foundation': it is the 'tragic conflict'.[35] Nietzsche therefore is concerned with truth, but not with metaphysical truth—he is rather concerned with truth as the 'human economy of living' and as a 'product of perspectival conditioning', of 'impulses and drives'.[36] Truth is a 'belief that has become a condition of life', and in that case 'strength is a criterion … truthfulness is only a means to a higher power of falsehood'.[37]

Nietzschean genealogy therefore refuses to tell the metanarrative of the Kantian or Hegelian (or socialist or Marxist) transcendent, constant human subject, and instead seeks to articulate the different 'fictions of subjectivity' over history.[38] Nietzsche's *Genealogy of Morals* is subtitled 'an attack', by which he means 'an attack on Christianity, and the illusion of eternal moral values'.[39] This exposes the nature of all genealogy—it is not disinterested, but specifically seeks to expose or undermine what it views as an underpinning societal fiction which has come to be viewed as 'eternal truth'.[40] However, both Nietzsche and Foucault view their genealogy not just as another interpretation, but as an authoritative narration—which nevertheless is intimately related to a question of value.[41] For in describing the 'truths' of human history as mere 'ruse[s] of power' and human history itself

[31] ibid 46–47.

[32] F Nietzsche, 'On Truth and Lies in a Nonmoral Sense' in D Breazeale (ed), *Philosophy and Truth: Friedrich Nietzsche* (Humanities Press International, 1979) 81.

[33] ibid 84.

[34] ibid.

[35] ibid 92.

[36] K Pearson and D Large, 'Introduction' in K Pearson and D Large (eds), *The Nietzsche Reader* (Blackwell Publishing, 2006) xxxix–xl.

[37] F Nietzsche, 'The Will to Power' in J Medina and D Wood (eds), *Truth: Engagements across Philosophical Traditions* (Blackwell Publishing, 2005) 24.

[38] Milbank, *Theology and Social Theory* 2nd edn, above n 1, 280.

[39] ibid 281; *cf* F Nietzsche, *A Genealogy of Morals* (Vintage, 1967).

[40] Milbank, *Theology and Social Theory* 2nd edn, above n 1, 281.

[41] ibid.

as a field of battle (or as power relations), this also apparently opens the space for humanist liberation ('apparently' because Milbank ultimately disagrees that genealogy is more than interpretation or that the story told is truly liberating), or, for Nietzsche, the 'emergence of an *ubermensch*, or a post-humanist human creature'.[42]

In Nietzsche, we see evidence that for him the violence which is said to be a part of truth and power relations ultimately stems from the rejection of Christianity's transcendent values. For Nietzsche's entire point could be understood as: truth is simply a will to power because it is humanly situated (or a striving for human dominance) rather than divinely situated. However, it is not a pure rejection of theology, for Milbank identifies intrinsically mythic and neo-pagan elements to Nietzschean thought. In particular, it is a rejection of Christian theology and a distortion of true theology, which replaces the Christian ontology of peace with a violent, neo-pagan mythos. It is the fact that this 'secular theology' is nevertheless a distorted theology which gives Christian theology the scope to critique it.

Milbank argues that if Nietzsche is correct, and all events are plays of power, then the cultures closer to realising this truth are more 'natural'.[43] In articulating this view, Nietzsche therefore 'celebrates a Homeric [pagan] nobility delighting in war, trials of strength, spectacles of cruelty, strategies of deception'.[44] But unless it is clear that such really is a more natural form of life, this pagan perspective must be called into question. Indeed, it is far from clear, for Nietzsche founds his account on the proclivity for human self-assertion, which is simply a matter of taste predicated on Nietzsche's own unfounded hierarchy of values which venerates the strong dominating the weak. Rather, the Christian perspective of sacrificial love and peace can be proposed as the more natural and desirable account.

B. Foucault, Nietzsche and Power

Similarly, Michel Foucault views truth as an instrument of oppression or power. In 'Truth and Power', some ideas are not preferable to other ideas because they are true or more true.[45] Rather, claims to truth 'perpetuate an exclusion where power hierarchies are strengthened'.[46] Truth cannot be refuted because, following the genealogy of Nietzsche, truth was hardened into an 'inalterable form' through history, the 'history of the error we call truth'.[47] Foucault argues in 'The Discourse on Language' that the division between true and false is a 'historically constituted

[42] ibid 282.
[43] ibid.
[44] ibid.
[45] M Foucault, 'Truth and Power' in L Cahoone (ed), *From Modernism to Postmodernism: An Anthology* (Blackwell Publishing, 2003) 252–53.
[46] ibid.
[47] M Foucault, 'Nietzsche, Genealogy, History' in Cahoone, n 45 above, 243.

division', and the will to truth, as a system of exclusion (of the false), relies on institutional support which exercises a pressure or power of constraint on other forms of discourse.[48] Ultimately, the abstraction of truth has 'masked the will to truth and its associated desire and power at work'.[49]

Foucault consequently defines truth as the 'ensemble of rules according to which the true and false are separated and specific effects of power are attached to the true'.[50] Truth therefore is not outside power or lacking in power: truth is a thing of this world, produced by multiple forms of institutional constraint and inducing regular effects of power. Each society has its regime of truth and its institutional criteria for determining between truth, which is sanctioned, and falsehood, which is excluded. Foucault's hypothesis is this: that truth is a 'system of ordered procedures for the regulation, distribution and operation of statements', and is 'linked in a circular relation with systems of power which produce and sustain it' and to 'effects of power' which it induces and which extend it.[51] In other words, truth is not about the revelation (transcendent or immanent) of reality. Rather, truth is an organised system sustained by the mechanisms of power for the purpose of furthering that power. So, following Nietzsche, Foucault states that the essential problem is to acknowledge truth's relationship with power and devise a new 'politics of truth' which 'detaches the power of truth from the forms of hegemony' (social, economic and cultural) within which it currently operates.[52]

Foucault argues that in a society there are permeating relations of power which are shaped by discourse. In particular, we are 'subjected to the production of truth through power' and we cannot 'exercise power except through the production of truth … the rules of right and the mechanisms of power' are equated to the 'effects of truth', particularly the power of true discourses.[53] Foucault also illustrates the will to truth as an operating principle of power through exclusion as legal discourse, which has progressively abandoned a theory of justice as its justification and moved towards externally guaranteed 'truth' of sociological or medical knowledge—so that even law cannot be authorised except by a discourse of truth.[54] Foucault defines power in *Power/Knowledge*, not as an individual or class of individuals dominating others, but as something which 'circulates and permeates', as a 'web … individuals are the vehicles of power, and also an effect of power', through systems of practice.[55] In *Discipline and Punish*, Foucault illustrates the way this power is displayed through Bentham's concept of the Panopticon, a picture of society as containing inmates who are constantly observed in order to 'induce … a state of conscious and permanent visability that assures the automatic functioning

48 M Foucault, 'The Discourse on Language' in Medina and Wood, above n 37, 318–19.
49 ibid.
50 M Foucault, 'Truth and Power' in Medina and Wood, above n 37, 333.
51 ibid 334.
52 ibid 333–35.
53 M Foucault, *Power/Knowledge* (Harvester Press, 1980) 93–94.
54 See M Barrett, *The Politics of Truth: From Marx to Foucault* (Polity Press, 1991) 142.
55 Foucault, *Power/Knowledge*, above n 53, 98.

of power'.[56] That is, since the inmates do not know precisely when they are being observed (it could be at any given time), they act as though they are being observed at all given times. In this way, power is maintained constantly without being constantly exerted.

Milbank critiques Foucault's stage of society as spectacle, a pure object of observation for the functioning of power, as essentially violent. For Milbank, 'looking at violence is actually *more violent* than participating in violence—that to be violent *is* actually to survey in a detached, uninvolved fashion a scene of suffering ... gazing at violence is the greatest violence, indeed the very essence of violence'.[57] In the passive, voyeuristic observation of violence, violence can flourish. If violence is unappealing, it would not be gazed at. Hence, looking at violence in a condoning fashion creates a space where violence is embraced and can flourish, and so is even more fundamentally violent than the action of violence itself. Milbank implicitly connects this to the pagan celebration of violence through the Colosseum: 'the modern "society of the spectacle" retreats from the pure liturgy of monotheism to a pagan theatricality. And like paganism, it invests its hopes in a controllable economy of violence.'[58]

Foucault ultimately tells a similar (pagan) story to Nietzsche, for he traces the growth of Western society in terms of the development of disciplinary power, which permeates and regulates individuals through constant observation.

Having defined Nietzsche and Foucault's genealogy in terms of power and violence, Milbank sketches a counter-genealogy, which views Christianity not as weak in relation to other individuals in terms of power, but weak in relation 'to God, the source of all charity'.[59] Indeed, if we allow the presupposition of Christianity that the charitable will is to promote human flourishing rather than to stifle and dominate, in contrast to the Nietzschean presupposition that love is the greatest mechanism of power and dominance, it follows that there can exist an 'analogical relation', a harmonious and peaceful coexistence of differences.[60]

Since this is the realm of non-absolute genealogy, the Christian presupposition is as equally valid as the Nietzschean presupposition and equally as rational. However, the love and peace that follows from the Christian presupposition is infinitely more desirable than the power and dominance that follows from the Nietzschean one. As such, it makes sense to choose Christianity. This move inverts genealogy from stating that the natural act is the will-to-power to stating that the 'natural act might be the Christian (supernatural) charitable act'.[61] In other words, since nihilistic genealogy cannot properly position Christianity, there remains possible

[56] M Foucault, *Discipline and Punish: The Birth of the Prison* (Pantheon, 1977) 201.

[57] J Milbank, *Being Reconciled: Ontology and Pardon* (Routledge, 2003) 28–30 (original emphasis). One also may think of the crucifixion of Christ in this context.

[58] ibid 33.

[59] Milbank, *Theology and Social Theory* 2nd edn, above n 1, 289.

[60] ibid 290.

[61] ibid.

a Christian (Augustinian) conception or genealogy of history which reads war 'as an absolute intrusion, an ontological anomaly'.[62]

In saying all this, Milbank does not categorically reject Nietzsche. Indeed, Milbank agrees with Nietzsche's critical insight—that the foundationalism of modernity and the bastion of objective, autonomous reason must be overthrown, and in its place lies nothingness—the void of nihilism. And it is uniquely Nietzsche who helps point the way forward, for he acknowledges that two of the 'truest' things in the world are love, for it 'penetrates the core and suffers with the individual', and religion, which 'offers another world to console the sufferer'.[63] So to arrive at the return of faith and theology, we must traverse the nihilistic, and rather than reinscribing the pagan violence of the heroic and powerfully victorious in its place (as Nietzsche does in the form of the *ubermensch*), one should instead seek the truth of Christian theology, which through Christ's crucifixion suffers with the individual, and through his resurrection allows the conception of a heavenly, life-giving peace.

IV. The Truth of Theology: Producing Peace through Trinitarian Correspondence

A. Understanding Milbank and Correspondence

In the most fundamental way, Milbank takes Christianity to be the 'absolute truth'.[64] This is because he sees truth as 'uniquely generated' through the 'tri-personed love of the Trinity'.[65] Because he positions truth relationally, in terms of the fundamental interaction of relationship in the Trinity, truth itself can never be interpretively exhausted—it continues through the ongoing love relationship both within the Trinity and between the Trinity and the world. In situating the truth within the Christian concept of the Trinity, of particular importance is the function of the third member, the Holy Spirit, who produces and sustains the bond of love between the community of believers. The love between Father and Son is 'perfect and infinite', and the Holy Spirit allows 'participation' in this perfect and infinite (true) love through producing and sustaining the 'bond between those of faith'—both with each other and with the Father and Son.[66] Since faith and reason are united in this participatory ontology, the bond of faith also includes the exercise of faith-enlightened reason. Therefore, Milbank endorses what may be termed a 'Christian' or Trinitarian correspondence theory of truth, where it is

[62] ibid 295, *cf* Augustine, *Concerning the City of God Against the Pagans* (Penguin, 2008) 861–62.
[63] Nietzsche, 'On Truth and Lies', above n 32, 95.
[64] Milbank, 'Double Glory', above n 19, 131.
[65] ibid 145.
[66] ibid 175–76.

this truth which can produce the necessary identity between human aspirations and existing reality. Indeed, the 'quest for a more human(e) world' is the 'quest for a world where human aspiration for peace and existing reality can be brought into a state of identity', and human aspirations are only viable if they correspond with the way things ultimately are—that is, with the relationship between Father and Son.[67] On this basis, Milbank argues that Trinitarian theology is the best source for a political critique. Such a critique is grounded in 'truth' as correspondence and produces peace.

To understand further the foundations of this Trinitarian Correspondence theory of truth, it is necessary to explain what precisely is meant by a correspondence theory of truth in philosophy. The correspondence theory of truth is the view that a proposition is true only when it corresponds with reality. There exists a proposition in the mind, such as 'snow is white'. This proposition is 'true' if it is reflected by or 'corresponds' to a real or factual state of affairs—that snow is, in fact, white.[68] However, the correspondence theory defined in this way does not sit comfortably with some of Milbank's other statements. For example, Milbank is also clear that

> The human mind does not 'correspond' to reality, but arises within a process which gives rise to 'effects of [linguistic] meaning' ... which is also the event of a 'truth' which cannot 'correspond' ... Knowledge 'surfaces' as the process of learning, which is true if divinely 'illumined'—it is not a knowledge of an object outside that process.[69]

In this sense, Milbank's assumption is radically realist: there are no prior criteria for truth (such as correspondence to reality), since in that case truth would be governed by something other than truth, which would then be false. Since 'the truth is the truth', it 'declares itself', with an 'apparentness uniquely characteristic of truth', so that it is 'self-authenticating'.[70] There can be no method for seeking truth from the nature or structure of minds, for why should that be true and not an illusion? Instead, truth offers one some 'advanced glimmering of its own character ... truth must be a gift from truth itself', which one must love and have faith in, and is 'ontologically fundamental, principally personal' and a 'contingent gift'.[71] So truth, for Milbank, exists uniquely through the gift of divine illumination, and is more concerned with desire than pure intellect:

> The mind is only illumined by the divine *Logos*, if also our 'preceding' energies, and ... desires, correspond to the Father and the Spirit respectively. We know what we want to know ... if all that 'is' is good and true, then no positive reality can be false as a 'mistake', or as 'noncorrespondence', but only false as deficient presence, embodying the shortfall of an inadequate desire. Now desire, not Greek 'knowledge', mediates us to reality.[72]

[67] ibid.

[68] M Lynch, 'Realism and the Correspondence Theory' in M Lynch (ed), *The Nature of Truth: Classic and Contemporary Perspectives* (MIT Press, 2001) 9.

[69] J Milbank, 'Postmodern Critical Augustinianism: A Short *Summa* in Forty-Two Responses to Unasked Questions' in G Ward (ed), *The Postmodern God: A Theological Reader* (Blackwell Publishers, 1997) 275.

[70] J Milbank, *The Future of Love: Essays in Political Theology* (Cascade Books, 2009) 176.

[71] ibid 178.

[72] Milbank, 'Postmodern Critical Augustinianism', above n 69, 275.

This is another way for Milbank to say that pure, secular reason cannot attain truth in the correspondence sense. It is desire for pregnant being, awakened by faith in conjunction with reason, which enables us to fully participate in and correspond to the divine being—or to apprehend truth.

B. Articulating a Genuinely Milbankian Correspondence

(i) Being and Participation

For Milbank, truth is not correspondence (in the sense of mirroring between a proposition in the mind and the facts of reality), but participation of the beautiful in the graciously revealed beauty of God. The measure of truth is likeness to the form of divine beauty, of which our soul has some recollection through desire and which has given or declared itself in a self-authenticating way rather than having been discerned in the mind.[73] This concept of participation is clarified by Aquinas. Etymologically, Aquinas defines participation as simply 'taking a part' of something.[74] More rigorously, he states that 'when something receives in particular fashion that which belongs to another in universal (or total fashion), the former is said to participate in the latter'.[75] Thus, when we find a quality or perfection possessed by a subject in only partial rather than total fashion, the subject is said to participate in that perfection. Appeal to a participation structure also accounts for the fact that a given perfection may be shared to various degrees by different subjects, alluding to the problem of unity in diversity, or the one and the many.

The final point in particular is instructive when one applies this Thomist notion of participation to human participation in the Trinitarian relationship. Not only is the problem of unity in diversity paradigmatically resolved in the community of the Tri-Unity, but the perfect quality of love and peace present in the divine relationship is imparted to the community of believers to the extent that they also exhibit these qualities of love and peace, albeit imperfectly.[76] The Incarnation can allow human or finite participation in the infinite relation (Trinitarian love) through the believing community partially apprehending the quality of this love, opening the possibility for an ontology of peace and reconciliation. Milbank has consequently attempted to recover a truly Christian correspondence theory through a more specific analysis of Aquinas, arguing that truth is 'accessible to the simplest apprehension' and yet 'amenable to profound learned elaboration'.

[73] Milbank, *Theology and Social Theory*, above n 20, 434.

[74] T Aquinas, 'Commentary on *De Hebdomadibus*', cited in J Wippel, *The Metaphysical Thought of Thomas Aquinas: From Finite Being to Uncreated Being* (Catholic University of America Press, 2000) 96.

[75] ibid.

[76] Milbank, 'Postmodern Critical Augustinianism', above n 69, 274.

'The notion of truth as correspondence is in crisis only because it is taken in an epistemological rather than ontological sense.'[77]

The detractors argue that the correspondence theory must be abandoned since we have no unmediated access to reality, and instead disquotational or deflationary correspondence must be embraced, which essentially reduces propositions of truth to that of being. Deflationary theories state that truth has no inherent nature. The basic intuition is that the proposition *p is true* is superfluous, since *p is* and *p is true* are equivalent. Truth is equated with being, and the notion of truth can be discarded and requires no explanation. Milbank and Pickstock identify two primary problems with this position. The first is that deflationists claim this is how truth really is, which would imply an inflationalist correspondence: 'it is true that p is true', where p = the correspondence theory of truth. This makes no sense on a deflationist view. Moreover, it leads to a contradiction, for this formulation nevertheless assumes correspondence to an (admittedly unverifiable) reality, and so is self-defeating.[78]

The second problem is that such a theory of truth implies that truth is merely instrumental, and this is analogous to the reduction of truth to relations of power and violence, which Milbank firmly rejects as a secular position. Such detractors are embracing a secular conclusion, so only a Thomist theological approach can save the correspondence theory of truth. Milbank notes that outside this theological framework the redundancy theorists are correct, but any notion of redundancy ultimately reduces to correspondence anyway, so that it is the theological which must be the case.[79] Indeed, correspondence must resurface, since the Christian seeks to imitate Christ, who is the Truth. So Aquinas's account of truth is the 'incarnate Christ's embodiment of the eternal truth' (a Christological mode of correspondence, where Christ the God-man is true in his imitation of, or accurately follows, the life of the eternal Trinity), and our participation in this is by 'imitation of Christ'.[80]

However, in Aquinas we also see correspondence as a 'real ontological proportion between thought and being', where these are regarded as transcendentally convertible in the sense that our mind apprehends the divine mind and therefore the divine being—truth does not simply reduce to our mode of apprehension of what actually is the case, but truth as correspondence is salvaged in the strong sense of participation in the divine being.[81] Recall the earlier point that in Aquinas being and essence are identical (or 'convertible'); the divine mind is of the same essence as the divine being, so that participation in the divine mind through thought is also participation in the divine being. One can only have correspondence

77 J Milbank and C Pickstock, *Truth in Aquinas* (Routledge, 2001) xiii.
78 ibid 1–2.
79 See Milbank, *Future of Love*, above n 70, 304–05.
80 Milbank and Pickstock, *Truth in Aquinas*, above n 77, 1–3.
81 ibid xiii.

at all if one has God, for truth as correspondence must be convertible with ultimate being. Secondly, and in addition, such a correspondence theory is equally to be seen as a coherence theory, since the ultimate true 'being of things' is their 'supreme intelligibility in the divine mind'.[82]

On this point, correspondence and coherence do not apply in the same way as they do in analytic philosophy. For correspondence, it is not simply a mirroring or reflection of reality in propositions ('true to the facts'), but there is an analogy between the way things are materially and the way things are in our minds. According to the coherence theory in analytic philosophy, a belief is true if and only if it coheres with the entire set of one's beliefs, assuming that the set itself is a strongly coherent one. Thus the truth or falsity of a belief is not a function of its match with a real, external world, but of the belief's relationship with other beliefs within one's web of beliefs. In other words, a proposition is true if it coheres with a system of propositions whose members cohere with one another, and coherence means that there must be both consistency and connectedness between the set of propositions.[83] By contrast, theological coherence refers to the ultimate truth of the being of things in terms of their supreme intelligibility in the divine mind, and therefore in this sense coherence is intrinsically connected to Thomist correspondence.

Since truth is primarily in the mind of God, then, Aquinas's realist theory of truth as correspondence of a mind to a thing is qualified by the 'subordination of all things to the divine mind'.[84] The referral to the divine intellect entails that the 'idea is oriented towards the reality of things', so the 'truth of God as contained in the divine mind' is expressed in the 'reality of the created world produced from the divine mind'.[85] It is real because truth, which exists in the mind, is convertible with being, the reality. Milbank and Pickstock ultimately conclude that:

> What all this suggests is that correspondence in Aquinas's theory of knowledge means something far more nuanced than a mere mirroring of reality in thought … there is an intrinsic analogy between the mind's intrinsic drive towards truth, and the way things manifest themselves, which is their mode of being true … if there can be correspondence of thought to beings, this is only because … both beings and minds correspond to the divine being and intellect.[86]

Therefore, rather than correspondence being 'guaranteed by its measuring of the given', it is 'guaranteed by its conformation to the divine source of the given'.[87] In this formulation we can clarify Milbank's various statements regarding the correspondence theory of truth. His notion of truth as correspondence consists not in a mirroring between propositions and the facts of reality, but in the unique,

[82] ibid 5.
[83] N Rescher, *The Coherence Theory of Truth* (Oxford University Press, 1973) 32.
[84] Milbank and Pickstock, *Truth in Aquinas*, above n 77, 8–9.
[85] ibid.
[86] ibid 15.
[87] ibid.

self-authenticating gift of the revelation of Trinitarian being and the divine mind through the Incarnation, which is participated in by humanity through imitation of what has been graciously revealed.

(ii) Revelation and Persuasion

Since the truth of the divine being is the good, and the good in Christian thought is peace and harmony (the perfect existence of the Tri-Unity), truth is thus an ontology of peace which persuades people and results in a harmonious community. To opt for truth and peace is also to opt for the ultimate reality of reason, for reason then seeks roots in being. Rather than reason being secular and a mere projection over the nihilistic void, reason is founded in Christianity—the divine ontology. However, if there is no ultimate source—if there is no transcendence and violence is ontologically intrinsic within the void of nihilism—this implies reason itself is not sacred, but is instead unreason or nihilism—a mere projection or illusion. As such, Milbank argues that only the 'persuasion to the ultimate truth of reason is rational'.[88] However, it is important to emphasise that Christianity does not claim that the true is self-evident to merely 'objective secular reason', but instead first qualifies 'philosophy as rhetoric in contending that the true are those things of which we are persuaded'.[89] A rhetorical path to the true leads to the following implication: only 'persuasion of the truth can be non-violent', but 'truth is only available through persuasion'.[90] Therefore truth and non-violence (or peace) must be recognised as that by which we are persuaded (rhetoric or faith).[91] Indeed, the very foundational Christian notion of faith is the Greek *pistis*, which means to have a conviction or trust in, and its root means to be persuaded. Thus, in Christian theology, to have faith is (at its most basic) to trust (in Christ) and be persuaded.

This notion of truth as persuasion alludes to the discursive theory of truth promoted by Jürgen Habermas. Habermas summarises his own position as a proposition being true if it could win argumentatively reached agreement in an ideal speech situation. In other words, truth is what may be accepted as rational under ideal conditions.[92] We can imagine what such an ideal situation would look like with regard to argumentative presuppositions of general inclusiveness, equal rights to participation, freedom from repression and orientation towards reached understanding.[93] Acceptance of the validity of the proposition in question in such a situation constitutes truth, and argument remains the only available medium of ascertaining truth.[94]

88 Milbank, *Future of Love*, above n 70, 219–20.
89 Milbank, *Theology and Social Theory*, above n 20, 401.
90 ibid.
91 ibid.
92 J Habermas, *Truth and Justification* (MIT Press, 2003) 36–38.
93 ibid.
94 ibid.

However, this leads Habermas to conclude that there is now a supposition of an independently existing reality about which we can state facts, and the truth of these facts is tested discursively. It follows that 'a proposition is agreed to by all rational subjects because it is true; it is not true because it could be the content of a consensus attained under ideal conditions'.[95] Hence, Habermas seems to be articulating a realist theory of truth at least compatible with analytical correspondence if not itself correspondence, in conjunction with his epistemic view that this truth may be verified through argumentation.[96] In short, under the assumption of ideal conditions, all available arguments are considered and exhausted, and this entitles us to take a proposition as true. However, 'the proposition's truth signifies a fact—the obtaining of a state of affairs'.[97]

This implies a fundamental problem with adopting Habermas's theory of discursive truth in conjunction with Milbank's correspondence theory. Milbank states that the notion of 'dialogue being a privileged mode of access to truth' (in terms of mirroring between propositions and reality) is a 'presupposition of liberalism', which he firmly rejects as 'secular' or even 'neo-pagan'—certainly not Christian.[98] Since dialogue as a privileged mode of access to truth essentially characterises Habermas's theory, it must be rejected on pain of inconsistency with 'true' truth: Trinitarian correspondence.

We are then entitled to ask what exactly Milbank means by characterising truth as that of which we are persuaded, and the exact mechanism of this persuasion. The best interpretation seems to be that persuasion is apparently not that one is persuaded of truth by open intersubjective discourse, but rather that one is persuaded through faith based on an unmerited revelation of the divine word. In other words, it is the revelation of the divine word that persuades, or produces faith, and faith properly and peacefully animates persuasion. In particular, God himself reveals truth through the Incarnation by demonstrating the Trinitarian relationship, that eternal relationship of love and perfect peace between Father, Son and Holy Spirit—or that law of love which corresponds with the created order through participation in the divine mind by faith or persuasion. Truth is understood, then, as both love and correspondence.

Theology understands itself as studying objects which are absolutely real, in that they take their source in original, indefeasible actuality of being. Theological reason, if it is true to itself, contends that all other disciplines which claim to be about objects, regardless of whether those objects are related to God, are really about 'nothing at all'—indeed, 'such disciplines are atheistic', and atheism is really a 'polite name for nihilism', absolute nothingness or void.[99] Only theology alone

[95] ibid 100–01.
[96] ibid 102.
[97] ibid 257.
[98] Milbank, *Future of Love*, above n 70, 290.
[99] ibid 303–04.

can 'remain with the question of truth'.[100] Truth is an 'adequation' or 'correspondence of knowledge with the real', since the one 'entirely real reality', God, is himself both 'infinitely real and infinitely knowing'.[101] As real, he is also manifest and self-aware, or truthful. To express a truth, then, means to correspond in our being to God (to a degree) via an awareness of aspects of the creation to whose lesser reality we also correspond, since creation is sustained by God and has its being in God.[102] From this theological perspective alone it makes sense to say that knowing corresponds to being, even if this cannot be validated. Hence a claim to know truly or to know at all amounts to a 'faith and participation in that which is the origin of all things and the depth of all things': the divine God.[103]

It follows that unless secular disciplines are explicitly ordered to Christian theology, they can be seen as intrinsically impaired, altogether lacking in truth, which to have any meaning must consist of correspondence between knowledge and the real in the fashion described. The fact that secular disciplines are not ordered to Christian theology (and so have an ontology of violence through nihilism rather than an ontology of peace through divine being) is therefore Milbank's primary reason for rejecting them.

V. Rejecting Secular Reason

Since secular reason is disengaged from faith and is a mere projection covering over a uniform void of being, the secular means the nihilistic. This nihilism is also violent because a pure reason, lacking truth or the good, is just the struggle of difference. Milbank suggests that this nihilistic violence can be resolved by a recovery of what secular reason initially refused, a 'social order grounded on virtue', or being incorporating the good.[104] However, virtue of the Platonic/Aristotelian type, though correctly oriented, is insufficient due to antinomies which arise in their accounts—such as peace being a 'merely suspended violence'.[105] Christianity provides a superior account based on its consistency, which 'links the particular to universal' by 'conceiving its relationship as transcendence', and so provides true peace.[106]

Milbank illustrates this contrast between secular or pagan violence and a social order grounded on virtue by referring to Augustine. Augustine demonstrates that pagan ontology is inherently violent (for even the 'Roman peace' is violence suspended by violent domination), as opposed to the City of God,

[100] ibid.
[101] ibid.
[102] ibid.
[103] ibid.
[104] Milbank, *Theology and Social Theory*, above n 20, 327.
[105] ibid.
[106] ibid 330.

which is ontologically peaceful. For example, he argues that the earthly (secular/pagan) city was 'founded on violence', and will 'continue in violence that leads to death': even victory in war will lead to death through 'arrogance inviting a violent overthrow'.[107] He acknowledges that even the earthly city ultimately aims for peace, even if it cannot be attained. However, the heavenly city or the City of God possesses 'eternal and perfect' peace intrinsically since God is our peace, and this peace is the 'final fulfilment of all human virtue'.[108]

Therefore, in Christianity and the City of God, one has a virtue which cannot be deconstructed to mere difference as antagonism and domination, but also allows analogical difference as participation in the very being of God, since Christian virtue ultimately seeks peace.[109] So the rejection of secular reason is provided through faith's explications, the arguments of theology which are a violent critique on what is false: the 'autonomous, exclusive citadel of reason'.[110] However, this violence is not received from theology itself, but from 'reason's implosion and self-dissolution as a function of the undoing of its violent self-assertion'.[111] Hence, pure secular reason in its final form is still 'pagan and cultic', as it 'trades life for the nothing and only returns at the price of the obscuration of nothing'.[112] In other words, the secular separation of faith from reason rejects the real life of truth and the good, substituting it for nihilism. The 'reason' that is left has no being, but is a mere illusion that obscures the nihilistic void—and this Milbank unequivocally rejects.

Modern secularity can thus be viewed as a mix of the heterodox, neo-pagan and anti-religious. It is heterodox in the sense that it promotes a distorted and non-Christian theology, neo-pagan in the sense that it promotes violent ideological struggle, and anti-religious in its rejection of faith in favour of a pure reason. Milbank claims that with the distortion and rejection of these faith elements the pure reason of secular modernity is revealed as an illusion disguising the nihilistic—and therefore an endless violence of biopolitics. Such a position is no more inherently reasonable than Christianity, and Christianity is preferable since it allows differences to coexist peacefully. The separation of reason and faith is a modern secular construct, not a Christian one—theology must not and cannot conform to secular reason, but nor is it fideism, a 'blind' faith which is against or contrary to reason/evidence.[113] The appropriate middle ground is a reason connected to the transcendent, participating in the divine intellect and illumined by faith.

[107] Augustine, above n 62, 599–600.
[108] ibid 865–66.
[109] Milbank, *Theology and Social Theory*, above n 20, 332.
[110] ibid 165.
[111] ibid.
[112] Milbank, *Future of Love*, above n 70, 167.
[113] J Milbank et al, 'Introduction' in J Milbank et al (eds), *Paul's New Moment: Continental Philosophy and the Future of Christian Theology* (Brazos Press, 2010) 11–13.

VI. Promoting Faith and the Reason of Theology

A. Faith and Reason in Christian Thought

Milbank, despite his trenchant criticisms of pure, cold, secular reason, which he equates with the 'perversity of rationalism' (mere discursivity and intellect which lacks desire or imagination), nevertheless boldly proclaims the

> grandeur of reason in its unlimited reach, beyond the transcendentalist confines of the finite, which can only be insinuated by a philosophy that is 'metaphysical' in the bad sense of reducing the ontological to the univocal and ontic and finally the epistemological and thereby seeking to corral it against theology. A true metaphysical confidence in reason, on the other hand, only enjoys this confidence because it has a *faith* in the infinity of reason beyond our grasp—the infinity of the *Logos* which is participatively mediated to us … the grandeur of reason is therefore also the nobility of faith … and … is … anything but rationalism and is severely impaired and undermined by the latter.[114]

Indeed, throughout the history of the Christian faith, its proponents have always seen themselves as simultaneously faithful and reasonable, and have seen their faith and reason as fundamentally intertwined.

(i) The Historical Catholic Perspective

Saint Augustine viewed truth as something progressively discovered by faith in conjunction with reason. As a foundation, Augustine argued that, according to the etymological definition of philosophy ('love of wisdom'), since wisdom is 'identical with God' and wisdom personified is God, 'lovers of God' are the 'true philosophers' and come nearest to the truth.[115] It is by reason that humanity is separated from the brute animals, and is alone among the creation able to appreciate the Creator God. However, the fact that human reason has been corrupted by sin necessitates that reason must be initially 'purified' by faith as humanity proceeds along the journey to truth, ultimately to God himself. Hence, for Augustine, faith is required for the proper operation of reason, since trust in and love for Jesus Christ, the Word and Truth of God, is the foundation for true knowledge. Otherwise, the 'powers of natural reason are prone to deception and error', rather than truth.[116] Although faith is a necessary condition for understanding religious truth, it is not a sufficient condition since reason is also required. Hence, neither faith nor reason alone is sufficient but both are necessary, and together they are

[114] Milbank, 'Grandeur of Reason', above n 18, 392.
[115] Augustine, above n 62, 298.
[116] R Cushman, 'Faith and Reason in the Thought of St Augustine' (1950) 19 *Church History: Studies in Christianity and Culture* 271, 279, 282–83.

sufficient. Faith is eminently reasonable because faith prepares the mind to fully perform its proper functions of reason.[117]

In Augustine's view, then, faith precedes reason, because unless one believes they will not understand. Consequently, 'the faithful shall at last see God by the instrument of reason; but reason cannot attain the vision of God unguided by faith'.[118] Augustine, however, does not advocate fideism: his is a faith seeking understanding. Faith is required a priori due to the internally contradictory nature of a rationalistic, secular approach: 'it cannot reach God because it does not want to have God. It withholds commitment until it has sight; but it cannot achieve sight until it yields commitment.'[119] The purely secular rational approach underestimates the sinfulness of the human heart and is ultimately against true reason, according to Augustine. Indeed, 'faith and reason are required one of the other. They are co-implicates; and it is error, in Augustine's view, to divorce them. Faith presupposes reason; reason urgently requires the correction of faith.'[120]

Thomas Aquinas, following Augustine, defines belief or faith to be 'thinking with assent ... to believe is an act of the intellect', and the 'formal object of faith is the first truth'.[121] An act of faith is 'related to the object of the will' (the good) and the 'object of the intellect' (the true).[122] Importantly, the truth of reason is not opposed to the truth of the Christian faith, for 'God himself is the source of all truth', and these truths do not contradict as there is 'no error or falsity in truth'.[123] For Aquinas, it is the very notion of faith that the intellect should always tend to the true, since nothing false can be the object of faith. However, Aquinas notes that the human intellect cannot know God 'naturally', but must be 'illuminated' by his grace through the divine spark or 'light' of participation.[124] Thus, Aquinas contends that faith is, by definition, in the intellect, it inclines towards the truth and is the most 'certain of the intellectual virtues', for it is based on divine truth.[125]

According to Aquinas, reason and faith only represent 'different degrees of intensity' of 'participation and divine illumination'.[126] Reason itself requires faith since it 'presupposes the operation of faith', while faith still 'demands discursive argumentation' and is 'higher than reason' only because it 'enjoys a deeper participation in the divine reason', which is 'pure intellect'.[127] In other words, faith and reason are on the same plane and strengthen each other insofar as they

[117] J Rist, 'Faith and Reason' in E Stump and N Kretzmann (eds), *The Cambridge Companion to Augustine* (Cambridge University Press, 2001) 38.

[118] Cushman, above n 116, 271, 273.

[119] ibid 284–85.

[120] ibid 294.

[121] Aquinas, *Summa Theologica*, above n 23, vol 1, 391–92.

[122] T Aquinas, 'Summa Contra Gentiles' in P Helm (ed), *Faith and Reason* (Oxford University Press, 1999) 109–11.

[123] ibid.

[124] Aquinas, *Summa Theologica*, above n 23, vol 1, 54–55.

[125] ibid 406, 409.

[126] Milbank and Pickstock, *Truth in Aquinas*, above n 77, xiii–xiv.

[127] ibid.

take part in the divine intellect—though faith is closer to the divine mind than reason is. So 'good reason' is an 'attentive reception', via the 'mediation of the senses and discursive operations', of the 'divine light of the *logos*', through faith.[128] Aquinas offers no support to those who claim there can be a philosophical approach to God independent of theology, or to those who demand confinement to Scripture without metaphysical reflection. Revelation supplements metaphysical reflection and enables the theoretical ascent to truth.

(ii) The Protestant Perspective

A central aspect of truth as revelation of the divine is the fact that it points to the beyond. In other words, the very notion of revelation directs us to what is not-yet-revealed. This lack of knowledge, which is nevertheless trusted based on what is known and has been revealed, is the essence of faith. So truth as revelation which is certain produces faith, since it points towards a lack of knowledge to be trusted. This means that merely secular reason cannot arrive at truth, for faith is required to supplement and transform reason to yield truth. This was the fundamental Protestant insight—the need for faith to purify and supplement reason in order to produce truth. For example, John Calvin agreed that faith must be 'preceded by a work of grace in the heart', due to the 'sinful propensity' of human reason alone.[129] However, for Calvin, faith is a 'certain belief in the divine veracity', not discernment taught by any 'demonstration of reason'.[130] Faith is something 'higher than human understanding', for without divine illumination faith cannot be produced—faith then 'purifies the mind', giving it a 'desire for divine truth' and 'establishing it in that truth'.[131]

Karl Barth argues that faith believes in the Word of God, Jesus Christ. That is, faith is trust or reliance on the faithfulness of the divine.[132] Importantly, Barth rejects the notion of faith based on pure human reason—we never believe 'because of' [reason], but 'in spite of' [reason], and we do not believe based on the proofs of reason.[133] Barth does not mean Christian faith is irrational, anti-rational or supra-rational, but rather it is rational in the 'proper sense' that 'human reason is illuminated by the divine reason', the *logos*.[134] In this sense, faith is belief based on the revelation or truth of the glory of Christ, and is fully compatible with reason. Similar to Augustine, faith precedes but aims for understanding. It is based on the truthfulness of God in the sense of his revealed fidelity, faithfulness and reliability; it is not irrational. As such, the orthodox Christian position (both Catholic and

[128] Milbank, *Future of Love*, above n 70, 323–24.
[129] J Calvin, *Institutes of the Christian Religion* (Hendrickson Publishers, 2008) 42.
[130] ibid 365.
[131] ibid 376–77.
[132] K Barth, *Dogmatics in Outline* (SCM Press, 1966) 18–20.
[133] ibid.
[134] ibid 22–25.

Protestant) involves an affirmation of truth as the divine revelation of Christ, and that both faith and reason are instrumental in apprehending this truth.

So Milbank fundamentally claims that the very notion of a divide between revelation and reason, far from being an authentic Christian legacy, itself results only from the rise of a questionably secular mode of knowledge. In the orthodox Christian position, both faith and reason are included in the more general framework of participation in the mind of God. For Aquinas, the key example, all human rationality is the participation in the divine reason, and therefore all knowledge requires faith. The light of revelation thus 'strengthens our grasp of natural principles'.[135] What this means is that 'theology [also] mediates knowledge' in all other disciplines.[136] To 'reason truly one must be already illumined by God'. Revelation, then, is 'just a higher measure of illumination', which is 'conjoined' intrinsically and inextricably with a 'created event which symbolically discloses that transcendent reality', and to which 'all created events to a lesser degree point'.[137] This 'created event' is the incarnation, crucifixion and resurrection of Jesus Christ, the God-man. Hence there can be no separation of reason and revelation, for 'true reason anticipates revelation' in the sense that a reason illumined by faith will always point towards revelation—the arrival of true reason in the event of Christ the Word.[138]

B. The Limits of 'Secular' Reason

It may even be contended that faith is actually a presupposition of reason, which implies that the notion of secular reason is inherently problematic. For if reason is viewed as independent of or autonomous from faith, and reason has no absolute foundations based in faith, then argument between different positions is precluded and pragmatically absurd. Any arguments which seek to go beyond tautology have to 'assume areas of given agreement', and to 'win an argument means to show the contradiction of alternative positions'—outside a 'horizon of shared faith' (or 'common feeling') no arguments would get off the ground.[139] Beyond the level of formal logic there is no single 'reason' without presuppositions, there are only many different, complexly overlapping traditions of reason (such as practical reason or speculative reason). It follows that if theology is to be a *logos*, its own Word or reason which has a right to speak, it must in some fashion be convincing in itself, rather than a mere expression of a 'faith' wrongly thought of as 'preceding a rational and linguistic reflection'.[140]

[135] Milbank, *Theology and Social Theory*, above n 20, 252.

[136] ibid.

[137] J Milbank, 'Knowledge: The Theological Critique of Philosophy in Hamann and Jacobi' in J Milbank et al (eds), *Radical Orthodoxy: A New Theology* (Routledge, 1999) 24.

[138] ibid.

[139] J Milbank, 'Hume vs Kant: Faith, Reason and Feeling' (2011) 27 *Modern Theology* 276, 278.

[140] Milbank, *Future of Love*, above n 70, 35, 77.

This means theology will have to provide an account of human history on the basis of its own particular and historically specific Christian faith. Theology may do this in an intrinsically convincing way by refusing to treat reason as an ahistorical universal, instead asking how Christianity has affected human reason. Such a theology turns to the patristics and goes beyond them to elaborate a Christian *logos*, or a reason which fundamentally bears the marks of the Incarnation, for Christianity ultimately claims that only the Incarnation of Christ fully restores truth and reason.

C. An Incarnational Reason

The contrast here is between a cold, pure, abstract reason, which cannot apprehend reality because it does not have its foundation in true being, and a reason combined with faith through the Incarnation. In particular, there is an element of feeling, desire and love which consists in faith united with reason, in contrast to a uniform and purely rational reason. The qualification of reason by myth and poetry (the dimension of feeling or affection) ensures that reason will not degenerate into pure abstraction. This alludes to the notion that revelation should be understood in its aesthetic as well as logical and ethical dimensions. The revelation of Christ through the Incarnation is not merely propositional with moral import, but is also an event which displays the beautiful and evokes the affections, especially love.

In particular, Milbank places emphasis on the imagination and the 'poetic moment', which is the 'realisation or manifestation of the Beautiful', an integral part of our 'poetic existence in Christ'.[141] This metaphysics of the person points the way to 'understanding humanity as fundamentally poetic being', which is fully participated in through the revelation of Beauty in the Trinitarian relations.[142] 'Poetic existence can then be described as a fundamental [Christian] activity and as a fundamental mode of knowledge.'[143] Ultimately, then, charity (love) or 'doing good' requires a 'free, gratuitous response to God's free gratuitous gift' as something beyond boundaries or precedents, something 'creative'—and this requires an engagement with the poetic and a 'discovery of true poetic bounds of possibility'—ultimately modelled by the love of the Trinity of God displayed in the Incarnation of Christ.[144] This insight provides the basis for a peaceful legal community; conduct ought not to be limited by the boundaries and precedents artificially constructed through cases and legislation, but may transcend these possibilities by creative participation in divine love as a free response to God's grace.

In contrast, pure or secular reason results in a form of paganism, since its absolute abstraction disguises the struggle of difference through violent regulation.

[141] J Milbank, *The Word Made Strange: Theology, Language, Culture* (Blackwell, 1997) 123.
[142] ibid 124.
[143] ibid 129.
[144] ibid 134.

The Bible, especially the New Testament, 'resists this advance to pure abstraction by reinvoking the poetic', yet in a nonpagan way which seeks a 'positive relationship to the properly vague abstraction of nondogmatic reason' (seen through the wisdom literature and the New Testament engagement with Greek philosophy). For example, the Apostle Paul quotes the Greek poets in his preaching to the Gentiles in Acts 17, seeking to teach them about the nature of the true God and our ontological connection (that in him we live and move and have our being) through poetic discourse. The balance is proclaimed paradoxically in the idea that reason itself (*logos*) becomes incarnate, which means the 'rational is fully and only accessible by the indirectness of a poetic discourse concerning this event'; reason thus is more 'realistically rational' as disclosing a 'rational though mysterious universe'.[145] As such, reason is uniquely accessed through faith in the divine, and faith involves both the intellect and the affections.

This is in fact central to the Christian concept of faith. Milbank defines faith (*pistis*: to trust or be persuaded) and trust interchangeably: to trust is to have faith in, and to have faith is to trust.[146] Faith includes both the affective element of trust and the intellectual element of persuasion through a reason specifically based in Christ, the divine Word. It follows that there are not 'many faiths' but 'one faith'—a 'trust in the transcendent God that involves being persuaded by the divine word beyond the scope of secular reason'.[147] It is a trust in 'specifically disclosive sacramental processes of mediation between the universal and the particular, mind and reality, the intellect and the senses'.[148] Thus, in the final analysis, faith in the Triune God is a recognition of and trust in the 'transcendental/ontological possibility of participation' in the infinite/divine.[149] Since this faith 'construes the universal sway of difference as analogical', by faith the proclamation is made that 'theology is a meta-discourse', and 'pure reason is viewed as private reason'.[150]

In short, pure secular reason (even when modest) always courts danger and drives us to the accomplice of violence in knowing, and to dread in ignorance. Secular reason itself is finally 'uncertain'.[151] This is the conclusion which pure reason must reach, while the intersection of reason by faith establishes common-sense reason and allows the progression of philosophy through establishing reason in true being. In this way, 'theology may outwit secularism and nihilism'.[152] It is not that the object of metaphysics (being) is denied, but instead the philosophical pursuit of being by pure reason will reach aporetic and nihilistic conclusions—that,

[145] Milbank, 'Double Glory', above n 19, 217–18.

[146] J Milbank, 'Sublimity: The Modern Transcendent' in R Schwartz (ed), *Transcendence: Philosophy, Literature and Theology Approach the Beyond* (Routledge, 2004) 230; Milbank, *Future of Love*, above n 70, 150–53.

[147] Milbank, *Future of Love*, above n 70, 150–53.

[148] Milbank, 'Double Glory', above n 19, 16.

[149] Milbank, 'Hume vs Kant', above n 139, 277–78.

[150] Milbank, 'Double Glory', above n 19, 162.

[151] Milbank, *Future of Love*, above n 70, 150–153.

[152] Milbank, 'Knowledge', above n 137, 32.

for example, reason itself is an illusion and there is nowhere for secular philosophy to proceed. Reason therefore cannot ground the rational disclosure of being, but by faith (truth as revelation of divine being), disclosure remains possible. Thus, theology 'saves reason and fulfils and preserves philosophy', but 'secular philosophy left to its own devices brings itself ... to an end'.[153]

To conclude, then, discursive reason should recognise that it operates within strict limits and is therefore not competent to pronounce judgment against metaphysical or religious positions. A certain stance of faith is involved. Hence, if one 'restricts reason to the formal' and 'insists it only operates in knowable boundaries', one may 'encourage entirely irrational and emotive political movements' that exhibit violence.[154] The converse implication of this is that the combination of reason and faith opens the possibility for a theological ontology of peace through revelation of Trinitarian relations and the Incarnational Paradox.

Further, any sharp separation of reason and faith is 'dangerous' because it implies that 'faith at its core is non-rational and beyond the reach of argument', while simultaneously implying that 'reason cannot impact on issues of substantive preference'.[155] In reality, however, reason and faith are always intertwined in a beneficial way. Reason has to make certain assumptions and must trust in the reasonableness of reality. Faith has to continuously think through the coherence of its own intuitions in a process that often modifies those intuitions. Thus, 'critical faith becomes a more reflective mode of feeling' and 'reason has always to some degree to feel its way forward'.[156]

Some might ask whether a sound basis has been provided for rejecting secular foundations and pure reason in favour of Christian theology and a faith united with reason. I have argued that for reason to effectively operate a certain stance of faith is always involved, and so the more appropriate approach is faith and reason working together. However, for those entrenched in the secular setting who may reject faith a priori, perhaps there is no possible argument that will be convincing from a faith perspective. In such a case, I ask the reader to be patient and to reflect on the arguments of Chapter 6, which suggest the particular value of the Christian tradition within the context of modern secular jurisprudence, and consider why the Christian heritage might be worth advocating from the perspective of the secular.

The rejection of hegemonic secular reason does not result in fideism, where faith is antithetical to or divorced from the operations of reason. Rather, faith is trust in and persuasion of the truth, and occurs through the gracious disclosure of this truth by the truth—namely, the Trinitarian relation of love and peace revealed in the Incarnation. This faith both illumines and is articulated by reason through participation in the divine reason, which allows both critical reflection and a

[153] ibid 37.
[154] Milbank, 'Hume vs Kant', above n 139, 276–277.
[155] ibid 277.
[156] ibid.

reliant trust in God. The articulation of reason is found in the incarnated Christ, the *logos* which is the sum and genesis of all reason as it is the divine reason, and reason is therefore the recognition of God as visible in the world.

Truth, faith and reason are mutually interdependent, so that each entails the others and one cannot exist without the others. Truth assumes participation in the divine mind by faith, and participation in the divine mind constitutes reason. Faith depends on being persuaded by the revelation or truth of the Trinitarian relations and the Incarnational Paradox, which reveals the divine mind and demonstrates the *logos* as the divine reason. And reason only achieves truth through the creative expression of its recognition of God in the world by faith. Reason consequently requires the persuasion of faith by the truth to avoid becoming secular or 'pure' reason. In this way, truth, faith and reason are theologically foundational for creating a peaceful legal community.

2

Secularising Science: The Divorce of Reason and Revelation

I. Introduction

The first chapter claimed that the secularisation of reason, or the separation of faith and reason, results in violence. This chapter explores that claim in the context of scientific discourse. I argue that the understanding of Aquinas as dividing faith and reason and a view of God as pure sovereign will form the theological framework undergirding the early modern scientists, as well as the institution of the church—and that these perspectives produce violence. Therefore, recognising Aquinas as articulating a united faith and reason with a view of God as participatory being is essential for articulating a Christian theology which leads to a peaceful community.

Section II of the chapter considers the development of science. The first sub-section explores the theological characteristics of the early modern scientists Galileo, Kepler and Newton, identifying their view of God as a type of pure will or sovereign architect. The next sub-section argues that such views of God are related to a scholastic misinterpretation of Aquinas on faith and reason, which subsequently allows the separation between faith and reason. In other words, science as knowledge may be apprehended by pure reason, without faith—in effect allowing the possibility for reason to become the autonomous foundation for scientific inquiry. This distinction, noted by Laplace, allowed the redundancy of theological considerations in scientific analysis, eventually leading to the evacuation of theology and methodological naturalism in scientific endeavour.

Section III examines the Reformation and Counter-Reformation, which parallel the development of modern science. This analysis argues that the respective theologies of these movements further entrenched a view of God as pure sovereign will, and the separation of faith and reason. The emphasis on the sovereignty of God in conjunction with the approach of faith alone and Scripture alone espoused by the Reformers isolates reason from faith through confining faith to theology, as well as preventing recourse to natural revelation for knowledge of God. This notion of God as sovereign, in conjunction with the Catholic Counter-Reformation response of more stringently regulating the pursuit of knowledge, fostered a community of imperialisation and struggles for dominance.

Since such science or knowledge resulted from the initial divorce of reason and revelation (or faith), I propose in section IV that the way to restore certain, true science which pursues peace is through uniting reason and faith through the model of Christian Trinitarian theology, and allowing Christian theology to reign with its ontology of peace. There exists a counter-narrative which views God not as pure sovereign will, but as a participatory being or loving community. Furthermore, in such a framework we see a more charitable interpretation of Aquinas which unites reason and faith. This opens the possibility for a future vision, where the pursuit of knowledge is no longer antagonistic but where faith is united with reason and science is a peaceful participation in the divine being.

II. The Theological Genesis and Subsequent Secularisation of Science

Milbank claims that modern science was 'intended to promote objective truth' and was essentially 'positivist in character', relying upon 'indefeasible sense-impressions of external facts of reality' governed by an immutable system of natural laws.[1] However, rather than providing a 'true ontology', in reality it only provides a 'very limited disclosure of certain aspects of reality lending themselves to manipulation and prediction'.[2] The only 'possibly universal truth' that science can entertain is the rule of contingency, or uncertainty.[3] Thus, due to the foundational emphasis on God's will and the separation of faith and reason, science is 'indifferent to anything but abstract power', and does not merely 'override past attachments or theoretical prejudices, but keeps them in reserve', so it can potentially 'recruit them to the interests of domination'.[4] In other words, science is not absolutely objective, but assumes a certain kind of theology which ultimately displays itself in the violent manipulation of the limited knowledge gained. Moreover, in the end, the removal of faith from reason in the context of science also results in uncertainty—a blind faith.

A. Voluntarism and the Early Scientists

This theology is an understanding of God as pure sovereign will, as the great divine architect—or what is otherwise known as theological voluntarism. Various sociological and historical analyses have revealed the extrascientific influence

[1] J Milbank, *Theology and Social Theory: Beyond Secular Reason* (Blackwell, 1990) 264.
[2] J Milbank and C Pickstock, *Truth in Aquinas* (Routledge, 2001) xii.
[3] Milbank, *Theology and Social Theory*, above n 1, 259–60.
[4] ibid 274–75.

undergirding the so-called scientific revolution, particularly this Christian theological framework of God as the Creator and Institutor of natural laws.[5] The following analysis will focus on the early modern scientists Galileo, Kepler and Newton, for two reasons. First, they are foundational in terms of the development of modern science as part of the scientific revolution. Secondly, and more importantly, I will argue that forthright in their thinking was a particular theology. This theology was fundamentally influenced by the scholastic emphasis on the will of God and the corresponding separation of reason and faith; these beliefs were also the primary motivation for their scientific pursuits.

(i) Galileo and the Unity of Truth

Galileo Galilei was a famed though notorious physicist and astronomer of the sixteenth and seventeenth centuries, whose predictions and discoveries allegedly contradicted the theological teaching of the Roman Catholic Church. For Galileo, the foundation for his unpopular espousal of Copernican cosmology was the fact that 'God is omnipotent and can do anything'.[6] This focus on the power and will of God in the creation and function of the universe caused Galileo to praise the 'marvelous construction of the vast celestial sphere'.[7] In this sense, God was viewed as the all-powerful designer or architect, one who is able to construct the universe by virtue of his incontrovertible, sovereign freedom. Moreover, Galileo believed that 'God acts, not through miracles, but in the most natural, simple, direct way'.[8] This acknowledgement of God working through natural rather than supernatural means enables, in principle, an analysis of the physical world without reference to God or special revelation.

In this context, Campanella, a clergyman who defended Galileo at the time of the controversy, advocated what is termed the doctrine of the unity of truth—that religious truth cannot contradict truth discovered by natural reason in any discipline, including science. This is expressed through the metaphor of God's double gift of truth—the Book of Scripture (special revelation) and the Book of Nature (general revelation). Since the same good and truthful God is the author of both books, they cannot disagree with each other, assuming both books are properly understood. This allows an a priori guarantee that religion (faith) and science (reason) will not disagree—the problem is the correct understanding of both.[9]

[5] D Griffin, 'Introduction: The Reenchantment of Science' in D Griffin (ed), *The Reenchantment of Science: Postmodern Proposals* (State University of New York Press, 1988) 10. See also M Osler (ed), *Rethinking the Scientific Revolution* (Cambridge University Press, 2000); R Giere and R Westfall (eds), *Foundations of the Scientific Method: The Nineteenth Century* (Indiana University Press, 1973); J Hannam, *God's Philosophers: How the Medieval World Laid the Foundations of Modern Science* (Icon Books, 2009).

[6] Galileo, cited in WL Wisan, 'Galileo and God's Creation' (1986) 77 *The History of Science Society* 473, 484.

[7] ibid 475.

[8] ibid 482.

[9] R Blackwell, 'Introduction' in T Campanella, *A Defense of Galileo* (University of Notre Dame Press, 1994) 24–25.

According to this view, allowing the study of the physical world apart from God's special revelation is not ultimately problematic, for it is all God's truth. Any attempt to forbid Christians to study the Book of Nature is a crime against Christianity itself, for if Christianity is true, it should not fear the discovery of other truths in nature which will provide greater insight into the wisdom and goodness of God. Hence Christian belief provided a unique foundation for exploring the natural world, since neglecting this cut off access to learning about God through understanding his creation. This is reflected in the significant scientific progress in the Middle Ages, actively supported by the church as long as it did not endanger accepted theological teachings.[10]

(ii) Kepler and the Precision of God's Decree

The medieval Christians expected that God had arranged things in an elegant way, without restricting his sovereign decree, and although this was the presumption, one still had to confirm empirically to see if God had in fact operated this way. For them, the desire to worship God by actively studying his creation is a distinctly Christian imperative, for when we observe the orderly causes of the world, it drives us to know the first cause of all other causes: God. For example, the most important fact about the world for Johannes Kepler, the celebrated German mathematician and astronomer of the seventeenth century, was that God had created it. In his eyes, the structure of the heavens should reflect the perfection of the Creator, and this perfection would reveal itself through the precision of geometry.[11]

For Kepler, 'God himself the Creator has adjusted ... the operations of the world' and the 'celestial motions'.[12] God 'assigned the motions of the heavens in harmonic proportions'.[13] 'The harmonic faculties explained ... [and] have been breathed out by that essential harmony, God himself, in the act of creation, inasmuch as he is "existence in activity"'.[14] So God is viewed again as the sovereign divine architect who freely and precisely designs the structure of the universe. Kepler goes even further, equating the nature of God's being with this precise mathematical structure, and emphasising the accomplishment of His will and activity. He extends this character to the rest of creation, arguing that

> indeed all spirits, souls and minds are images of God the Creator if they have been put in command each of their own bodies, to govern ... they also observe the same patterns along with the Creator in their operations, having derived them from geometry.[15]

If we are images of God insofar as we command and govern ourselves according to the patterns of geometry, what we are reflecting is the idea of God as one who commands and wills according to precise rules.

[10] Hannam, above n 5, 1–2, 7–8.
[11] ibid 227.
[12] J Kepler, *The Harmony of the World* (American Philosophical Society, 1997) 129.
[13] ibid 147.
[14] ibid 311.
[15] ibid 146.

It follows that the world's

> construction is not arbitrary, as some may suppose, not a human invention which may also be changed, but entirely rational and entirely natural, so much so that God Himself the Creator has given expression to it in adjusting the heavenly motions to each other.[16]

All has been 'arranged by God the supreme Regent', who is the 'eternal craftsman'.[17] Once again, there is an emphasis on God as the sovereign designer who accomplishes his will through intricate construction of the natural laws. In Kepler's view, God was exalted through his study of astronomy—for God was not imprecise and did not make mistakes. Kepler then completed the link between religion and science, for his ideas about God provided him with a hypothesis, he had the mathematical ability to systematise his findings and the progress of previous medieval scientists enabled him to check whether this system was empirically accurate—and for the most part, it was.[18]

For these scientists, the emphasis on God's nature and his decree implies that the starting point for all natural philosophy (science) was that nature had been created by God. That foundation rendered it a legitimate area of study, for through the study of creation humanity could learn about its Creator. Because God was consistent and not capricious, these natural laws were constant, orderly, immutable and worth scrutinising. The way to find out which laws God had chosen to use was from experience and observation. Such motivations and justifications were maintained almost uniformly by the pioneers of modern science; they assumed that scientific inquiry is a religious duty because nature reflects the creativity of its maker.[19]

(iii) Newton and the Sovereign Architect

The close relationship between nature and divinity further underscored the importance of religious belief in scientific study for the early modern scientists. Faith was an important prerequisite for reading the Book of Nature, and knowledge of God provided the reason to study nature. Each science provided a different means of understanding God's wisdom through discerning the patterns that linked all forms of knowledge to its original source. For example, Isaac Newton, the celebrated English physicist and mathematician of the seventeenth and eighteenth centuries, claimed that 'we can know by natural philosophy [science] what is the first Cause'.[20] Some early scientists, such as Newton and Robert Boyle, were voluntarists who emphasised God's freedom and omnipotence, and believed

[16] ibid 158.

[17] ibid 279. 139.

[18] P Barker, 'The Role of Religion in the Lutheran Response to Copernicus' in Osler, above n 5, 85–86.

[19] Hannam, above n 5, 340–41.

[20] Isaac Newton, cited in E Strong, 'Newton and God' (1952) 13 *Journal of the History of Ideas* 147, 157.

that a priori knowledge of nature was impossible.[21] As such, since God had freely chosen to create this particular world, the only way to learn what kind of world God had created was to study it empirically.

Newton attributed the order of creation to the 'counsel and contrivance of a voluntary Agent'.[22] 'To compare and adjust all these things together in so great a variety of bodies, argues that cause to be not blind and fortuitous, but very well skilled in mechanicks [*sic*] and geometry.'[23] For Newton, then, the design apparent in creation implied a sovereign designer acting freely, a divine architect. In other words, 'such a wonderful Uniformity in the Planetary System must be allowed the Effect of Choice'.[24] Therefore, to adequately understand and appreciate the subtlety of Newton's method in science, one must take into account his metaphysical considerations: acknowledging the Lord God who designed and is in control of the universe through general established laws of nature and special intervention at will, and the blending of the Books of Nature and Scripture.[25] The whole of creation is subordinated to God and his will, for God is 'omnipotent' and 'governs all things' with 'true dominion'.[26] This is the proper theological and metaphysical background for Newton's opinion that scientific laws articulated by virtue of observing the natural world are true reflections of reality; God has created the world with orderly, constant natural laws which may be discovered and expressed.

Through this reasoning, the scientists of the Middle Ages made modern science 'conceivable' and 'safe', even an imperative, in a Christian context. Without the belief that all nature was created by God, modern science would not have happened.[27] More specifically for my purposes, the particular theology which undergirded the development of modern science involved an emphasis on God's sovereignty and will in design and providence as a divine architect. It also involved a particular theology of the relationship between faith and reason.

B. Aquinas, Faith and Reason

The cornerstone of modern science was a widespread acceptance of reason as a valid tool for discovering truth about the world. It was initially required for the church, as the guardian of almost all intellectual endeavours in the Middle Ages, to approve this use of reason. The relationship between faith and reason are important parts of the narrative. The rationalisation was that since one truth cannot

[21] J Wojcik, 'Pursuing Knowledge: Robert Boyle and Isaac Newton' in Osler, above n 5, 184.
[22] Newton, above n 20, 151.
[23] ibid 153.
[24] ibid 162.
[25] J Force, 'The Nature of Newton's "Holy Alliance" between Science and Religion: From the Scientific Revolution to Newton (and Back Again)' in Osler, above n 5, 257–258.
[26] Newton, above n 20, 153.
[27] Hannam, above n 5, 336.

contradict another truth, human science cannot contradict divine revelation, nor can the works of God contradict the Word of God. Theology consequently does not need proofs taken from the sciences, yet it does take those proofs so that faith can be strengthened by understanding the supernatural in terms of the sensible and the natural. This is allowed since the root of wisdom, understanding and reason (particularly in regard to scientific inquiry) is God and from God, and those Christians who are wise and rational are so through him. Christ, the Word of God, is the highest reason, and we are called rational by participation in Christ. Therefore Christ wishes us to be rational by being as similar to him as we can in action and truth.[28] In this sense, God's existence (or at least the belief in God's existence) is foundational to the development of science and the scientific method operating as a function of reason. Since human reason is a dim reflection of divine reason, and nature is constructed according to divine reason, human reason can comprehend nature. All this makes scientific sense because there is a God who acts reasonably.[29]

(i) The Initial Misconception

These notions of participation, human reason and the distinction between the truths of faith and the truths of reason ultimately have their foundation in the work of Thomas Aquinas. In particular, it was Aquinas's five proofs of God's existence allegedly by reason apart from revelation which demonstrated to Christians that reason was their ally and not something they needed to be afraid of, because if rational arguments could be mustered to demonstrate what was believed by faith, such reason was worth pursuing. However, certain interpretations of Aquinas (for example, that of John Duns Scotus) took this notion of reason apart from revelation too far. According to these interpretations, Aquinas espouses a full divide between faith and reason, theology and philosophy. However, John Milbank argues that this dualistic reading of Aquinas is false, and actually emerges from later theological tendencies and readings.[30] In particular, Milbank claims that Aquinas's focus on God as 'analogical' Being was transformed through Duns Scotus redeploying the notion of God as pure 'act' or 'will', and, together with Duns Scotus's emphasis on God's being metaphysically identical to human being, this implied that there is 'purely natural access' to knowledge of God and the world, and the exclusion of subjective participation by faith.[31]

Duns Scotus's view stems from bad theology and involves the entrenchment of secular reason. Although passages can be ostensibly cited from Aquinas in support of a position which divides faith from reason, and although he distinguishes

[28] T Campanella, *A Defense of Galileo* (University of Notre Dame Press, 1994) 55–56, 70.

[29] L Williams, 'Kant, Naturophilosophie and Scientific Method' in R Giere and R Westfall (eds), *Foundations of the Scientific Method: The Nineteenth Century* (Indiana University Press, 1973) 9–11.

[30] Milbank and Pickstock, *Truth in Aquinas*, above n 2, 17.

[31] ibid 22, 106–07.

between reason and faith, it is rather the case that faith and reason represent for Aquinas 'differing degrees of divine enlightenment'—they are intrinsically united and involved in the creature's participation in and understanding of the divine creation.[32] It is worthwhile briefly examining this misinterpretation of Aquinas to observe how it arose.

According to Aquinas, there are two types of truth: that which is 'accessible by human reason' and that which is 'above reason' and must be 'received by faith'.[33] Both are 'divinely revealed', since 'human reason is prone to error', and as such even those truths which are 'demonstrable by reason' may be 'held in faith'.[34] Importantly, the truth of reason is not 'opposed' to the truth of the Christian faith, for God himself is the 'source of all truth', and these truths do not contradict, for 'there is no error or falsity in truth'.[35] However, if one does not hold to Scripture, there is no longer any means of proving the articles of faith by reasoning, but only of answering objections against faith—'arguments from human reason cannot avail to prove what must be received on faith'.[36] In saying this, human reason may be used to prove those elements of Scripture which may be known by natural reason, for 'sacred doctrine makes use also of the authority of philosophers in those questions in which they were able to know the truth by natural reason'.[37]

Hence, Aquinas agrees that it is necessary to also accept by faith those things which may be proved by natural reason. This allows people to 'arrive more quickly at divine truth', so that the 'knowledge of God may be more general', and it is also for the sake of 'certitude', since 'human reason is very deficient'.[38] For example, God's existence can be demonstrated by reason, being understood 'through the things that are made'.[39] That is, God's existence may be perceived and demonstrated through the effects of him as the first cause. Aquinas goes on:

> The existence of God and other like truths about God which can be known by natural reason, are not articles of faith, but are preambles to the articles. For faith presupposes natural knowledge, even as grace presupposes nature … Nevertheless, there is nothing to prevent a man who cannot grasp a proof accepting, as a matter of faith, something which in itself is capable of being known and demonstrated.[40]

From this, it could seem that, in principle, though natural human reason is deficient and in some sense needs faith, it is also the case that truths can be naturally known through pure proof or demonstration.

[32] ibid 18–19.

[33] T Aquinas, 'Summa Contra Gentiles' in P Helm (ed), *Faith and Reason* (Oxford University Press, 1999) 106, 108.

[34] ibid.

[35] ibid 109–11.

[36] T Aquinas, *Summa Theologica* (William Benton, 1952) vol 1, 8.

[37] ibid.

[38] Aquinas, *Summa Theologica*, above n 36, vol 2, 393–94.

[39] ibid vol 1, 12.

[40] ibid.

Despite Aquinas apparently being anxious to combine reason and faith in a mutually beneficial way, it was his desire to affirm that truth could be independently known by both reason and faith which not only allowed the use of pure reason in science to become acceptable, but also allowed a fundamental divide to be made between reason and faith. Aquinas states that

> it was necessary for men's salvation that there should be a knowledge revealed by God, besides the philosophical sciences built upon human reason … because man is directed to God as to an end that surpasses the grasp of his reason.[41]

First, Aquinas appears to implicitly acknowledge that the philosophical sciences (which include the natural sciences) are built upon human reason, and he in particular seems to acknowledge that truths about God are discoverable by reason through the philosophical sciences. Adopting this view rendered acceptable the use of human reason alone, without faith, in the pursuit of truth in the natural sciences. Aquinas then appears to further distinguish between truths about God which human reason can discover through the philosophical sciences and the knowledge or truth revealed by God through faith, or 'sacred science obtained through revelation', which 'surpasses the grasp of … reason'.[42] Since these truths of faith cannot be accessed by natural reason, according to this interpretation, the unity of faith and reason is sundered and faith and reason begin to operate on separate planes.

(ii) The Laplace Transform(ation): Collapse of the Architect

The fact that Aquinas allegedly permitted truth to be demonstrated apart from faith allowed the possibility for faith and theology to be entirely excluded from scientific endeavour. This can be observed through Campanella advocating that truth may be discovered in the natural world purely by reason. Consequently, if a truth such as God's existence, or even a general knowledge of the natural world, can be demonstrated by human reason alone, it follows that the possibility remains for faith and theology to become entirely redundant and irrelevant. This possibility was subsequently actualised, particularly with the advent of Newtonian physics. For those Christians (such as Galileo, Kepler and Newton) who were scientists and embraced nature as governed by a series of invariable physical laws discoverable by reason, this demonstrated the power and omniscience of God, who willed and designed these laws. However, what they did not realise was that, by removing God as an active agent and relegating him to a deistic author of immutable and independent laws, they were inadvertently constructing the way for his complete expulsion from science.

This can be illustrated by a conversation said to have taken place between the then French Emperor, Napoleon Bonaparte, and the eighteenth/nineteenth-century

[41] ibid 3.
[42] ibid.

French mathematician Pierre Laplace. Napoleon asked Laplace about his apparent omission to mention the role of God in his deterministic physical theory, to which Laplace is said to have replied that he 'had no need of that hypothesis'.[43] Whether historically accurate or not, the prominence of that account indicates the rise of completely secular or non-theological accounts of the world.[44] Thus, allowing the assumption that it is possible for reason to discover truth about the world apart from faith effectively enabled faith and theology to be vanquished as explanations or considerations, resulting in the fundamental secularisation of science. Obviously this secularisation did not mean that theists could not also be scientists. The secularisation operated at a meta-conceptual level, where the use of reason separated from faith (secular reason) became the very basis of scientific enquiry.

One way this secularisation of science has been manifested is through the notion of methodological naturalism. Methodological naturalism argues that the goal of natural science is to explain contingent natural phenomena strictly in terms of other contingent natural phenomena. Explanations should therefore refer only to natural objects and events, and not to the personal actions and choices of divine agents. This notion of seeking explanations only within the natural order is to be contrasted with philosophical naturalism, which states that the natural world is all that exists and that there is no spiritual realm where God or other beings exist. Methodological naturalism does not assume the non-existence of God or any metaphysical reality, but it does resist ascribing metaphysical explanations for physical events, similar to the statement by Laplace. However, it goes further than this by contending that any scientific explanation must be a priori natural, and not supernatural. God, faith and theology are excluded from science by definition. Therefore, by initially viewing God as pure will and a sovereign architect, divorcing reason from revelation and allowing scientific discovery of divinely constructed immutable natural laws by reason alone, the way was made for the complete secularisation of science.

III. (No) Salvation by Faith Alone: How the Reformation Further Divided Faith and Reason

A. Reformation: God as Sovereign

However, it is not only secular reason that divides faith and reason. The Reformation, and in particular its theology of God as executing pure sovereign will (which

[43] Pierre Laplace, cited in G Stent, 'Epistemic Dualism of Mind and Body' (1998) 142 *Proceedings of the American Philosophical Society* 578, 583.

[44] S Meyer, 'The Return of the God Hypothesis' (1999) 11 *Journal of Interdisciplinary Studies* 1, 1.

results in salvation by faith alone and the authority of the Scriptures alone), provided further artillery for the divorce of faith and reason. The Reformation of the sixteenth century marks one of the great epochs in the history of Western civilisation. Its pioneer was Martin Luther, who published his 95 theses mainly in response to the Roman Catholic doctrine of indulgences, and one of its most prominent minds was John Calvin, who published and continually revised his magnum opus, *Institutes of the Christian Religion*.[45]

Reformation theology can be generally summarised into a series of *solae*, which is Latin for 'alone'. The first is that we are saved *sola fide*, or by faith alone. A person's reconciliation with God is based purely on that person's faith or trust in the divine offer of forgiveness through the life, death and resurrection of Christ. Knowledge of this is based on *sola scriptura*, or on the Scriptures alone. According to this teaching, there is no source of Christian truth apart from the Bible, and the Bible is the final authority for determining truth about God. From these follow *sola gratia* and *solus Christus*: that a person is saved purely by God's grace alone through the person and work of Christ alone. Finally, since a person contributes nothing to their salvation, the final result is *soli Deo gloria*—glory to God alone. In other words, God alone, by sovereign decree or the exercise of his incontrovertible will, arranged for people to be saved, and so it is God alone who gives the gift and receives glory. By examining the doctrines of faith alone and Scripture alone as articulated by Luther and Calvin under the assumption of God's sovereign decree, I will argue that they allowed the further separation of reason and faith.

As the foundation for all his theology, Luther held that the Scriptures were the supreme authority. All Christian doctrine was to be traced back to the Scriptures, and in the event of dispute between the patristic writings, papal authority or any other man-made proclamation, the Scriptures were to be the deciding factor. When asked to justify the authority of his teachings, Luther stated that 'unless I am convicted of error by the evidence of Scripture, or … by manifest reasoning I stand convicted by the Scriptures to which I have appealed … I cannot and will not recant anything'.[46] For Luther, it is the Scripture which authenticates and validates itself as the authority in all matters of Christian truth—all must submit to and obey it.[47] Luther also emphasises that we are 'saved by faith alone' in response to Scripture, trusting in Christ and his work. It cannot be 'seen or reasoned or conjured by human effort', but is something 'granted' by God as a matter of sovereign decree.[48]

Luther holds this faith to be in explicit contrast with human or secular reason, which is unacquainted with heavenly things. Indeed, he states that 'faith must believe against reason … and against its understanding which grasps and admits

[45] B Reardon, *Religious Thought in the Reformation* (Longman, 1981) 47, 164–65.
[46] Martin Luther, cited in H Hillerbrand, *The Protestant Reformation* (Walker and Company, 1968) 68.
[47] P Althaus, *The Theology of Martin Luther* (Fortress Press, 1966) 75.
[48] M Luther, 'Commentary on St Paul's Epistle to the Galatians' in Hillerbrand, above n 46, 102.

the validity only of that which is empirical'.[49] Luther further disparages reason, saying that 'she talks nothing but follies and absurdities, especially … on sacred subjects'; reason is 'perverse', 'foolish' and 'blind', for she seeks to 'measure divine things by the concepts of men'.[50] However, Luther implicitly distinguishes between this human or secular reason, which he rejects, and reason that is the servant of faith and based in faith, as well as operating with faith. Secular reason is a reason that is based in the immanent and only accepts the validity of the empirical or physical; it rejects faith and God at first instance.[51] So, for Luther, the use of this type of reason in the attempt to comprehend divine things is absurd. Conversely, discursive reasoning based in the acceptance of faith which is used to understand God's revelation in the Scripture is part of the process of knowing God.

Similarly, John Calvin affirms the authority of Scripture alone and salvation by faith alone. Calvin argues that since the Scripture is God's Word and God is the absolute Sovereign will, it is invested with inherent and ultimate authority.[52] Attacking those who claim that the authority of the Scripture is based in the authority of the church, Calvin scoffed at the notion that 'the eternal and inviolable truth of God could depend on the [relatively impotent] will of men'.[53] Instead, Scripture is self-authenticating, 'carrying its own evidence along with it'.[54] 'It does not submit to proofs and arguments, but judges them, as from the very mouth of God.'[55] So Scripture as the Word of God is the supreme authority and source of Christian truth, and Calvin concludes:

> Such, then, is a conviction which asks not for reasons; such, a knowledge which accords with the highest reason, namely, knowledge in which the mind rests more firmly and securely than in any reasons; such, in fine, the conviction which revelation from heaven alone can produce.[56]

Calvin defines this conviction, or faith, as the 'firm and sure knowledge of the divine favour towards us, founded on the truth of a free promise in Christ, and revealed to our minds, and sealed on our hearts, by the Holy Spirit'.[57] It is this faith alone which saves us, apart from works. This faith 'is higher than human understanding', for 'such is the proneness of our mind to vanity, that it can never adhere to the truth of God … without the illumination of the Spirit'.[58] The Spirit originates faith and gradually increases it, 'purifying the mind to give it a relish for divine truth'.[59] In contrast, reason or mere human discernment is 'defective and

[49] Althaus, above n 47, 57, fn 42.
[50] M Luther, 'The Bondage of the Will' in P Helm (ed), *Faith and Reason* (Oxford University Press, 1999) 140–41.
[51] Althaus, above n 47, 57, fn 42.
[52] J Calvin, *Institutes of the Christian Religion* (Hendrickson Publishers, 2008) 30–31.
[53] ibid.
[54] ibid 33–34.
[55] ibid.
[56] ibid 34.
[57] ibid 360.
[58] ibid 377.
[59] ibid.

lost', for 'neither the eye sees nor the mind comprehends'.[60] Hence, Calvin distinguishes human reason from faith, arguing that human reason is too corrupted by sin to attain the things of God. Instead, faith alone is required to comprehend the divine.

On the basis of God's sovereign will, Luther and Calvin proffer a framework which fundamentally isolates faith from human or secular reason. It is faith alone which saves, and faith alone which can attain to the knowledge of God. Although faith is in accordance with the highest reason found in the divine mind, the notion of a faith distinct from human reason allowed theology to be based on faith at the expense of reason, for human secular reason is rejected as blind and lost. As such, science is left free to appropriate this secular reason and completely reject faith. The doctrine of *sola scriptura* also contributed to this isolation of faith from reason by rejecting the Book of Nature as an authority, effectively forcing the operating process of science to be non-theological and reject faith, embracing reason without faith. Thus, through emphasis on God's sovereignty, faith alone and Scripture alone, the Reformation further contributed to the divorce of reason and faith by continuing to allow for a space devoid of faith. Not only this, but the almost dogmatic alienation of faith from reason in this theology indicates a type of violence in its structure of knowledge—a violence that was followed through in the reaction to the Reformation parallel to the development of the scientific discipline.

B. Counter-Reformation: Imperialising Knowledge

The Catholic response to the Reformation (known as the Counter-Reformation) was a period of spiritual revival for the Catholics, an opportunity for them to continue reform and to purify their church. It was also a period of doctrinal debate, in terms of both confronting Reformed theology and jurisdictional controversy over the disciplinary implications of practical reform. These debates culminated in the Council of Trent, where the official Catholic doctrine was settled and promulgated.[61]

However, as well as being remedial, this move was also repressive, for in response to the Reformers the church sought to militarily enforce the papal monopoly of doctrinal determination by declaration. While the Reformers emphasised the sovereignty of God's will and unique authority, the Catholics retained this idea but transformed it in terms of replacing the sovereignty of God with the imperialism of the papacy or the magisterium of the church. The attempt by Tridentine Catholicism to gain a monopoly on human thought also extended into philosophical inquiry, and most significantly the developing discipline of the natural sciences. The typically cited case of Galileo indicates that the church monopolised authority both to approve and to condemn. Although approving of scientific

[60] ibid. See, eg, 1 Corinthians 2:10–14; Matthew 11:25; Matthew 16:17; Romans 11:34; John 6:44–46.
[61] A Wright, *The Counter-Reformation* (Weidenfeld and Nicolson, 1982) 35.

experiment by Galileo (or anyone), they did condemn works of theory which contradicted Catholic doctrine, such as Copernican cosmology as opposed to the prevailing Aristotelian–Ptolemaic system. This control further extended to papal regulation of the materials contained and taught within the universities and the libraries.[62]

Intimately involved in the Catholic arrogation of authority and promotion of imperial rule was the continued divide of reason and faith, for the consequence of separating reason and faith

> was not benign, but instead itself encouraged, with and not against early modernity, a theocratic and hierocratic authoritarianism. For the more science and politics were confined to immanent and autonomous secular realms, then the more faith appealed to an arational positivity of authority invested with a right to rule, and sometimes to overrule, science and secular politics.[63]

In other words, the creation of an apparently autonomous secular realm of science and politics caused theocratic faith (now devoid of reason) to exert its authority over this secular realm through violence. This clash of authority between the secular and the various manifestations of the sacred was not merely institutional. In the previously mentioned events surrounding Galileo, for example, we see that the church sought to forcibly prevent Galileo from publishing scientific work it viewed as contradicting its teaching regarding the structure of the universe.[64] Far more severe than this, the clash between the Reformation and Tridentine Catholicism resulted in open warfare over the sixteenth and seventeenth centuries, sickening both the people and the rulers in Europe, killing thousands and displacing many others. MacCullough grimly concludes that the 'Reformation and Counter-Reformation thus shed much blood and shortened or ruined countless lives in the course of their warfare'.[65]

The Reformation and Counter-Reformation emphasised the absolute voluntaristic sovereignty of its authority, whether God or the Pope as the Vicar of Christ, and therefore solidified the divide of reason and faith. This was manifested in the attempt to increase the regulation and control of science and reason in the institutional context of the church, and featured the most undesirable characteristics of totalitarian dogmatism and a lack of charity. Ultimately, the particular focus on will and sovereignty in conjunction with the separation of reason and faith produced violence. The use of violence to regulate knowledge effectively meant that belief was coerced, rather than persuaded using reason.

Hence, violence exists in the institution of knowledge, particularly science, following from the Scotian emphasis on God as a pure sovereign will. For, as the early scientists advocated in accordance with Duns Scotus, we are in the image of

[62] ibid 85–87.
[63] Milbank and Pickstock, *Truth in Aquinas*, above n 2, 17.
[64] Blackwell, above n 9, 24–25.
[65] D MacCullough, *Reformation* (Penguin, 2003) 670–73.

God—and if we are in the image of God as absolute sovereignty and pure will, we too are characterised by will, unanchored from the good; and it is the clash of wills which produces antagonism. Present too in the ostensibly noble aim of learning more about God through discovery of the natural world constructed according to his sovereign decree is the imperialisation of knowledge, the dogmatic alienation of those with differing views. However, there is one more element central to this ontology, an element which reinscribes it as characterised by a distorted theology: the presupposition of a secular reason which eventually becomes a blind faith.

C. From (Pure) Reason to (Blind) Faith

The removal of reason from faith exacerbates the violence of knowledge and effectively renders faith 'blind', or without reason. The concept of reducing secular reason to blind faith can again be traced to a misinterpretation of Aquinas, who seems to distinguish between the science of natural reason and the science of sacred doctrine, while simultaneously implying that their respective processes are based on faith. He states that:

> Sacred doctrine is a science. We must bear in mind that there are two kinds of sciences. There are some which proceed from a principle known by the natural light of the intellect, such as arithmetic and geometry and the like. There are some which proceed from principles known by the light of a higher science. Thus the science of … music proceeds from principles established by arithmetic. And in this way sacred doctrine is a science, because it proceeds from principles established by the light of a higher science, namely, the science of God and the blessed. Hence, just as the musician accepts on authority the principles taught him by the mathematician, so sacred science believes the principles revealed to it by God … the principles of any science are either in themselves self-evident, or reducible to the knowledge of a higher science.[66]

Aquinas attempts to demonstrate that the process of the natural sciences and the process of sacred doctrine both rely on faith, for both are either self-evident or reducible to the knowledge of a higher science which is self-evident, and simply accepted on the basis of that authority. Nevertheless, on this interpretation the natural sciences and sacred doctrine remain distinct. This distinction provided the foundation for the eventual rejection of Christian theology in the sciences under the masquerade of operating with reason separated from faith. However, an interpretation which separates reason and faith while also understanding that reason and faith are in the above sense based on faith ultimately leads to a pure reason which reduces to irrational or blind faith. In other words, according to this (mis) interpretation, both matters of reason (science) and matters of faith (doctrine), though operating on different planes, are based in faith—but this becomes a blind faith, one without reason.

[66] Aquinas, *Summa Theologica*, above n 36, vol 1, 4.

IV. Uniting Faith and Reason to Restore True *Scientia*: The Participation Model

A. Illuminating Aquinas

The key to articulating a reason combined with faith is found through properly interpreting Aquinas. It was the movement of Duns Scotus to focus on God's will rather than his intellect, combined with the separation of reason and faith, which resulted in the loss of the idea of the understanding subject discovering the world through participation in the divine. Instead, in the face of a universal sovereignty and cosmic geometry, science is resigned to a cold, pure, 'mathematical' reason. This is a fundamental misunderstanding of Aquinas, a distorted theology centred about a pure will unanchored from the good, which consequently results in antagonism and imperialism, characterised by a blind faith. Based on the need to reinvigorate reason and pursue peace, this part proposes a different kind of theology through a 'proper' return to Aquinas—us as participating subjects, inquiring and understanding the diversity of Being, embracing the divine mystery. This allows the return of an authentic Christian faith and restores reason as true participation in the divine, which then leads to harmony rather than strife.

An initial aspect is the previously discussed interpretation that results in faith and reason beginning to operate on separate planes. An implication of this can be observed in Aquinas explicitly distinguishing between faith and the natural sciences. According to Aquinas, 'all science is derived by principles self-evident and therefore seen; and therefore all objects of science must be, in a fashion, seen … the object of faith is unseen … consequently faith and science are not about the same things'.[67] Science is derived by self-evident principles, where self-evidence means to be seen. Since God, the object of faith, is unseen, faith and science operate on different planes. This presents a problem in terms of my claim that faith and reason may operate on the same plane, in a united front. Aquinas recognises this and clarifies that theology is in fact a science 'because the articles of faith are self-evident to the faithful as revealed by God'.[68] Since the faithful have their reason purified by faith and see God, the truths of faith are self-evident to them as revealed by God. Hence, faith and science (or natural reason) are not mutually exclusive, but operate to sharpen and extend one another. Faith and reason must be combined for true knowledge (or 'science') to be apprehended. For, as Aquinas clearly states:

> To see the essence of God belongs to the created intellect by grace, and not by nature … it is impossible for any created intellect to see the essence of God by its own natural

[67] ibid vol 2, 383–84.
[68] ibid 384.

> power … to know self-subsistent being is natural to the divine intellect alone … for no creature is its own being but rather has participated being. Therefore the created intellect cannot see the essence of God unless God by his grace unites Himself to the created intellect, as an object made intelligible to it.[69]

Our human intellect and our human ability to discover truth are based purely in God's grace, his gift of participation in the divine being. We cannot see God by our own 'natural' power because to see God is exactly to participate in his being, which is a matter of grace rather than nature. So the grace of God giving Himself so that we can participate in His being makes Him intelligible to our human intellect. This participation amplifies our already existing (natural) rational powers to properly comprehend the things of God and His creation:

> Our intellect … because it is elevated above matter in its own nature, can be raised above its own nature to a higher level by grace … now this increase of the intellectual powers is called the illumination of the intellect … by this light the blessed are made 'deiform'—that is, like to God … hence the light of glory cannot be natural to a creature unless the creature has a divine nature, which is impossible. But by this light the rational creature is made deiform.[70]

Thus, by grace, which is the light of participation in God's nature, our intellect is illuminated to become 'deiform', or like God. By grace, we as rational creatures participate in the very divine nature of God.

This implies that, even though there is natural reason which can observe the material (what one might call 'science'), no 'pure scientific cognition is ever exercised by us without discursive mediation'—that is, without divine illumination through the *logos*.[71] It follows that Aquinas's entire treatment of truth (including what is observed in relation to the physical sciences) must be brought within his philosophical theology, for

> were one to attempt to comprehend a finite reality not as created, that is to say, not in relation to God, then no truth for Aquinas could ensue, since finite realities are of themselves nothing and only what is can be true.[72]

Our rational comprehension of physical reality, expressed as 'truth', is predicated on the fact that this reality is created by God and our understanding of it is on the basis of participating in what 'is': the divine being. By the same token, even as faith 'involves an intensification of participation in divine intellectual intuition', this can only be disclosed through 'acts of interpretation … as essential for faith as for reason'—which is the same 'discursive mediation' given through the *logos*, or reason.[73]

[69] Aquinas, *Summa Theologica*, above n 36, vol 1, 53–54.
[70] ibid 54–55.
[71] Milbank and Pickstock, *Truth in Aquinas*, above n 2, 19.
[72] ibid 20.
[73] ibid 21.

It follows that faith and reason are intrinsically united in Aquinas; indeed, one cannot have true knowledge without faith and reason working together, based fundamentally on participation in the divine. More specifically, in combining metaphysics with theology, Aquinas demonstrates that there is a kind of continuum where reason (metaphysics), empowered ultimately by faith, allows some limited and uncertain knowledge, while at the other end there is purely intuitive faith or revelation, which is absolutely certain and true. So reason and faith are united in producing truth, metaphysics cannot be separated from theology, and science (true knowledge of the physical world) cannot be attained except by acknowledging the physical as created by God, with the emphasis being on us as knowing subjects participating in the divine nature. As Aquinas receives from Anselm and Augustine, reason is faith seeking understanding, because for thought to begin it must trust and believe its first sight. Just as reason is at first faith, faith can only develop its insights rationally. Faith and reason can never be separated. Reason must have faith that it is correctly apprehending the divine, and faith needs reason to develop its primitive gaze into the transcendent.

B. Seeking a Science of Peace

This notion of faith and reason as partners in the process of participating in the divine being also allows a movement from 'science' as the systematic pursuit of natural or immanent knowledge towards science engaging in the quest of comprehending and replicating the divine nature of love and peace. True science does not merely seek its purpose and fulfilment in discovering the nature of physical reality, but also as ultimately reaching for higher things, beginning to better grasp the nature of divine reality through participation in the reality of ubiquitous creation. It is precisely this *telos* which reveals true science not just as the pursuit of knowledge (in the pure or abstract sense), but also as revealing the good through seeing God. As Aquinas argues:

> Hence the intellect which participates more of the light of glory will see God the more perfectly. And he will have a fuller participation of the light of glory who has more charity, because where there is the greater charity, there is the more desire, and desire in a certain way makes the one desiring apt and prepared to see the thing desired. Hence he who possesses the more charity will see God the more perfectly, and will be the more happy.[74]

The person who has more charity (as opposed to the 'secular' science of dominance) will see God the more perfectly and will increase one's desire to see God. This beautiful cycle of increasing charity, desire and knowledge of God opens

[74] Aquinas, *Summa Theologica*, above n 36, vol 1, 55.

the possibility for redeeming not only the scientific community, but the entire human community as characterised by interacting relationships. It points the way forward towards a proper knowledge of God by grace, the reanimation of reason through faith and an ontological community of peace through participation.

Returning to an authentic Christian theology in Aquinas allows one to focus on the intellect rather than the will, on peaceful participation rather than violent sovereignty. In particular, when we, as knowing subjects, participate in the divine nature, reason is strengthened and united to faith, and we pursue charity and the good. Within the divine (Trinitarian) nature, the Father is faith, the trust that exists between the divine persons and is granted to the faithful by participation, that they may know the Father. The Son is reason, the divine *logos* or Word, who was with God and is God, and made his dwelling among us, enlightening our natural rationality. And the Holy Spirit is love or charity, the binding force of the church community and the divine relationship, which elevates knowledge and belief, reason and faith. These are three, and yet one, so they are distinct but united. This unique formulation allows true ontological peace in science, the Trinitarian uniting of reason and faith through love.

So the invocation of the transcendent, Triune God (in which the divine persons love, trust and reason themselves) permits one to think of reason itself as unknown and yet real—that is, of an infinite reason in which we faintly participate by faith working through love. Through uniting faith and reason, and seeking Trinitarian theology to rein in the harmony of the objective universal of truth and the subjective particular of faith, trusting and participating in the divine reason revealed by God, both matter and reason are saved, and a foundation is provided for a true, certain science with an ontology of peace.

3

Deconstructing Derrida: Law, Spirit, *Logos*

I. The Postmodern and the Pagan

This chapter continues to articulate the way in which Christian theology may allow the possibility for harmoniously coexisting difference by specifically presenting itself as a genuinely postmodern theology (in the sense of rejecting the secular reason of modernity), existing as a metanarrative which is more desirable than the narrative of paganism or nihilism, yet one which is at least as electable. Centring upon an analysis of Jacques Derrida, the chapter argues that in his deconstruction there is a type of theological metanarrative with particular Christian elements. I focus on Derrida for two reasons. First, the work of Derrida aims to deconstruct the bastion of pure, objective rationality or reason characteristic of modernity. Second, he does this in a way which is similar to the work of Christian theology in the sense of rejecting a secularised reason through displaying its nihilistic end. Thus, in Derrida we find the tools necessary for articulating a postmodern Christian theology—the deconstruction of secular reason as producing a nihilistic violence of difference—which may then be appropriated to finalise the construction of a Postmodern Critical Christian (Augustinian) theology, or a theology which unites faith with reason and creates a space for the peaceful coexistence of difference.

Section I of the chapter briefly notes Derrida's philosophical background and context. It also proposes that Derrida's 'post-modern' deconstruction of reason is indispensable for the return of Christian theology, since the exposure of secular reason's end implies that the only way to save reason is through reinstating a Christian theology of peace. Section II considers Derrida's seemingly conflicting atheist and Jewish heritage, indicating the ways in which Derrida propounds a type of Christian theology. However, section III shows that this theology is distorted and contains specifically pagan elements, namely an ontology of violent difference associated with the destruction of reason. Section IV therefore acknowledges that the movement from violent paganism (the end of secular reason) to the equally electable Christian peace is the desirable one. Following Derrida but ultimately departing from him, section V argues for the need of a developed, genuinely postmodern theology: an authentic Christian theology which goes beyond a reason of pure rationality and allows for the harmonious existence of difference without the violence of pagan agonism and strife. Section VI briefly considers how the construction of this theology through the book so far will be critically deployed in relation to jurisprudence.

A. Derrida and the Text

For Derrida, all readings of a text are misinterpretation as well as interpretation because all terms are devoid of meaning except the meaning constructed for them. There is always more to the text that our interpretation fails to appropriate, and there is 'nothing outside the text' in the sense that the words do not refer to what they signify and there is no purely objective or neutral perspective: all meaning is in the text itself.[1] These claims stem from Ferdinand de Saussure, a linguist who was foundational for Derrida. Saussure argues that words as linguistic signs are arbitrary. For example, regarding a 'tree', there is nothing that connects the sign of a tree with any particular tree, or the concept of tree-ness. The signifier is the sound pattern or written form of the word, the signified refers to the concept itself, and the sign is the combination of the signifier and signified, so it follows that the signifier is arbitrary. The meaning is conferred by virtue of the difference between any one signifier and all other signifiers. In other words, tree is defined by what it is not, and as such, in language there are only differences.

Derrida proceeds from this point, claiming it follows that there are signifieds apart from signifiers, which he calls the transcendental signified (or master-signifiers, such as 'God', 'truth' or 'consciousness'). In reality, such things do not exist but are constructed through language—they are only defined by what they are not. Meaning is present only as the effect of linguistic difference. Here Derrida defines a new term, *differance*, which, following Saussure, is not an entity, but that which makes concepts possible in linguistic expression. No single element can be simply present or absent itself, for any element achieves meaning precisely by what it is not. Derrida consequently comes to two crucial conclusions: first, one should elevate the written word above the spoken word because the written word connotes absence or difference; and second, that all language refers only to other language, and it is incapable of referring to anything other than language.[2] Derrida thus uses Saussurean linguistics to argue that the presence of a philosophical concept is not pure or fully comprehensible, but is qualified by the construction of the concept through the things which are absent from it (differences). This *differance* indicates the conceptual instability in language which differs and defers.

[1] J Culler, *On Deconstruction: Theory and Criticism After Structuralism* (Routledge, 1983) 96–97.

[2] See J Derrida, 'Difference' in L Cahoone (ed), *From Modernism to Postmodernism: An Anthology* (Blackwell Publishing, 2003) 225–40.

The concept of deconstruction has been variously presented as a philosophical strategy or position and as a mode of reading texts. In particular, Derrida understands deconstruction to be the reversal of a textual hierarchy in which there is a violent hegemony of oppositions and ideas. To deconstruct a text is to expose and remove those philosophical assumptions and displace the prevailing system, privileging aspects previously dominated. This is one of the senses in which Derrida states that deconstruction is justice.[3] In the history of Western metaphysics, speech has been set over the written word and incorrectly privileged. However, deconstruction exposes the fact that speech depends upon the very qualities predicated of writing, and theories grounded in presence (speech) are ultimately inconsistent with themselves as their foundations are difference (absence). Conversely, the written word as containing absence is consistent.[4]

Hence, for Derrida, deconstruction breaks down traditional interpretations of texts, which may be nothing more than instrumental use of power to manipulate the community. The purpose of deconstruction is to expose the superfluous meaning attributed to texts and demonstrate the way in which the text fails to communicate what some might think it communicates. Although it might be concluded from this that Derrida is merely advocating a relativistic nihilism, it is important to note that deconstruction is not an abandonment of philosophy, but alerts reason and philosophy to its own limitations and latent motives, contingent metanarratives and ideological oppressions. Deconstruction does not reject reason as a groundless will to power or nihilistic rhetoric, but continues to question the reasons of reason and the role of epistemological institutions.[5] For example, Derrida does not deny that truths are needed, but emphasises truth in terms of required vigilance to reverse the persecution of dissidents. Deconstruction shows how the other is inevitably installed in the self, and that there is a proliferation of meanings, and meanings of meanings, so that no one meaning or metanarrative should dominate another.

B. The Necessity of Postmodernism for Theology

In this regard, postmodernity can mean 'a philosophy of alterity, an incredulity towards metanarratives' which seek to violently dominate.[6] It is 'expressing the self without limitation, without closure', with a focus on the Other (as opposed to the self).[7] 'It is perhaps by definition, indefinable', and there are 'some tensions, if not

[3] Culler, above n 1, 85–86.

[4] ibid 108–09.

[5] R Warrington et al, *Postmodern Jurisprudence: The Law of Texts in the Texts of Law* (Routledge, 1991) 11.

[6] J Thacker, *Postmodernism and the Ethics of Theological Knowledge* (Ashgate, 2007) 5.

[7] ibid 6.

outright contradictions, contained within', because there is no established canon of postmodern thought.[8] Such a canon would tend to reinscribe a dominant paradigm of thinking and marginalise the 'Other' differing views.

As pure reason is turned against itself through deconstruction and it is found that there is apparently no universal foundation for reason, the question may legitimately be asked whether there is anything at all. It is the nihilistic gesture of this question which ultimately leads to a pagan postmodernism, for if there really is a metaphysical nothing then there is only an infinity of warring perspectives in the void. If we concede that deconstruction tends to expose this nihilistic and violent limit of pure secular reason, it follows that postmodernism is a necessary step in returning us to theology and a more fundamental truth.

In particular, deconstruction exposes the fact that 'modernist pure atheism' actually 'echoes theology by beginning with an unadulterated nothingness', in the sense that 'reality is derived in an ordered series from pure nullity (or pure divine simplicity)', in such a way that 'all of reality can be logically situated with respect to this nothing'.[9] Similarly, 'entirely rational metaphysical theology', without faith, always 'proves to be exercising some arbitrary subjective preference'.[10] Milbank argues that this pagan, nihilistic type of postmodern thought actually represents a 'heightened form of rational discourse', or the end of secular reason.[11] A 'legitimate postmodern critique of negative dialectics as dogmatically metaphysical' therefore points the way to resolution by 'newly legitimating a belief in transcendence'.[12] In other words, a postmodern critique of the true lack of foundation undergirding a purely rationalist metaphysics (whether theological or atheological) exposes the fact that at its core is really a nihilistic violence—a nothingness which operates through coercion and the force of an arbitrary preference. This, in turn, opens reason to a theological critique, and an alternative Christian metaphysics based in faith and divine peace.

There seems to be some similarity here between the rationale of deconstruction and the pursuit of Christian theology for, just as deconstruction proclaims the 'end of modernity', which 'means the end of a single system of truth based on universal reason, which tells us what reality is like', so theology 'no longer has to measure up to accepted secular standards of scientific truth or normative rationality'.[13] However, in the extreme relativist or crude nihilist versions of postmodernity, 'there are infinitely many possible versions of truth, inseparable from particular

[8] ibid 5.

[9] J Milbank, 'The Double Glory, Or Paradox versus Dialectics: On Not Quite Agreeing with Slavoj Žižek' in C Davis (ed), *The Monstrosity of Christ: Paradox or Dialectic?* (MIT Press, 2009) 158–59.

[10] ibid.

[11] J Milbank, *The Future of Love: Essays in Political Theology* (Cascade Books, 2009) 156.

[12] ibid.

[13] J Milbank, 'Postmodern Critical Augustinianism: A Short *Summa* in Forty-Two Responses to Unasked Questions' in G Ward (ed), *The Postmodern God: A Theological Reader* (Blackwell Publishers, 1997) 265.

narratives'.[14] This kind is really about a 'thoroughgoing perspectival historicism', and it seems to follow that

> if Christianity is just one of many possible perspectives, then why believe any of them? Is not each perspective a strategy of power, every discourse but a means to assert that discourse? [This] Postmodernism seems to imply nihilism, albeit of a 'positive' kind, embracing contingency and arbitrariness as the real natural good.[15]

Thacker indicts such a mode of thinking as pagan postmodernity, because it is a fractured multiplicity in conflict, and only a violently imposed metanarrative can resolve it.[16] This is where Christian theology comes to the fore. By faith (with reason), Christianity can propose its own metanarrative as one option among many, yet as the most desirable one, since it can instantiate peace—the harmonious ordering of difference, rather than the violent striving between differences. Here also we can make an important distinction: there is a pagan postmodernism which, having rejected pure reason, is left with nothing but nihilistic struggle between equally competing perspectives. However, there is also a Postmodern Critical Augustinianism which rejects a pure secularised reason, yet by faith proposes Christian theology as the desirable metanarrative, and claims to give peace. Derrida articulates some of these valuable elements of Christian theology, but also seems to mix it with the pagan idea of violent difference. Seeking the justice Derrida too desires, I therefore move to untangle the pagan from the Christian, and pursue with Derrida a metanarrative which is not dominant or violent—one which rejects the hegemony of pure reason and trusts in a Christianity of peace.

II. Different Perspectives: The Metanarratives of Jacques Derrida

A. The Atheist Derrida

It is possible to read the trace pagan elements in Derrida's deconstruction as symptomatic of the competing metanarratives which constitute his personal background, views and work. It may at first seem problematic to label Derrida in this way, particularly given the postmodern distaste for labels and categories. The point is that Derrida's thought possesses characteristics of atheism, paganism, Judaism and Christianity, paradoxically passing through them all yet not reducible to any. The labels are not intended to be categorical, but merely to denote ideas which have their culmination in a postmodern Christian theology—a paradoxical system of unity in difference. This is indispensable for the development of

14 ibid.

15 ibid 266–67.

16 Thacker, above n 6, 27–35.

a Postmodern Critical Augustinianism which argues for a fundamental unity in difference through the law of love.

For example, it seems that he fundamentally rejects Western metaphysics, and in particular Christian theology. Derrida himself states that he 'quite rightly passes for an atheist'.[17] Furthermore, he rejects the notion of logocentrism as the self-presentation or presence of meaning in writing, and similarly as 'the belief that the first and last things are the Logos, the Word [of God], the Divine Mind, the infinite understanding of God ...'[18] He denounces the concept of writing containing the fullness of metaphysical presence as 'vulgar', thus conflating and rejecting metaphysics and a Christian theology of divine presence in the Word.[19] This atheist Derrida appears to be against the Being of God and his metaphysical presence in writing (such as Scripture or Christ as the divine Word).

B. The Jewish Derrida

(i) Law and Book

However, Derrida's deconstruction and emphasis on the law and the book (or text) is also due to his Jewish genealogy of life and thought. For example, Ofrat contends that Derrida's Jewish upbringing and culture and his Jewish identity are the ultimate source of his writings. Derrida's philosophy is the corroboration of the fragments of Jewish identity from which it grew, and Judaism or Judeo-centrism may be there 'as essence, logocentric substance, primary source of truth' in this philosophy.[20] In addition, Bass notes that Derrida tends to adopt Hegel, who articulates the notion of the unhappy consciousness which is always divided against itself. Its paradigmatic figure is Abraham, 'the prototype of the "Jewish" consciousness for which there is an intrinsic conflict between God and nature'.[21] This theme runs throughout Derrida's work, where he opposes the Greek 'happy' (at one with nature) with the Hebraic 'unhappy' consciousness.[22] The inherited opposition is programmed by a logic of presence which demands a resolution to the conflict, and Derrida pushes it to the limit where it becomes irreducible. Derrida's interrogation of the Jewish divided consciousness is thus particularly poignant as the experience of the people of the Book.

[17] Jacques Derrida, cited in J Caputo, 'Adieu-sans Dieu: Derrida and Levinas' in J Bloechl (ed), *The Face of the Other and the Trace of God: Essays on the Philosophy of Emmanuel Levinas* (Fordham University Press, 2000) 278.

[18] G Spivak, 'Translator's Preface' in J Derrida, *Of Grammatology* (Johns Hopkins University Press, 1976) lxviii; B Johnson, 'Translator's Introduction' in J Derrida, *Dissemination* (University of Chicago Press, 1981) ix.

[19] M Dumitrescu, 'Derrida vs Saussere: Two Ways of Looking at the Linguistic Sign' (2007) 3 *Cultural and Literary Studies* 118, 119.

[20] G Ofrat, *The Jewish Derrida* (Syracuse University Press, 2001) 2–3.

[21] A Bass, 'Translator's Introduction' in J Derrida, *Writing and Difference* (Routledge, 1978) xix–xx.

[22] ibid.

Moreover, Derrida's notion of deconstruction as justice carries in its roots the Jewish conception of divine violence as justice articulated by Walter Benjamin.[23] In 'Force of Law', Derrida specifically examines a paper by Benjamin which distinguishes between the mythic or founding violence of law and the divine or annihilating and destructive violence of law.[24] According to Benjamin, mythical violence is a manifestation of the (pagan) gods because God opposes myth. But divine violence is the antithesis of mythical violence and confronts it. Mythical violence brings guilt and retribution, while divine violence expiates, the former threatens and the latter strikes, the former is bloody while the latter is lethal but bloodless. The pagan legend of Niobe (mythical violence) may consequently be confronted with God's judgment on the company of Korah: 'it strikes them … and does not stop short of annihilation. But in annihilating it also expiates, and a deep connection between lack of bloodshed and the expiatory character of this violence is unmistakeable.'[25]

Hence, 'mythical violence is bloody power over mere life for its own sake, divine violence pure power over all life for the sake of the living. The first demands sacrifice, the second accepts it.'[26] Benjamin's mythical violence appears to be fundamentally pagan. Similarly, divine violence, despite its claim to be divine, always inaugurates a new law with violence. In other words, it replaces violence with violence. Consequently, Derrida has received some (pagan) elements of this cycle of violence into his concept of deconstruction being justice.

(ii) Justice, Spirit and Revelation

In leading up to his famous phrase 'deconstruction is justice', Derrida argues that the origin or foundation of the law is mystical in the sense that it is essentially neither legal nor non-legal, but a positing by force—and that laws maintain their authority not because they are just, but simply because they are laws. This normative proposition is therefore essentially deconstructible, and it is this deconstructible nature of law that ensures the possibility of deconstruction itself.[27] For Derrida, it follows that 'justice in itself, if such a thing exists, outside or beyond law, is not deconstructible. No more than deconstruction itself, if such a thing exists. Deconstruction is justice.'[28]

Derrida's deconstruction may actually have more in common with Christianity than it appears. In a practical sense, Derrida's process of deconstruction is also justice because (like Christianity) it essentially involves exposing and reversing

[23] A Hirvonen, 'Promising Justice: Derrida with Jewish Jurisprudence' (2001) 12 *Law and Critique* 159, 159–60.

[24] J Derrida, 'Force of Law: "The Mystical Foundation of Authority"', paper presented on Deconstruction and the Possibility of Justice, Cardozo Law School (1989) 31.

[25] W Benjamin, 'Critique of Violence' in M Steger and N Lind (eds), *Violence and its Alternatives: An Interdisciplinary Reader* (St Martin's Press, 1999) 66–67.

[26] ibid 68.

[27] See J Derrida, 'Force of Law: The Mystical Foundation of Authority' in M Davies, *Asking the Law Question: The Dissolution of Legal Theory* (Law Book Company, 2002) 349–53.

[28] Derrida, ibid, 14–15.

the hierarchical and violent assumptions of Enlightenment reasoning and argumentation, usually in the context of removing binary oppositions and demonstrating the dependence of binaries on each other. Deconstruction, then, does not eradicate established realities, but generates alternative understandings of dominant views, as well as enabling transformation through detailed and particular questioning and reconstruction.[29]

This can be observed in Derrida's explicit discussions of deconstruction, justice and law. 'Justice is an experience of the impossible … law is the element of calculation … but justice is incalculable, it requires us to calculate with the incalculable; and aporetic experiences are the experiences, as improbable as they are necessary, of justice.'[30] Justice is 'infinite, incalculable, rebellious to rule and foreign to symmetry, heterogeneous and heterotropic', while law is 'stablizable[*sic*] or statutory, calculable, a system of regulated and coded prescriptions'.[31] Justice must go through 'the ordeal of the undecidable', and therefore requires 'fresh judgment' which is

> both regulated and without regulation: it must conserve the law and also destroy it or suspend it enough to have to reinvent it in each case, remystify it, at least reinvent it in the reaffirmation and the new and free confirmation of its principle.[32]

Hence, for Derrida, at the moment of justice there is a paradoxical or aporetic place of undecidability where a decision must be made. This opens the space for a new judgment that in some novel way reinvents law. There is, in other words, a *revelatory* moment, where a renewed legal principle emerges or is revealed by virtue of interpretation, the outcome of deconstruction and justice. It is an intrinsically creative process, a process of redemption whereby the old has gone and the new has come. In the arrival of this particularly Pauline space there exists an incalculable spirit of decision, unbound by rules and outside of statutory categories, yet also within the letter or regulated system of law itself. So it may be that Derridean deconstruction is redeemable as a fundamentally Christian endeavour.

C. The Christian Derrida?

(i) A Theological Language

We can also see Derrida the Christian in his explicit employment of theological language, and he even implicitly or inadvertently utilises theological concepts.

[29] See M Davies, *Delimiting the Law: Postmodernism and the Politics of Law* (Pluto Press, 1996) 341–48.

[30] Derrida, 'Force of Law', above n 27, 16.

[31] ibid 22.

[32] ibid 23–24.

This is because deconstruction also renders God and theology possible as discourses.[33] Indeed, when articulating the limits and subjectivity of language and representation in *Writing and Difference*, Derrida's words are replete with theological references, such as Bible, the one true established text of the earth (but not referring to the Christian Bible), God (as its author), Father and *logos*.[34]

Derrida's emphasis on this text of the earth is understood against the background of his theory of language. He argues that all language necessarily refers to other language—it does not refer to some external reality independent of language. The meaning of a word is defined by other words which have always been defined by other words and previous structures. Hence, there is an infinite regress of language having been defined by always-existing prior structures, and so it is impossible to determine the creation of language as an 'event', as such. This nonsynthetic alternation between structure and event is what Derrida terms *differance*. In this linguistic system, there are only differences and absence, no present external referent. So for Derrida in this sense the world could be viewed as a text. The notion of the world as a text has a certain affinity with Christianity.[35] Viewing the world in this way is an entirely Christian approach, for God has revealed himself in creation through the 'book' of Scripture and the 'book' of nature, encapsulating all of reality in the text. The fact that there is no creative event for language may also allude to the divine *logos*, Christ, as eternal and uncreated.

Another parallel element of Christianity and Derrida's deconstruction is its rejection of the purely rational metaphysics of the Western enlightenment. Litowitz observes that Derrida deconstructs 'all asserted metaphysical foundations as logocentric fictions'.[36] Hence, Derrida's deconstruction is anti-foundationalist, 'a sustained argument against the possibility of anything pure and simple which can serve as the foundation for the meaning of signs'.[37] It strikes at the very idea of a transcendental phenomenology or a transcendental signified. What Derrida rejects is the notion that experience can be pure in the sense that it can be fully understood as it is found in our private mental life, without reference to transient circumstances or actual empirical objects. Similarly, John Milbank argues that the strength of Christian theology lies in its independence from a modern secular reason, and this Christian view may be affirmed all the more strongly if its 'purely rational demonstrability is denied' and it is believed through faith, for only then can it be 'undergirded by belief in a transcendent, creator God'.[38]

[33] K Hart, 'Jacques Derrida' in Ward, above n 13, 163–64.

[34] See, eg, Derrida, *Writing and Difference*, above n 21, 9–11.

[35] See, eg, J Caputo, *The Prayers and Tears of Jacques Derrida: Religion Without Religion* (Indiana University Press, 1997). In particular, the 'world as a text' does not just mean relativistic nihilism, but an openness to the Other.

[36] D Litowitz, *Postmodern Philosophy and Law* (University Press of Kansas, 1997) 107–08.

[37] N Garver, 'Preface' in J Derrida, *Speech and Phenomenon* (Northwestern University Press, 1973) xxii.

[38] Milbank, 'Double Glory', above n 9, 175–76.

(ii) The Three Become One: Derrida's Trinity

Even more significantly, Derrida's broader concepts are distinctly comparable to central tenets of Christian theology. Consider Derrida's own definition of *differance* in *Dissemination*:

> Differance differs from itself. On the one hand, it indicates difference as distinction, inequality, or discernability; on the other, it expresses the interposition of delay, the interval of a spacing and temporalisation that puts off until later what is presently denied, the possible that is presently impossible … in the one case to differ signifies non-identity; in the other case it signifies the order of the same.[39]

Thus, *differance* is both difference and sameness, to differ and to defer, a 'sameness which is not identical'.[40] *Differance* as simultaneously difference and sameness, or unity and diversity, carries the import of the Christian Trinity, or Tri-unity. For in the Trinitarian nature, God is one, the unity and uniquely divine being or essence. However, this one God also exists in diversity through three divine persons: Father, Son and Holy Spirit. In addition, according to Derrida, 'to differ is to temporalise, to resort, consciously or unconsciously, to the temporal … mediation of a detour that suspends the accomplishment or fulfilment of desire or will'.[41] This difference component of *differance* may be observed in the Trinitarian relationship through the Incarnation of Christ, where the transcendent, eternal God temporalises in Christ and mediates between humans and God. However, in this process Christ 'detours' from his presence in heaven and suspends his own will for the sake of dying on the cross to save humanity from their sin, since he says to the Father 'not as I will, but as you will'.[42]

This may be further demonstrated through an analysis of his concepts of presence and absence, as well as trace. According to Derrida, a sign is put in place of the thing itself, the present thing. Indeed,

> signs represent the present in its absence … the sign would thus be a deferred presence. This classical determination presupposes that the sign (which defers presence) is conceivable only on the basis of the presence that it defers and in view of the deferred presence one intends to reappropriate.[43]

This sign is both secondary, in the sense that it is second in order after an original and lost presence, and provisional with respect to this final and missing presence. Consequently, one can see Christ as the sign of Trinitarian presence, Christ as the divine presence on earth representing the Trinity in their absence from earth. In addition, the Incarnation is only conceivable on the basis of the deferred presence of the Trinity, a final heavenly presence provisionally represented by Christ on earth which will be reappropriated by believers in heaven. However, one may well

[39] Derrida, *Dissemination*, above n 18, 129.
[40] ibid.
[41] ibid 136.
[42] Matthew 26:39.
[43] Derrida, *Dissemination*, above n 18, 138.

question the designation of Christ as 'secondary', for 'in Him all the fullness of God was pleased to dwell'.[44] Derrida notes that if one does question this secondary and provisional character of the sign, a particular consequence follows: 'we question the authority of presence or its simple symmetrical contrary, absence or lack. We thus interrogate the limit that has always constrained us ... to form the sense of being in general as presence or absence.'[45] Similarly, to question Christ's character as secondary and provisional, or to affirm Him as the God-man, implies that He is both present and absent, for he died and was resurrected, dwelling in heaven and in believer's hearts.[46]

Regarding trace, Derrida states that 'the trace is not a presence but rather the simulacrum of a presence that dislocates, displaces, and refers beyond itself'.[47] What is perceptible and imperceptible about the trace of difference is that 'it is lost in an irretrievable invisibility, and yet even its loss is covered, preserved, regarded and retarded. This happens in a text, in the form of presence.'[48] Hence Derrida's trace is the mark of the absence of a presence, an always already absent present. This can be compared to the work of the Holy Spirit, who refers beyond Himself to Christ, for Christ says 'He will glorify me, for He will take what is mine and declare it to you'.[49] In addition, the Holy Spirit covers the loss of the presence of Christ by being present in the believer, and marks the absence of Christ by his presence.[50] Bringing the concepts together, the structure of presence is thus constituted by difference and deferment, and through trace indicates the suspended status of the subject as neither absent nor present. Therefore, there seems to be a Christian dimension to Derrida's deconstruction, one which indicates some of the commonality of goal and method.

III. The Pagan Differ(a)nce

There is also a strong pagan dimension to Derrida's ontology. For example, Derrida claims that '*differance* is not, does not exist, has no being-present' and consequently has no existence or essence. He emphasises that '*differance* is not theological ... (and is) irreducible to every ontological or theological ... appropriation'.[51] Yet, he equivocates and concedes that '*differance* remains a metaphysical name'.[52] So there is some conflict or strife within Derrida, where he expresses his discourse in terms

[44] Colossians 1:19.
[45] Derrida, *Dissemination*, above n 18, 138–39.
[46] Acts 1:11; Ephesians 3:17.
[47] Derrida, *Dissemination*, above n 18, 156.
[48] ibid 157.
[49] John 16:14.
[50] John 16:7.
[51] Derrida, *Dissemination*, above n 18, 134.
[52] ibid 158.

of theological concepts and admits some aspect of metaphysics while simultaneously insisting that his deconstruction is not theological. Moreover, the fact that *differance* is endless difference and deferring calls to mind the endless difference and warfare of the ancient pagans, particularly the continual flux and becoming advocated by Heraclitus in pre-Socratic Greek philosophy.

Heraclitus fundamentally argues that 'everything moves on and nothing is at rest'.[53] Jantzen proceeds to explain that 'it is evident from his fragments that he does not consider the continuous reciprocal exchange of elements to be a matter of smooth transition but of opposition and war'.[54] Indeed, Heraclitus states that 'it is necessary to understand that war is universal and justice is strife, and that all things take place in accordance with strife and necessity'.[55] He thus 'assimilates the transformation of the elemental opposites with war and conflict between people; violence is a fundamental principle of the universe'.[56] In this sense, the ancient pagan philosophy presents a foundational ontology of violence through the agonism of endless difference.

Other pagan similarities in Derrida's work can initially be observed in his analysis of Western theatre, where he argues that it is inherently cruel, and describes it as declining, decadent and negative, for it is made to do that for which it is not made. The theatre destroys representation and imitation. Furthermore, it expels God, for the theatrical practice of cruelty inhabits and produces a non-theological space. The stage is theological when it is dominated by speech or representation, a *logos* which governs from a distance in the sense that an objectively removed author constructs the performance to represent their own thoughts. With the removal of the objective author and their intent, representation and the spoken word, the *logos*, comes the violence and non-theological status of theatre.[57]

Derrida further notes in *Writing and Difference* that at the origin of cruelty is a 'murder', and 'firstly a parricide'—the murder of the 'Father of the word', the 'author-God', with the following murder of speech, text and representation.[58] If we understand the murder of the Father of the word and the author-God as a rejection of theology, we see not only that Derrida invokes the violence of murder, but that this violence explicitly rejects and destroys God, theology and the word (*logos*) as representation while simultaneously adopting theological language such as *logos* and the parricide of the author-God to describe it. In other words, Derrida's deconstruction associates the rejection of theology (or the invention of the secular realm) with violence while maintaining a distorted theological account of that rejection. This implies the account can be theologically critiqued. Furthermore, in his usage of the term *differance*, Derrida links it with wordplay on totalitarianism

[53] Heraclitus, cited in G Jantzen, *Foundations of Violence* (Routledge, 2004) 156.
[54] Jantzen, ibid, 157.
[55] Heraclitus, cited in Jantzen, ibid, 157.
[56] Jantzen, ibid, 157.
[57] Derrida, *Writing and Difference*, above n 21, 233–35.
[58] ibid 239.

and solicitation. He views structuralism as a form of philosophical totalitarianism, and submits this violent structural project to the counterviolence of 'solicitation', which derives etymologically from the latin word meaning 'to shake'.[59] As such, Derrida's identification of violence is (not) resolved by violence, for his deconstruction rejects Christian theology.

Derrida further argues in *Acts of Literature* that the dispossession of presence in language is a law of language, and operates as a 'power of death in living speech' because it 'threatens the possibility of the spoken word' and 'dislocates the subject'—in other words, it is a 'violence done to the natural destiny of language'.[60] It follows that there is no transcendental signified, no outside the text in the sense that nothing in reality escapes the features of textuality. Context is not determined by a transcendental signified such as God, so context has no discernible boundary. This is what motivates deconstruction. Any talk of God or theology is shaken and blocked by difference, for the sign is essentially theological, and difference rejects the sign. Thus, since the sign is theological and difference rejects the sign in conjunction with the transcendental signified (of which God is the paradigm), it follows that theology is rejected from deconstruction (and this secularist conclusion makes sense in light of Derrida the atheist). In addition, since the features of textuality are inherently violent (ie writing) and nothing in reality escapes these features, this implies that Derrida articulates a fundamental ontology of violence.

This ontology of violence in the deconstructive process may be seen in Derrida's deconstruction of Levinas, where Derrida argues that Levinas's contention that we must break with Parmenides signifies a parricide, the 'murder of the Greek father who is dominating us', the 'killing of a speech'.[61] Language 'cannot lend itself to inclusion in or modification by the object without violence'—language is limited.[62] Language can only infinitely tend towards justice by acknowledging and practising the violence within it, as violence against violence, or an economy of violence. Violence did not exist before the possibility of speech, the *logos*—on this view, it is transcendental or ontological.[63] The finite totality is inherently violent, unlike the infinite totality, and according to Derrida totality is a theological notion.[64] Juxtaposing these characterisations is Derrida's ultimate failure to engage with and resolve the 'contestation, antagonism, struggle, conflict, and dissension' of politics.[65]

Derrida's inadvertently violent engagement due to traces of paganism appears even more fundamental when one considers his further statements on the violence of writing. According to Derrida in *Of Grammatology*, writing is the dissimulation

[59] Bass, above n 21, xvi.
[60] J Derrida, *Acts of Literature* (Routledge, 1992) 78, 82.
[61] Derrida, *Writing and Difference*, above n 21, 89.
[62] ibid 95.
[63] ibid 117, 125.
[64] ibid 141.
[65] S Critchley, *The Ethics of Deconstruction* (Blackwell, 1992) 199–200.

of the natural, primary and immediate presence of sense to the soul within the *logos*, and its violence befalls the soul as unconsciousness. Indeed, 'metaphysics has constituted an exemplary defense against the threat of writing'.[66] Writing is aggressive, a disease, the defeat and fall of innocent language, and consists of relations of power and violence.[67] In the final analysis, 'writing cannot be thought of outside the horizon of intersubjective violence'.[68] Derrida therefore states in *Margins of Philosophy* that philosophical language is a fund of forced metaphors, and this is how philosophy has traditionally understood meaning and reference in language—the twisting return of the already there of a meaning and production, but also as revelation or unveiling, as truth. As such, forced metaphors must be correct and natural.[69]

A written sign carries with it a force of breaking with its context, and this force of breaking is inherent in the very structure of the written. The force of rupture is due to the spacing which constitutes the written sign, which separates it from other elements of the internal contextual chain and from all the forms of a present referent, whether objective or subjective.[70] Once again, the ontological relationship between violence and pagan mythology emerges, with the notion of a forced metaphor combined with the theological language of 'revelation'. More importantly, however, Derrida's indictment of writing as inherently violent and the fact that he advocates the privileging of writing over speech puts him in the unenviable position of appearing to advocate and participate in the very violence he is insightfully identifying.

Derrida himself testifies that deconstruction does not consist of removing violence from writing and reversing this process, but aims to show why the violence of writing does not befall an 'innocent' language—there is an originary violence of writing because 'language is first writing', and it is 'mythological and usurpatory'.[71] According to Derrida, then, 'deconstruction is the overturning and displacement of a conceptual order which is an organisation of forces that has constituted the remainder of the dominant force which organised the logocentric hierarchy'.[72] Critchley notes that deconstruction is characterised by the traversal of the space between commentary and interpretation, which he calls a 'violation and transgression'.[73] Thus, what we ultimately see is that Derrida's deconstruction, despite its positive Christian elements and the way in which it incisively exposes the limits and end of secularised reason, also contains pagan elements which violently and transgressively expose originary force, mythology and usurpation—unfortunately assuming a primordial violence and promoting an ontology of violence.

[66] Derrida, *Of Grammatology*, above n 18, 101.
[67] ibid 106.
[68] ibid 127.
[69] J Derrida, *Margins of Philosophy* (University of Chicago Press, 1982) 257.
[70] ibid 317.
[71] Derrida, *Of Grammatology*, above n 18, 37.
[72] Derrida, *Margins of Philosophy*, above n 69, 329–30.
[73] Critchley, above n 65, 129.

Indeed, Milbank notes that there is a 'hidden connection between premodern pagan dualism and postmodern dualism', for the latter's 'self-proclaimed paganism is a kind of deconstructed paganism' since the 'real pagans were always hoping to subordinate that admitted conflictual diversity of the gods to a harmonious order', and the open celebration of violence was latent.[74] Christianity, which admits difference and is therefore not dualistic, is already beyond the reach of Derridean deconstruction. Though there is this pagan emphasis on regulating difference through violence in Derrida's work, let us not throw out the baby with the bathwater: Derrida's deconstruction also has much in common with Christianity in the way that it foregrounds an ontology of difference and deconstructs the pure reason which is the secular foundation for a violent modernity.

Derrida's work is therefore indispensable for articulating the end of secular reason and an ontology which incorporates difference. The question then is how to remove the pagan emphasis on violent difference while maintaining the perceptively critical elements which undermine secular reason and finally arrive at a Christian theology beyond secular reason, one which peacefully admits difference in the community. In other words, I propose now to move from a nihilistic, pagan postmodernity of violence to a Postmodern Critical Augustinianism of peace.

IV. Moving Perspectives: From Secular Reason to Christian Theology

Milbank acknowledges that religions may 'conceal historical contingency and human invention', but this is 'just as true of modern secular systems of thought', which are unable to admit their own choice of values with respect to the 'conjunction of an empty freedom with instrumentalist reason'.[75] Such an admission requires on the part of secular thought a nihilistic courage (for example, Nietzsche and the original movement to postmodernism from modernity). However, it is 'much easier for religions to admit this', for they 'admit that they are not fully explicable but shrouded in mystery and the requirements of faith'.[76] 'Religion is more forthright regarding the inexplicable character of cultural existence than science dares to be.'[77] Indeed, 'Nietzsche himself advocated the inevitability of myths, and the need for a mythology embodying the nihilistic realisation that we always construct on mythical truth'.[78] 'Every secular positivism is therefore also revealed to be a positivist theology, and it is impossible to explain theology either scientifically or humanistically' (in other words, non-theologically).[79]

[74] Milbank, 'Postmodern Critical Augustinianism', above n 13, 270.
[75] J Milbank, *Theology and Social Theory: Beyond Secular Reason* (Blackwell, 1990) 140.
[76] ibid.
[77] ibid.
[78] ibid.
[79] ibid 143–44.

Indeed, the faith of humanism has become a substitute for transcendent faith, and the associated genealogies reveal a world inevitably dominated by violent difference, yet without a solid ground in historicism. It presents this knowledge as more than mere perspective, but the question is raised whether such a claim can be sustained without reference to metaphysics. If it cannot, this differential ontology is but one more mythos, and it follows that the realisation that discourses of truth are so many incommensurable languages does not inescapably lead us to the conclusion that society is the combination of force, fate and chance. In other words, nihilism cannot exceed a merely mythical status.

Consequently, the ontology of the secular is inherently violent; this ontology is only mythology, and it results from the contingent embrace of pagan violence through the refusal and rejection of Christianity. There remains an alternative to escape the violence: propose Christianity as an equally selectable mythos (by faith), yet one which is infinitely more desirable since it embraces an ontology of peace where differences are conceived as analogically related, rather than equivocally at variance. Moreover, this faith is not against reason, but, through the peace of analogical participation in divine being, reason and faith work together in the revelation of the Trinity—the paradigm of harmonious unity in diversity.

V. A Genuinely 'Postmodern' Theology

We have seen that Christianity and Derrida's postmodern deconstruction have a common emphasis on a linguistic ontology of difference which attempts to subvert Enlightenment foundations of secular reason. However, we have also seen pagan elements to Derrida's deconstruction, which arguably lead to violence. Christian speech 'fades to make way for the arrival of a new sign and a new speaker, or a new speaking-event'—the person and work of Christ.[80] This grants difference a known content, whereas Derrida's difference is always deferred 'and therefore nothing, no-difference'.[81] Writing tends to abstract, so it is more the text that appears ideal and empirical, rather than the voice as Derrida claims. Through deconstruction, Derrida merely reveals that the 'nothing' at the heart of the text is 'death'. He preserves the 'formalism and 'manipulative tyranny' of writing precisely by revealing its nothingness, which can be more specifically defined as nihilism. Milbank then presses the point, arguing that in nihilism

> the flux is a medium of perpetual conflict, a pagan *agon* where the most powerful rhetoric will temporarily triumph, only to succumb to an apparently or effectively more powerful discourse in the future. Because there are no fixed categorical areas for different discourses/practices, they ceaselessly overlap and contest for influence. Lyotard and others rightly do not envisage a peaceful coexistence of a plurality of discourses alongside

[80] J Milbank, *The Word Made Strange: Theology, Language, Culture* (Blackwell, 1997) 70.
[81] ibid.

each other, without mutual interference. The best that can be hoped for is some mitigation of the severity of conflict, a set of formal rules of engagement ... for this reason, postmodern nihilism remains in continuity with liberalism and the Enlightenment.[82]

Therefore, though Derrida is on the right track, the pagan elements of his deconstruction yield troubling results. His emphasis on *differance*, the infinite difference and deferral of language, reveals that there is really nothing at the foundation of language—there is only the nihilistic void. But since there is always difference(s), in the nihilistic void the different rhetorics exist in a state of perpetual war by the exercise of pure power, and only the further exercise of power can impede the extent of this conflict. Conversely, 'Christianity can become "internally postmodern" in a way that may not be possible for every religion or ideology ... through its belief in creation from nothing' it is a 'reality suspended between nothing and infinity', and is 'a reality of flux ... composed only of relational differences ... like nihilism, Christianity can, should, embrace the differential flux'.[83]

Christianity uniquely provides 'an allowing, by faith ... that a lust for "present" knowledge does not refuse the guidance of desire (whereas a Derridean discovery that presence is absence still refuses this guidance) which will render, precisely, faith possible': that is, it enables us to trust our written narratives as realised through a transcendent linguistic encounter with Christ, the word of the speaking God.[84] Christian theology is able to 'think unlimited semiosis ... which articulates the deferrals of the sign ... where the nihilists seem only to think of signified absence in terms of a necessary suppression, betrayel or subversion'—that is, violence.[85]

For theology, and theology alone, difference remains real difference since it is not subordinate to immanent univocal process or the fate of a necessary suppression. Instead, the very possibility of substitutive transference is here held to be a peaceful affirmation of the other, consummated in a transcendent infinity.[86]

So in the new era of postmodernity, the human has become 'subordinate to the infinitely many discourses which claim to constitute humanity', and 'universality can no longer pose as the identical, but must be paradoxically invoked as the different'.[87] Radical postmodernity poses the challenge to theology that the ontology of difference is inseparable from an absolute historicism, a philosophy which only thinks truth as the narrative of the constitution of the strategies of power. Indeed, according to this critique, the many-varied nature of truth and truths reveal truths as arbitrary, the will-to-power. This postmodern suspicion is 'all-encompassing, leaving no residue of humanist meaning'.[88] 'Such an ontology of difference is found to be true, yet not just, which results in despair'.[89]

[82] Milbank, 'Postmodern Critical Augustinianism', above n 13, 267.
[83] Milbank, *Word Made Strange*, above n 80, 70.
[84] ibid 78.
[85] ibid 112.
[86] ibid 113.
[87] Milbank, 'Postmodern Critical Augustinianism', above n 13, 260.
[88] ibid 261–62.
[89] ibid 262.

More moderate forms of postmodernism, which admit irreducible difference and the historical/contextual nature of truth claims without lapsing into denials of absolute truth and value, may be of use. Indeed, the 'tradition-governed inquiry is rational and makes objective progress', and so it seems that the 'response to nihilism is to adopt a tradition and derive an ontology from the implicit assumptions of its narrative forms'.[90] Christianity is such an ontology, but it is unique in the sense that it alone presents an ontology of peace and 'refuses to submit ultimate reality to conflictual phenomena'.[91] Where Derrida's deconstruction submits that difference is intrinsically violent, Christianity submits that difference is intrinsically peaceful. Christianity is therefore a redeemed version of Derridean deconstruction: deconstruction is required to remove the secular reason founding society, leaving a space for faith to come to the fore; Christianity is required to construct this space as difference without violence. Nihilism 'sustains its ontology as another *mythos*', and therefore the 'critique beyond nihilism must be theological'.[92]

However, this is not to say that reason per se is rejected. We can appeal to a 'bias toward reason which is both innate and a post-Christian residue', in contrast to a 'pure, cold nihilistic vision', which concludes that 'in the end there is an incomprehensible springing of all things from nothing' and reveals its own 'illusory character as the covering of the void'.[93] Nihilism is the giving over of (secular) pure reason to the ontological reign of non-sense or unreason. By contrast, a Christian perspective 'saves the human bias toward reason', for reason in this framework is consistent with the infinite and 'leaves no residue of chaos'.[94] In other words, rationalism is linked to the biblical mythos alone, and to save reason in this fashion requires the supplementation of reason by faith, including faith in infinite reason.

After modernity lies a disappointment with pure reason, leaving only a formalistic nihilism as its pale echo. This nihilistic will to reject reason also promotes abstract difference as necessary conflict or ontological injustice. However, Augustinian Christianity promotes a more hopeful metaphysic of peace in the City of God. In the Trinity and the Incarnation there is an original difference without violence, so justice and an ontology of peace are possible, by faith. Christian reason recognises no such necessary or original ontology of violence, but recognises the infinite as peace, from which true theological reason which promotes peace may spring. Christian theology, with its ontology of peace, can then overcome nihilism.

If theology embraces a more thoroughgoing perspectivism, pragmatism and historicism in this sense, it can escape the modernist illusions that a purely finite, immanent science can give us a true ontology. Our thoughts depend entirely upon contingent, theoretically unjustifiable assumptions, and it is precisely this

[90] ibid 263.
[91] ibid.
[92] ibid.
[93] Milbank, *Theology and Social Theory*, above n 75, xvi–xvii.
[94] ibid.

historicist confinement of our thought which renders it irreducible to immanent process, and 'always dependent on divine participation and opening up to the transcendent'.[95] However, it is not merely that in a postmodern world every perspective is as good as any other and therefore a single Christian perspective remains possible. On the contrary, the postmodern valuation of the unsurpassability of plural difference or perspective is upheld—what is contested is the mode of this valuation or the precise construal of the transcendentality of difference itself. The nihilistic difference is the 'ultimately contested universal', the 'impenetrable flux of perspectives'.[96] This view cannot construe difference as peaceful and never describes it as analogical, but for Christianity difference can be construed peacefully through the theological virtues of faith, hope and love.

In this way, Christian theology, believed by faith, but in contrast to the postmodern nihilism of secular pure reason, imagines the temporal process in its very temporality as reflecting eternity, as the possibility of a historical progress towards God, and as something recuperable within memory whose ultimate purpose is forgiveness and reconciliation. Conceptions of the 'below' (human subjectivity and relationship) are only constituted within the narrative that simultaneously postulates the 'above' (transcendence). Christianity pursued from the outset a universalism which tried to accommodate rather than merely abolish difference: Christians could live in their different societies, yet are fundamentally united in the Body of Christ and as citizens of the eternal city, the City of God.

VI. The Threshold of Ontological Peace: Constructing a Christian Theology of Legal Community

Though correctly oriented, Derrida's ontology consists of difference as violence. However, it is the orientation of his ontology which opens the possibility for the recovery and restoration of true reason that leads to a Christian peace—difference without violence. The destruction of secular reason opens the space for the return of the theological, a reason reconciled with faith and theology which participates in the unique economy of the truth-disclosure of the Trinity through the analogical relation of difference.

This is because Christianity has a different kind of logic, one of peace: not to simply abolish the law, which would be replacing violence with violence akin to Benjamin's divine violence, but redeeming the law through the Spirit and love. This allows true justice—God as just and the justifier of the one who has faith

[95] ibid 219–21.
[96] ibid 145–46.

in Christ through doing away with the letter of the law and replacing it with the Spirit. It is justice not as de(con)struction, but as (de)construction, such that it combusts the violence of secular reason and constructs the peace of faith, thereby sublating both. Indeed, the event of Christ disrupts the false peace of pagan postmodernism, that there really is nothing external to language and all is warring perspectives—Christ cannot be covered over by language, but, as the Word or *logos*, He comes through language. He is outside the law of the letter, yet enables the law of the spirit, the law of God's love that brings peace.

Hence, a genuinely postmodern, Christian theology which allows the mutual coexistence of difference in an ontologically peaceful way provides an alternative narrative through which one can critique the development of law's distorted theology, secularisation and violence.

4

An Account of Secular(ised) Jurisprudence: Violence from Duns Scotus to Derrida

I. Law and Postmodern Critical Augustinianism

The following chapter engages with Postmodern Critical Augustinianism in a specifically jurisprudential space by narrating the contingent development of secular law and suggesting that this is associated with the emergence of ontological violence in the legal community. Section I outlines common ground for considering 'law', before section II establishes the theological nature of traditional natural law by examining the jurisprudence of Thomas Aquinas and some contemporary interpretations. Section III analyses the theology of John Duns Scotus, particularly his emphasis on the univocity of Being, God as pure sovereign will and purely natural knowledge of God, demonstrating that there is a theological shift characterising the development of jurisprudence from Aquinas to Duns Scotus which creates the space for a secular, violent posited law. The notion of God and humanity as pure will violently governed by a secularised reason is traced through to Machiavelli and Hobbes in section IV, before section V completes the narrative by arriving with the secular positivism of Austin and Hart.

Parts III–V argue that, according to these thinkers, notions such as pure reason, univocal being and sovereign will are foundational for law's formation, with the result that their respective legal communities are characterised by antagonism and alienation, a fundamentally ontological violence. In particular, what these thinkers have in common is their explicit or implicit emphasis on society governed by some type of concentrated sovereign authority exercising its will in the form of violence. Section VI explores the nature of this violence more specifically through Cover, Derrida and Benjamin, as prominent theorists of law and violence. However, section VII identifies that Cover and Benjamin may also allow for a counter-narrative of law, one which embraces peace rather than violence. Indeed, they signal an alternative Christian narrative which can positively reconfigure the ontology of law based on the harmonious existence of difference found and revealed in the relations of the Trinity.

We can perhaps initially understand 'law' as the attempt to justly govern human interactions in a community through a system of enforced principles. Such a definition is advantageous in the sense that it includes normal civil law (such as criminal, evidential, tort or contract, which are what one usually thinks of), yet importantly it is also potentially able to incorporate the theological notion of law found in the Pentateuch and the Pauline corpus. Further, the invocation of the Pauline law of Christ or the law of love removes the element of enforcement and therefore in principle removes the violence in favour of peace—in other words, law is a just government of human interactions in a community through a series of principles based on love for one's neighbour, rather than external enforcement.

So the answer to the question 'what is law' is deceptively easy, and in 2500 years of attempting to answer the question no consensus has been reached. The question also begs further questions, such as whether law is a discrete entity or a social process, or whether there is a range of intersecting disciplinary phenomena which may be properly termed 'law'. Law is therefore a complex, interwoven, dynamic system. Three functions of law are: to lay down the 'rules of organisation and function'; the 'facilitation of interpersonal transactions'; and the 'protection of the public interest'.[1] Apart from the nature and functions of law, there are various answers to the standard and central question of jurisprudence—the definition of law itself.

However, to have a theory of (the nature of) law presupposes that law itself is a distinct category to be theorised, and this is by no means clear. Some have advocated the unitary category of law, others have advocated that there is no substantive distinction between law and non-law, and yet others have advocated some type of combination of the two. Typically, there are two types of response to this issue of defining law. The first is that law is a set of universal moral principles in accordance with nature (natural law), and the second is that law is a collection of valid rules or norms which lack moral content (positivism). Correspondingly, law is defined differently according to particular jurisprudential schools and methodologies.

For example, schools of legal sociology focus on the social significance of law and its relation to politics, positivists focus on an examination of the framework of rules and regulations governing society, and natural law jurisprudence examines metaphysical issues associated with the essence of law and its connection with morality. For many positivists, law is simply the rules created and recognised by the legal institutions of the state and is a distinct category from other disciplines. This definition is anaemic, for at the heart of law lies paradox: it is separate from politics yet inherently political, different from morality yet broadly reflects social concerns, a constraint on power by the exercise of power, and is concerned with fair procedures yet is often inaccessible and sometimes unjust. It is this notion of the law as a complex, interwoven, non-unitary system incorporating various

[1] P Smith (ed), *The Nature and Process of Law: Introduction to Legal Philosophy* (Oxford University Press, 1993) 9–10.

disciplines with the most artificial of boundaries which gives it scope for critique by and through such disciplines. The critique this book undertakes is a theological critique, and I will now proceed to consider the theology which undergirds traditional formulations of (natural) law, before exposing the distortion of this theology.

II. Faith, Reason and a Theological Natural Law

A. Thomas Aquinas and the Classical Tradition

(i) The Thomist Framework

Thomas Aquinas, a thirteenth-century scholastic theologian and the classical proponent of natural law, defines law as 'a dictate of practical reason emanating from the ruler who governs a perfect community', so there is an eternal law, or *lex eterna*, which is God's law and which fulfils these criteria.[2] Since the eternal law of God is a subset of the content of the divine intellect and is therefore unchangeable truth, and to some extent people by grace know God and know truth, to this extent they know the eternal law. The 'divine law', or *lex divina*, allows people to participate 'more perfectly in the eternal law' through clarifying the eternal law against the limitations of pure human reason, and consists of the true revelation contained in Holy Scripture, the Old and New Testaments of the Bible.[3] Those who do not have this law of revelation nevertheless do by nature (illuminated by grace) those things which are of the law, and so know what is good and what is evil by conscience. This is the 'natural law', or *lex natura*, which humans apprehend through their possessing a 'share of the Eternal Reason' and so are able to 'participate in the eternal law through reason'; hence, the natural law is 'the rational creature's participation of the eternal law'.[4]

Through human reason (enlightened by grace as a subset of the divine reason or *logos*), the precepts of the natural law 'proceed to the more particular determinations', which are called positive or 'human laws'.[5] All human law, or *lex humana*, as it accords with right reason, ultimately derives from the eternal law. Hence, if a law deviates from right reason (implying it does not accord with the eternal law of God or immutable truth), it is necessarily unjust, and therefore lacks the requisite quality of law.[6] Aquinas's articulation of the natural law illustrates his understanding of the relationship between reason and faith (or grace)—namely, that divinely

[2] T Aquinas, *Summa Theologica* (William Benton, 1952) vol 2, 208.
[3] ibid 210–11.
[4] ibid 209.
[5] ibid 210.
[6] ibid 216–18.

illuminated human reason participates in the eternal law of God by faith (grace), and if human law does not accord with this eternal law, it is necessarily against reason.

(ii) The Thomist Context: Augustine, Cicero and the Stoics

This summary of the Thomist framework for law belies the extent of contemporary dispute over what precisely Aquinas meant in articulating this framework, and particularly just how theological the framework is. However, by briefly outlining the sources of Aquinas's thought and considering some contemporary perspectives, I can articulate a reasonably plausible foundation for understanding Thomist jurisprudence as intrinsically theological. Aquinas quotes Augustine as an authority for stating that 'there exists an eternal law', which is 'Supreme Reason' and 'Unchangeable'.[7] Similarly, Aquinas argues that Augustine 'distinguishes two kinds of law, the one eternal, the other temporal, which he calls human'.[8] Humans may access the eternal law through reason, which is sharing in the eternal reason, and this 'participation' is the natural law from which may stem human or positive law.[9] Hence, following Augustine, the eternal law is 'imprinted' in our nature by the 'Divine light'.[10]

Aquinas also cites Augustine's statement saying 'that which is not just seems to be no law at all' in order to justify his further contention that the force of a law depends on its justice or whether it is from God.[11] Aquinas, further using Augustine, argues that the 'new law is instilled in our hearts'; it is not written down, but 'inscribed on the hearts of the faithful'.[12] This is the law of faith and of the Spirit. This new law is also the law of love, which contains the old law and fulfils it. Ultimately, then, according to Aquinas and following Augustine, the laws of the secular state have their justification and authority from the fact that they are part of the eternal and natural law of love—or, in other words, that they are given by God.[13]

Given Aquinas's heavy reliance on Augustine, we should consider Augustine's own framework for natural law. Like Plato and Aristotle before him, Augustine contends that in order to live in peace, a person 'subordinates their primal tendencies to the rational soul'.[14] However, 'divine direction' is required to know what to do and 'divine assistance' is required to obey.[15] A person requires grace in order to apprehend obedience and consequent peace in the context of the everlasting law,

[7] ibid 208.
[8] ibid 210.
[9] ibid 208–10.
[10] ibid 209.
[11] ibid 227; *cf* ibid 233.
[12] ibid 321.
[13] C Anton-Hermann, 'The Fundamental Ideas in St Augustine's Philosophy of Law' (1973) 18 *American Journal of Jurisprudence* 57, 75.
[14] Augustine, *Concerning the City of God Against the Pagans* (Penguin, 2008) 873.
[15] ibid.

and to be 'in subjection to this law for the good of the society'.[16] The basis for this is 'two precepts taught by God'—to love God and to love one's neighbour as oneself. If one follows these, it will result in 'obedience to the law of society' and peace in that society.[17] For if the law of society is love of neighbour in the power and manner provided by Christ, this society will be characterised by selfless sacrifice, charity and generosity—a harmonious community.

From the Roman jurist Cicero particularly, Augustine adopted the Stoic notion of natural law and the eternal law (or, as he terms it, 'everlasting law') as the supreme moral norm, together with the sublime rational orderliness which characterises the universe and is instituted by God—in other words, the divine wisdom is the universal law. Augustine distinguishes between the human or temporal law and this eternal law, which is the supreme immutable reason and must always be obeyed. Hence, the eternal law is the ultimate norm or standard for the human law.[18] This theistic (in contrast to the Stoic) definition of the natural law became the basic concept and authoritative pronouncement of law for medieval jurisprudence. For the Stoics, the eternal law was god, so the Christian conception of natural law articulated by the likes of Augustine and Aquinas is a departure from the Stoic conception articulated by Cicero, yet it was this Stoic conception which was adopted and extended in a Christian context by Augustine and Aquinas. The eternal law thus manifests itself in the eternal reason of all created reason, so humans are governed by and are aware of this eternal law through the eternal reason. This participation of the rational person in the eternal law by the law of reason is the natural law, and even the person who does not acknowledge God may nevertheless appropriate the eternal law through rational participation enabled by grace.

Focusing on Cicero particularly as a major influence for Augustine, and therefore by extension for Aquinas, the natural law is the law of a harmonious Stoic universe which could be objectively perceived and is reflected in human nature.[19] This law is eternal and rational, immutable and supreme, part of the divine reason and from God. Furthermore, there is a plausible influence for the Apostle Paul in the Stoic philosophy of the natural law. In fact, the early church fathers, like Augustine, seemed quite satisfied to view Paul as articulating a theory of natural law similar to that of Cicero, which was subsequently put into a Christian framework by Paul and elaborated by Augustine and Aquinas. Consider, for example, Romans 2:14–15, where Paul argues that those who do not have the law do by nature what is required by the law (eg they are moral by a divinely enabled or enlightened conscience). In this sense, Thomist natural law considered in itself is theological, but there is one influential contemporary interpretation which has been perceived as questioning this designation: that of John Finnis.

[16] ibid.
[17] ibid.
[18] Anton-Hermann, above n 13, 59–62.
[19] R Brooks, 'Introduction' in R Brooks (ed), *Cicero and Modern Law* (Ashgate, 2009) xxxviii.

B. Thomism as a Theological Framework: Some Contemporary Interpretations

(i) John Finnis: Secularising Thomism?

John Finnis, a twentieth-century legal theorist who articulates a modern formulation and revivification of Thomist natural law, claims that Aquinas considers the natural law to be self-evident but that the existence of God is not self-evident, and that his will cannot be discovered without revelation. Finnis proceeds to arguably articulate a theory of natural law 'without needing to revert to questions of God's existence and will'.[20] He states that, according to Aquinas, 'a positive or human law is derived from the natural law by a deductive process' and 'obtains its force from the natural law', which Finnis defines as 'the set of principles of practical reasonableness which order human life and community'.[21] From a historical perspective, Finnis also alludes to the fact that Cicero, Augustine and Aquinas all espouse a principle similar to 'an unjust law is not law'.[22] Finnis further discusses the origin of the phrase 'natural law' in Cicero and the Stoics, emphasising that a primary use of *natura* refers to 'practical reason according to human nature'.[23] Hence, for Finnis, according to Aquinas, even though the eternal law is from God, human apprehension of the eternal law by the natural law is 'through human reason'.[24]

(ii) Re-establishing the Theological Tradition

However, Lloyd Weinreb and Jean Porter, as contemporary natural law theorists, reject this interpretation of Aquinas for, according to them, Finnis claims that the Thomist natural law theory is not ontological, and is severable from Aquinas's context of the eternal law of God. This is to 'radically distort the Thomist framework' and to 'misconceive' the fact that the 'natural law exists on the basis of the eternal law and eternal reason rationally ordering the universe'—in other words, for Weinreb and Porter, Finnis's account of natural law in Aquinas is not theological enough.[25] Jean Porter in particular argues that the 'usual approaches' to natural law, and 'particularly to Aquinas', are 'too focused on philosophy to the neglect of theology, the scholastics, and Scripture'.[26] To address this inbalance, she seeks to 'articulate a theological account of the natural law through the accounts of the scholastics' (and especially Aquinas) in order to 'properly incorporate Scripture', as well as provide a bridge to other perspectives.[27]

[20] J Finnis, *Natural Law and Natural Rights* (Oxford University Press, 1980) 48–49.
[21] ibid 280–81.
[22] ibid 363.
[23] ibid 374–76.
[24] ibid 400.
[25] See L Weinreb, *Natural Law and Justice* (Harvard University Press, 1987) 109; J Porter, *Nature as Reason: A Thomistic Theory of Natural Law* (Wm B Eerdmans, 2005) 38–39.
[26] Porter, ibid, 1–2, 5, 45.
[27] ibid.

Although Porter's perspective is correct and her critique of Finnis's account is appropriate given her characterisation of it, the fundamental claim that Finnis's account of Aquinas is not theological enough is overstated. Holistically considered, the account provided by Finnis is theological. The 'human reason' referred to by Finnis is not a secular reason, divorced from faith and God's grace, but actually illustrates the connection of reason to faith. According to Finnis, the term 'natural' law and the consequent distinction between 'natural' reason and revelation drawn by some theologians has given 'credence to the supposition that the term "natural" signifies immanence and secularism at the expense of transcendence or the supernatural'.[28] Finnis rejects such a supposition as 'muddled', arguing that what Plato, Aristotle and others mean by nature actually 'implies participation in the divine intellect and divine reason', entailing 'faith in the existence of God' (however one conceives God to be).[29] The 'assertion of objective norms of human flourishing and principles of human reasonableness' then leads to the 'affirmation' of some transcendent source of these, which the philosophers term God.[30] Reason is something God-given, and 'practical reasonableness entails the imitation of God' and forms the foundation for the civil legal system, where practical reason refers to the human reasoning process which considers what would be good for humans to do, have, get and be. Moreover, the 'basic values grasped by practical reason' gain an 'objectivity', 'constancy' and 'impartiality' reinforced by faith in God.[31]

Regarding Aquinas and natural law as divine participation in the eternal law, Finnis argues that, for Aquinas, it is 'necessary to postulate an intellect far superior to the human intellect', which has the 'power of understanding without imperfection', 'allows us to reason' and 'activates our individual intelligences through light or illumination'.[32] Aquinas then 'identifies this separate intellect as God', and God's grace is necessary for proper participation in the eternal law by divinely assisted human reason.[33] Finally, according to Finnis, Aquinas concludes that 'every activity of reasoning derives from nature'—which, bearing in mind Finnis's earlier definition of the term 'nature' as participation in the divine, puts reason and faith in the same dimension. This basis is logically, if not chronologically, prior to Finnis's articulation of the basic forms of human good, which form the first principles of natural law. In particular, the 'basic good of practical reasonableness shapes the relation with the other goods' by 'guiding one's commitments', 'selection of projects' and 'implementation'.[34] Therefore, Finnis, following Aquinas, utilises the interconnection of faith (or grace) and reason to articulate his version of a natural law.

[28] Finnis, above n 20, 394–95.
[29] ibid.
[30] ibid.
[31] ibid 397.
[32] ibid 399–400.
[33] ibid.
[34] ibid 85–90, 97, 100.

To this can be added John Milbank, for Milbank argues that the natural law of Thomas Aquinas is 'intrinsically theological and transcendent', in contrast with the secular modern law in its being 'positivistic and immanent'.[35] Indeed, Milbank's framework for understanding reality, and consequently for interpreting Aquinas, is that accounts of human life, law and nature must be integrally theological, and this entails the rejection of any recognition of the secular or a 'pure nature'—that is, a nature apart from the enlightenment of God's grace. For Milbank, 'medieval modes of governance' avoided the use of political power and external sovereign authority to govern all facets of life, since the 'resort to unlegislated power was seen as necessary in those instances where the written law no longer served justice'.[36] In other words, following the model of Aquinas, 'appeal was made to a natural law of equity rooted in an eternal, divine law', and this to an extent 'provides an escape' from violent coercion by an overwhelming political force.[37] Milbank thus concludes that a way out of this 'conundrum is through authentic Pauline theology', which 'provides the theological framework for Thomist natural law'.[38] Therefore, Aquinas's account of law has an integrally theological foundation. More precisely, law is founded upon faith united with reason, the rational creature's participation in the divine intellect enabled by grace. However, this theological foundation was distorted, and effectively created the notion of the 'secular'—an autonomous foundation for law governed and accessed by a pure reason, detached from faith and God's grace.

III. 'Creating' the Secular: Duns Scotus, Univocity and Separating Philosophy from Theology

A. Voluntarist Theology: The Univocity of Being

With the shift in theology following John Duns Scotus in the thirteenth and fourteenth centuries, a number of things changed. They included: the displacement of the Trinity as an essential relation of the divine persons; a loss of analogical participation through advocating the univocity of Being in the sense that God and humanity exist in a metaphysically identical way; prioritising the will over the intellect in God; and the denial of the Augustinian theory of illumination.[39] Duns Scotus's emphasis on the pure, singular will of God (a theologically voluntarist

[35] J Milbank, 'Paul against Biopolitics' in J Milbank et al (eds), *Paul's New Moment: Continental Philosophy and the Future of Christian Theology* (Brazos Press, 2010) 24.
[36] ibid 33, 36.
[37] ibid.
[38] ibid 33.
[39] J Milbank, 'The Grandeur of Reason and the Perversity of Rationalism: Radical Orthodoxy's First Decade' in J Milbank and S Oliver (eds), *The Radical Orthodoxy Reader* (Routledge, 2009) 379.

position) rather than the intellectual relations of the persons of the Godhead signalled the displacement of relationship as the paradigmatic Trinitarian theme, and (eventually) a denial of the participation of the creature in this divine relationship.[40] Associated with this singular, will Duns Scotus affirms the univocity or singular existence of all Being. He argues in *Philosophical Writings* that

> For whatever is of itself intelligible either includes essentially the notion of 'being' or is contained virtually or essentially in something else which does include 'being' essentially. For all genera, species, individuals, and the essential parts of genera, and the Uncreated Being [God] all include 'being'.[41]

'To put it briefly, then, "being" is univocal for all.'[42] Duns Scotus explains what he means by univocal being by saying that one can say that God is a being without knowing the quality of God's being, whether it is created or uncreated. The concepts of infinite/finite or created/uncreated being which are applied to God therefore have the concept of being in common. It follows that being is a universal in the sense that it is a shared, general concept of being possessed by all creatures—God, humanity, animals and the like. So Duns Scotus asserts that the mode of being for God and creation is exactly the same, implying that Being itself is an abstract or neutral category that is attached to God.

If Being is not something unique to God, but is shared in the same way by the creation, Being is a concept separate from God. It is a contingent attribute of God which is equally possessed by all creation. Since Being is then independent of God, it allows existence apart from God, as well as philosophical or metaphysical reflection apart from God. This opens the space for the world to be an autonomous realm, a realm of philosophy apart from theology—ultimately resulting in the emergence and eventual domination of the secular. Moreover, since Duns Scotus carries the assumption that God can be naturally known as the basis for his argument that being is univocal, it follows that this produces an associated 'natural' or secularised reason appropriate for approaching philosophy as separate from theology.

Duns Scotus's univocity of being can be contrasted with Aquinas's analogy of being, which understands the mode of God's being by analogy of the creation's being—they do not exist in the same way, but the creature's being is founded from or a participation in the 'ultimate' Being of God. As James KA Smith summarises,

> God's very essence *is* existence, whereas the creature 'is' only to the extent that it receives the gift of being from the Creator or, in other words, to the extent that the creature participates in ... or is suspended from ... the being of the Creator.[43]

[40] J Milbank, *The Word Made Strange: Theology, Language, Culture* (Blackwell, 1997) 177.

[41] J Duns Scotus, *Philosophical Writings: A Selection* (Hackett, 1997) 4.

[42] ibid 7.

[43] JKA Smith, *Introducing Radical Orthodoxy: Mapping a Post-Secular Theology* (Baker, 2004) 96–97 (original emphasis).

Indeed, Smith argues that 'for Milbank, following Aquinas, there is no metaphysics apart from revelation. This contrasts with the autonomous, non-revelational metaphysics of Scotus, who subjects God to a conception of being that is anterior to God's self-revelation.'[44] Where Aquinas's view of Being is grounded in God's self-disclosure through revelation, Duns Scotus evaluates the nature of God's Being on the ground of an autonomous, secular category of being apart from God's revelation. Aquinas unites faith with reason, while Duns Scotus invents a secular reason.

This also implies that Duns Scotus articulates a type of idolatry which elevates the created being to the same status as the Creator, granting finite creation intrinsic subsistence and autonomy at the level of the infinite, even venerating Being as possessing a greater ontological status than God.[45] In other words, 'finite and infinite being are seen as equally and univocally "in being"—hence *esse* threatens to become greater than God and God [is] idolatrously reduced to the status of a partner with his Creation in causal processes'.[46] The concept of univocal being equates finite and infinite being, reducing the being of God to equal that of the creation. Moreover, since God is understood according to this universal concept of being, Being (rather than God) becomes the entity which mediates knowledge and philosophical reflection, rendering Being greater than God and reducing God to just another category.

We may now move to consider specifically how Duns Scotus inaugurated this theologically distorted notion of purely natural knowledge, leading to a secular realm and reason. In the next part, we will also see that this theological distortion resulted in a violent (Hobbesian) conception of humans (and, for that matter, God Himself) as creatures of pure will who exist in purely logical or contractual interactions, enforced by some external power.

B. Knowledge by Pure Nature

For Duns Scotus, knowledge of God and His nature can come apart from God's direct revelation. Instead, it comes through pure human reason. Duns Scotus contends that:

> If there are some necessary reasons for what we believe, it is not dangerous to set them forth ... if you say, otherwise, that God gives such knowledge to whom he wills, then it would follow that we labour in vain in our study and inquiry into the truth. A far better and easier way of coming to theology would be to sit in church and ask God to give us this light.[47]

[44] ibid 98.

[45] Milbank, *Word Made Strange*, above n 40, 44; *cf* Smith, above n 43, 98.

[46] J Milbank, *Theology and Social Theory: Beyond Secular Reason*, 2nd edn (Blackwell, 2006) xxiv.

[47] Duns Scotus, cited in A Wolter, *Duns Scotus on the Will and Morality* (Catholic University of America, 1997) 6.

So we can use our reason to come to the knowledge of God, apart from God's grace. 'We can infer, then, in metaphysics from act and potency, finiteness and infinity, multitude and unity, and many other such metaphysical properties, that God or the First Being exists.'[48] Duns Scotus explicitly connects this idea of purely natural knowledge to his univocal theology and emphasis on God as pure will. In particular, if God exists as pure will, and we exist in a way that is metaphysically identical to God, we too are primarily characterised by will. So he says that God is the 'first efficient cause' who has 'infinite power' to cause all things through free and contingent 'volition'.[49]

Correspondingly, he says of humanity that 'the will is the motor or moving cause throughout the soul, and all else obeys it'.[50] For Duns Scotus, it follows that 'because of … conformity of the will to right reason … I concede the conclusion that by purely natural means any will could love God above all'.[51] Since our will by natural reason conforms to God's will as the ultimate will, it is purely by our natural will, apart from God's gracious enlightenment, that we can love God. So Milbank concludes that

> the [Augustinian] doctrine [of illumination] is rather finally abandoned by Scotus, who sees the divine influence, when seen in various ways as alienating human powers, as superfluous. This leaves 'illumination' as only applying to faith and helps encourage a nature/supernature duality'.[52]

Duns Scotus's univocity of Being and separation of theology from philosophy are related since the univocal nature of Being implies an a priori notion of being which is then applied to God (and equally to the creation), rather than considering God the very paradigm or distinctive pinnacle of being. This notion of Being detached from the divine nature and revelation therefore fundamentally separates ontology from theology, or metaphysics from revelation. Being can be apprehended by pure reason apart from faith.

All the preceding indicates a theology 'that emerges on the basis of "pure reason" which must rationally reduce revelation to that which concerns the only "extra-rational" which reason can recognise, namely the purely positive and "factual"'.[53] For in place of a Thomist participatory framework which understands the immanent as 'suspended from' the transcendent, Duns Scotus assumed an ontology based on a univocal or 'flattened' being, one which denied the depth of being and 'unhooked' it from the transcendent, allowing the emergence of a 'secular' plane and 'secular' reason which are completely independent of the transcendent.[54] This theological distortion led to particular political developments which undergird

48 ibid 7.
49 ibid 7–8.
50 ibid 38.
51 ibid 91.
52 Milbank, 'Grandeur of Reason', above n 39, 380.
53 ibid 385.
54 Smith, above n 43, 88–89.

our modern Western legal system, particularly the reduction of human being to the 'self', an 'isolated subject'—ultimately resulting in the Hobbesian 'picture of the social order as an aggregate of competing, atomistic, self-interested subjects … quasi-united in a supposedly neutral space called the "public", where relationships [are] no longer governed by charity, but by contract'.[55] The claim is that

> behind the *politics* of modernity (liberal, secular) is an *epistemology* (autonomous reason), which is in turn undergirded by an *ontology* (univocity and denial of participation) … Scotus's marking out of an autonomous creation opens up the space for a new emphasis on human autonomy in the political sphere.[56]

This emphasis on human autonomy in a secular political sphere, isolated from the foundation of true Christian theology, produces relations of violence in the legal community. Identifying this ontological distortion allows the alternative conception of the possibility of an ontologically redeemed legal system—one based in the theological peace of communal, harmonious participation in the divine being through the law of love.

IV. Machiavelli and Hobbes: Secular Legal Ontology and the Emergence of Governing Violence

A. Machiavelli, Dominance and Paganism

Before we arrive at the Hobbesian picture of social order, however, there is another historical occurrence which involves a different conception of the secular, one which (on the basis of Duns Scotus's separation of philosophy and theology) is premised on a purely philosophical (partial) rejection of Christianity and the substitution of pagan struggle, strife and competition to gain authority and power—a moment which is equally influential in the development of a modern Western legal system characterised by violence. This is the Machiavellian moment, which is important because it represents the space where the pure will of the ruler is connected with pagan 'virtues' of manipulation and dominance in order to maintain that rule. Not only is governance associated with violence, but violence is actually rendered desirable in this space. This pagan conception of violence as virtue forms the foundation for modern legal systems which regulate through violence; more importantly, it is antithetical to the Christian idea of virtue.

Milbank identifies the Machiavellian moment as the 're-emergence of pagan politic[s] and philosoph[y]' in the secular space as an 'alternative mythos',

[55] ibid 89.
[56] ibid 99–100 (original emphasis).

which rivalled Christianity by articulating a new kind of virtue based in violence.[57] There is a theological demarcation between the Hobbesian framework of distorted theology and the Machiavellian framework which rejects (Christian) theology, with a common source stemming from the secularisation allowed by Duns Scotus and a common convergence in providing the foundation for a pagan, ontologically violent legal system. The Hobbesian emphasis on sovereignty as the violently exerted pure will of the state has its genesis in Duns Scotus's conception of God, and the Machiavellian emphasis on secular governance through the virtues of manipulation and consolidating power has its genesis in the pagan idea of virtue within the framework of the secular as allowed by Duns Scotus. Hence, from the secular allowed by Duns Scotus, Hobbesian politics pursued this distortion of Christian theology and Machiavellian politics rejected the virtues contained within Christian theology in favour of the pagan; these culminated in a modern legal system characterised by violence.

Machiavelli fundamentally argues that, in order for a wise prince to function properly as the leader of the society and its members, and to appropriate and retain power, he must manipulate and dominate his competition. He argues that the lands of a prince, or 'these dominions … are acquired either with others' arms or one's own, either by fortune or virtue'.[58] Here Machiavelli claims that war and violence are necessary to establish a political system. His formulation is pagan in the sense that it equates the circumstances of acquiring the relevant lands either to fortune (ie 'fate') or to virtue, incorporating the pagan idea of military virtue where effectiveness in battle (here to acquire lands) is privileged. He further argues that 'diversities in the form of government spring up by chance … the vicissitudes of fortune', underscoring the emphasis on arbitrary fortune and fate as determining factors of governing success.[59] Fortune and (military) virtue are intimately related, for 'those princes or republics of the present day who lack forces of their own, whether for attack or defence, should take shame to themselves'.[60] In other words, what is followed is the ancient (pagan?) adage that fortune favours the brave, where the brave means those who are skilled in war.

Machiavelli approvingly cites the Romans as doing what

> wise princes must do … seeing inconveniences from afar, always remed[ying] them and never let them go on in order to run from a war, because they knew that one does not escape war, but one defers it to the advantage of others.[61]

The wise prince must also know to take advantage of the right opportunity to engage in war for his own advantage; he must be strategic and manipulate the situation to promote his own ends. This corresponds with Machiavelli's argument that

[57] Milbank, *Theology and Social Theory* 2nd edn, above n 46, 23–24.

[58] N Machiavelli, *The Prince* (Yale University, 1997) 5.

[59] N Machiavelli, *Discourses on Livy* (Federalist Papers, 2013) 13.

[60] ibid 47.

[61] Machiavelli, *The Prince*, above n 58, 11. Also see N Machiavelli, *The Prince* (Chicago University Press, 1985) 98–99, 103; N Machiavelli, *The Discourses* (Penguin, 1970) 15, 16, 118–26.

fraud is the indispensable companion of force, and both are necessary to achieve 'greatness' or military dominance:

> I hold it as most certain that men seldom if ever rise to great place from small beginnings without using fraud or force, unless, indeed, they be given, or take by inheritance the place to which some other has already come. Force, however, will never suffice by itself to effect this end, while fraud often will.[62]

The Machiavellian promotion of greatness is contrasted with humility. Machiavelli advises the wise prince that 'you shall often find that humility is not merely of no service to you, but is even hurtful'.[63] This is because humility (the centrally Christian virtue) will lead to thinking of others as better than yourself, to seeking the good of the other, and to loving and serving the other. Ultimately, it will lead to peace—and for Machiavelli, peace is antithetical to greatness, for greatness is fundamentally characterised by military prowess. We see this in his continued veneration of the Romans:

> having treated of the methods followed by the Romans for increasing their power, we shall now go on to consider those which they used in making war; and in all they did we shall find how wisely they turned aside from the common path in order to render their progress to supreme greatness easy.[64]

Thus, the wise ruler progresses to greatness by making war even more effectively, and greatness is really attained by the one who has the greatest violence.

Milbank in particular identifies this pagan, violent Machiavellian foundation and connects it to the modern political or legal system. For Milbank, 'the idea of the sovereign ruler able to manipulate internal conflicts in the interests of an outward-facing political strength is connected with the possibility of a political-economic surrogate for political *virtu*' and possesses a fundamentally 'Machiavellian colouring'.[65] 'In the Machiavellian mode', there is an 'irreplaceable role of war in maintaining internal solidarity'.[66] Furthermore, for Machiavelli there is a more explicit connection of such pagan virtues as heroic strength and glorious warfare with the individual pursuit of public repute as a civic virtue.[67] So this vision of the lawful conflict was embedded in a distorted Christian account of 'providence' (effectively 'fate' or 'fortune') which eventually produces order predicated upon the interaction of violent forces.[68] This led to the 'acceptance of a perpetual violence within the rules, that is sustained and re-created by the rules themselves'.[69] Ultimately, then, 'in the Machiavellian tradition, pagan chaos is … restored'.[70]

[62] Machiavelli, *Discourses on Livy*, above n 59, 128.
[63] ibid 129.
[64] ibid 116.
[65] Milbank, *Theology and Social Theory* 2nd edn, above n 46, 32.
[66] ibid 173.
[67] ibid 33.
[68] ibid 38.
[69] ibid 196.
[70] ibid 161.

In the final analysis, Machiavelli is integral to an account of the development of a secular and violent political system, because in his view the aim of political virtue is to manipulate and overcome fortune to create ruling strength displayed through war, and this makes 'Machiavelli a forebear of a modern and non-Christian politics'.[71] Machiavelli provides a foundation for the use of violence according to the will of the ruler in the maintenance of political power and control over society. The other part of this foundation is found in Thomas Hobbes, who articulated a view of society constituted of and by violence—and it is only through the violent exertion of concentrated political power that this violence may be stayed.

B. Hobbesian Legal Ontology: A Clash of Pure Will and Rule by Force

Hobbesian legal ontology is fundamentally characterised by antagonism, a clash of wills. Hobbes states that

> the right of Nature, whereby God reigneth over men, and punisheth those that break his Lawes [*sic*], is to be derived, not from his creating them, as if he required obedience as of gratitude for his benefits; but from his Irresistible Power.[72]

In other words, the pure sovereign power and will of God is the founding idea of the legal system. Hobbes continues the emphasis on clashing wills in his characterisation of the state of nature: 'the condition of man … is a condition of war of every one against every one, where everyone is governed by his own reason'.[73]

Contractual relationships between God and humanity, as well as among the members of humanity, are also paramount for Hobbes. These are presumably predicated on the priority of the will (to make agreements, and so forth). For example, 'God Almighty promised paradise to those men that can walk through this world according to the precepts and limits prescribed by Him'.[74] Hobbes proceeds to argue that there must then be some external power or authority to compel people to fulfil their obligations.

> There must be some coercive power to equally compel men to the performance of their covenants. This can be done by the terror of some punishment greater than the benefit they expect by the breach of their covenant … there is no such power before the erection of a commonwealth.[75]

So, with will as paramount, human relationships are characterised by the clash of these wills and contracts to restrain them. However, according to Hobbes,

[71] ibid 23–25.
[72] T Hobbes, *Leviathan* (Longman, 2008) 397. Also see 81–83, 271 (marginal summary).
[73] ibid 86–87.
[74] ibid 91.
[75] ibid 96.

there is only one way to construct a state power that will ultimately protect the citizens from actual or threatened internal or external violence and forsaking of covenants:

> This way is to confer all of their power and strength upon one man, or upon an assembly of men, that will reduce all of their wills, from a plurality of voices into one will ... Everyone thereby submits their wills to his will, and their judgments to his judgments ... when this is done, the multitude is united in one person that is called a commonwealth ... This is the generation of that great Leviathan, or rather, to speak more reverently, of that immortal god, to which we owe our peace and defense under the immortal God. By the authority given him by every particular man in the commonwealth, he has the terror derived from so much power and strength conferred on him, that he is enabled to perform the wills of all of them ... the essence of the commonwealth consists in this: By mutual covenant with one another, a multitude have made by their individual authority one person who can act for the ends of using his strength and any means he thinks is expedient for the multitude's peace and common defense.[76]

So, on the basis of a (fictional) state of nature characterised by violence, Hobbes proposes a contract between the members of this state of nature to submit all of their wills to one mammoth will, the Leviathan, which is charged with the protection of the society and its members through absolutely sovereign coercive force, or violence. It is precisely this fictional state and its corresponding interpretation of the legal society which warrants critique, for

> what Thomas Hobbes concluded as disclosed by mere reason—a fundamental war of all with all—is unveiled as a particular interpretive decision or commitment, not the self-evident truth of a universal logic. As such, this logic can be contested.[77]

This book contests that account of violent social relationships and immanent human nature by exposing its basis in secular rejections or distortions of Christian theology, and clarifies Christian theology as characterised by transcendent participation in the divine being, resulting in human relationships of love and peace. According to an ontology of immanence allowed by Duns Scotus's separation of human being from God's being, 'notions of human community reduce intersubjective relations to flattened, immanent relations of power', such as that provided by Hobbes.[78]

With Hobbes, political theory separated itself from theology. Unlike Thomist natural law, which is derived from transcendental equity surpassing human conventions, Hobbesian natural law articulates equity as a series of immanent rules based on purely philosophical reflections on the necessity of individual self-preservation.[79] So Duns Scotus's movement away from Aquinas's analogy of Being and allowance for the autonomy of philosophy from theology provided the conceptual ground

[76] ibid 116.
[77] Smith, above n 43, 145.
[78] ibid 188.
[79] Milbank, *Theology and Social Theory* 2nd edn, above n 46, 10.

for Hobbes to envisage the society as characterised by self-preservation from a purely natural perspective. Hobbes's emphasis on God's absolute power and the universal privileging of contractual will also represents a culmination, in two senses, of Duns Scotus's work. First, it ensured that the human exercise of absolute sovereignty was viewed as closest to being in the image of God. Secondly, by abandoning a participatory ontology for a covenantal bond, it provided a model for human relationships as merely contractual.[80]

Therefore, since Hobbes associates God with the 'operation of arbitrary and material power', 'the Hobbesian field of power seems to be constructed by a perverse theology'.[81] Hobbes consequently attempted to build social theory 'solely upon the rational calculation of self-interest', and the public interest is 'mostly confined to the securing of the private interests of life, property and contract'.[82] It is particularly significant that Hobbes characterises the Leviathan as a mortal god below the immortal god. This contingent theological interpretation and its subsequent societal implementation for Hobbes presupposed the mythical character of sovereignty, and in particular the view of God and humanity as existing discretely and functioning individually through the dominant exercise of will. And with the rise of more modern theories of sovereignty and the evacuation of theology from those theories, the 'real moment of mystification occurs, because here the "mythical" character of sovereignty is forgotten'.[83]

Given the Hobbesian legal system has a fundamentally (distorted) theological character and connotations, when this system is explicitly secularised, as in more modern articulations, the mythical and theological character of this kind of sovereignty is neglected. Reintroducing and exposing the theologically contingent character of the Hobbesian system opens such a system up for theological critique and the proposition of a different theological system—one of ontological peace in the political or legal community.

Ultimately, the Hobbesian political system gained traction because it was theologically promoted. After all, Hobbes drew upon the analogy of the 'immortal God'—in his view, an individual, absolutely authoritative sovereign will—in describing the 'mortal god', or the Leviathan, as an individual, absolutely authoritative sovereign will. However, the vesting of absolute power in the state meant there was no longer any need to appeal to the authority of God, giving birth to the modern idea of the secular state and providing the conceptual framework for modern secular positivism.

[80] ibid 16.
[81] ibid 55, 23–24.
[82] ibid 29–30.
[83] ibid 27.

V. The Final Stage: Austin, Hart and the Violence of Secular Positivism

Hobbes states that 'it is manifest that law in general is not a type of counsel, but a type of command … it is a command of one to another who has been formerly obliged to obey him'.[84] In this sense, Hobbes defines law in terms of the command of the sovereign, the entity which has been obliged to obey. John Austin, the eighteenth-century legal positivist, adopted this idea of law as command and explicitly articulated its secularist basis, excluding God from law in that, according to him, the 'laws of God' are not 'within the province of jurisprudence'.[85] For Austin, the 'province of jurisprudence' (ie the definition of law) is positive law or law that is 'posited by political superiors to political inferiors' (law by position).[86] In other words, it is a 'rule laid down to an intelligent being by an intelligent being having power over him'.[87] The 'political superior' with power is termed the 'sovereign'.[88] So every law, 'properly so-called', is a 'species of command' issued by the sovereign, which is the entity owed habitual obedience by the majority of the society.[89] Command is 'distinguished from wish or desire' by the fact that the party issuing the command has the 'power to inflict evil' or pain in the event that the command is not obeyed, and this 'evil incurred through disobedience' is called 'sanction', or enforcement of obedience.[90] Therefore, law strictly so-called according to Austin may be defined as a command from a sovereign enforced by sanction.

The very term 'positivism' itself connotes the violent positing of law, a use of force to establish and preserve the law, as well as to compel obedience to it. Integral to Austin's definition of law is this notion of sanction for disobedience, namely that obedience by which the legal subject is (en)forced through inflicted evil and pain. Furthermore, this violence is integrated with the use of theological language, such as 'sovereign' and 'command', for sovereign is an attribute traditionally ascribed to God, as it is (particularly in the Duns Scotian/Hobbesian framework for Austin) God who is a willing, superior being and has the power to enforce commands through the violent threat of punishments for disobedience. Austin explicitly admits this much when he notes that God is the ultimate sovereign.[91] Hence, not only is Austin's theory of law characterised by violence, but this violence is linked to a distorted (pagan) theology.

[84] Hobbes, above n 72, 183.
[85] J Austin, *The Province of Jurisprudence Determined* (Ashgate, 1998) 8–9.
[86] ibid.
[87] ibid.
[88] ibid.
[89] ibid 11–12.
[90] ibid.
[91] ibid 18–19.

In his critique of Austin, the twentieth-century legal theorist HLA Hart (a positivist himself) agrees, arguing that Austin's law of the sovereign giving coercive orders (commands enforced by sanction) is nothing more than the law of the gunman: 'A orders B to hand over his money and threatens to shoot him if he does not comply'.[92] Not only does this strengthen the contention that Austinian positivism is violent, but for Hart it also demonstrates the failure of Austin to give a proper account of the nature of the legal system as a series of rules producing obligations. In particular, Hart states that two types of legal rules exist. The first, or primary, rules are those under which people are required to do or abstain from certain actions. The secondary rules introduce, extinguish and modify the primary rules, and determine the nature of their operation. The most important of these is the secondary rule of recognition, which identifies and gives validity to the primary rules of obligation.[93] This obligation stems from what Hart terms the internal aspect of rules, where the citizen, as part of the society (internal to it), is under some duty or obligation to obey the rule through something like habit or social pressure to conform, as opposed to the external point of view, which merely views rules as predictors of human behaviour, with the external observer experiencing none of the obligation to comply.[94]

However, William MacNeil argues that Hart never really resolves the latent violence in the command theory of Austinian positivism—instead of replacing this violence with rules, Hart displaces the violence to the rule system itself, especially to the rule of recognition.[95] MacNeil also notes Hart's apparent indifference to the violence of law, symptomatic of his anxiety (as a positivist) to avoid invoking moral concepts of the good.[96] Even Hart's rule of recognition imbibes violence due to its circular nature (the officials recognise the rule that recognises them as officials), for it proclaims certainty when there is only ambiguity, and papers over what Derrida terms the 'mystical foundation of law'—that on this view, there is no foundation, only coercion.[97] Indeed, Hart ultimately appeals to law being recognised as that which Parliament enacts, which indicates no fundamental difference with Austin's theory.[98] But this is not quite so—MacNeil identifies that there is one problematic difference. Due to the internal aspect of Hart's rule system, the Austinian violence displaced there is no longer external, but internal. In other words, the gunman is now inside your head, so to speak; there is a mental 'shootout' between law and morality. Thus, MacNeil appeals for the return of Austinian positivism and the rejection of Hartian positivism, for at least Austin

[92] HLA Hart, *The Concept of Law* (Oxford University Press, 1994) 82.
[93] ibid 80–81, 100.
[94] ibid 86–89.
[95] W MacNeil, *Lex Populi* (Stanford University Press, 2007) 44.
[96] ibid 49–50.
[97] J Derrida, 'Force of Law: "The Mystical Foundation of Authority"', paper presented on Deconstruction and the Possibility of Justice, Cardozo Law School (1989) 10.
[98] MacNeil, above n 95, 53–54.

leaves room for inner thought and reflection, while Hart gives us a violence '(fascism) of the mind'.[99] The violence of secular positivism is maintained, and even intensified.

VI. Diagnosing Legal Violence: Cover, Benjamin and Derrida

So far, we have traced the development of the secularism and violence of law through its foundation in the theological natural law of Thomas Aquinas, its distortion in the voluntarism and univocity of Duns Scotus, its amplification in the paganism and conflict of Machiavelli and Hobbes, and its implementation in the secular positivism of Austin and Hart. This section elucidates the notion of contemporary law as violence using Robert Cover, Walter Benjamin and Jacques Derrida. This triad of thinkers are not only the key theorists of law and violence, but they can also show us what is missing from the violence of secular law and what ought to be recovered to redeem it—the love of Christ.

A. Law's Cover: *Logos*, *Nomos*, *Agon*

Robert Cover claims that law is not merely an external or categorical system of rules, but actually constitutes our existence. We inhabit a universe containing the narratives which give law meaning and construct the world in which we live. A legal tradition is part of a complex normative world governed by established narratives which set the paradigm for behaviour, and this affects even ordinary legal doctrine and procedure.[100] It follows that, insofar as law is constructed according to a mythical narrative of secularism and violence, so our world will be ontologically characterised by secularism and violence. Conversely, if law is constructed according to a theological narrative of peace, so our human relationships will consist of harmony.

Cover proceeds to argue that legal interpretation takes place in a 'field of pain, death, violence and suffering', for 'acts of legal interpretation occasion and signal the infliction of violence upon others'.[101] For example, a judge 'articulates their understanding of a text', and as a result people lose their freedom, property, children or lives. Interpretations can also constitute justifications for violence which has occurred or is about to occur, and this violence is intrinsic in organised social practice. The term 'interpretation' 'suggests a social construction of interpersonal reality through language', but 'pain and death together destroy one's ability to construct interpersonal realities', and even 'destroy language itself'.[102]

[99] ibid 58–60.

[100] R Cover, '*Nomos* and Narrative' (1983) 97(4) *Harvard Law Review* 4, 4–5, 9.

[101] R Cover, 'Violence and the Word' (1986) 95 *Yale Law Journal* 1601, 1601.

[102] ibid 1602.

Religious (and particularly Judeo-Christian) 'martyrdom' is the 'correct starting point for considering the nature of legal interpretation', because it is only through this 'extreme resistance against violence and commitment to uphold the law that law itself is constituted' and 'legal interpretation joined with systematic domination'.[103] A different but 'equally violent response' is that of revolution or rebellion, which 'forms the basis of American constitutional history'.[104] This produced the conditions for embedding the understanding of a political text (interpretation) in the institutional capacity to take collective action, which is precisely what distinguishes legal interpretation from other forms.[105]

Cover defines legal interpretation as a 'practical activity designed to generate credible threats and actual deeds of violence' in an effective way.[106] Legal interpretation is practical in the sense that it seeks to impose meaning on the legal institution and to restructure it in light of that meaning. In this way, legal interpretation also 'institutionalises particular language acts' so that they become social practice.[107] Ultimately, Cover concludes that violence in law is socially organised, for

> were the inhibition against violence perfect, law would be unnecessary; were it not capable of being overcome through social signals, law would be impossible … legal interpretation as a practice is incomplete without violence—because it depends upon the social practice of violence for its efficacy …[108]

The violence of law exposed by Cover is also associated with theological language. For example, Cover notes that the 'Word' (writing or the letter—the object of interpretation) is the site of violence in law, associating Christ as the Word or *logos* (the divine reason) with violence. He further uses the concept of Christian 'martyrdom' as the starting point for considering the nature of legal interpretation, since this symbolises resistance against violence. However, in Cover's framework, martyrdom connotes extreme violence, for it was the martyrs who suffered immensely torturous and excruciating deaths for the sake of upholding their faith. Thus, martyrdom is really a resistance against violence which in fact produces further dominance, implying that Cover's employment of the term demonstrates that the discourse and social practice of legal interpretation and law in general involves primary as well as tertiary violence.

B. Critiquing the Mystical Position of Law

(i) A Performative Force

This is further demonstrated by Derrida, who argues in *Force of Law* that the origin or foundation of the law is mystical in the sense that it is essentially neither legal

[103] ibid 1604–05.
[104] ibid.
[105] ibid 1606.
[106] ibid 1610–11.
[107] ibid.
[108] ibid 1613, 1628.

nor non-legal, but a positing by force—and that laws maintain their authority not because they are just, but simply because they are laws. Derrida notes that, through the language of 'enforcing the law', law is a 'force' that 'authorises or justifies itself', and raises the question of how we can distinguish between the (legitimate?) force of law and the 'originary violence that established that force of law as legitimate'.[109] Since justice is not necessarily law, it cannot become justice legitimately 'without recourse to force'—whether by withholding force or by appealing to force at its first moment—'at the beginning of justice there was *logos*, and force'.[110] 'The very emergence of justice and law implies a performative force', or a moment where the law is put down or 'posited'.[111] Since law 'prohibits individual violence in order to preserve itself', it actually 'monopolises violence', and there is a corresponding fascination with the person who exposes the violence of the legal system by defying the law.[112] The law is transcendent and theological, violent and non-violent, because it depends on who is before it or who institutes it.

Any expression of law shows itself to be violent through the making of a determination or the taking up of a position, for all law is dependent on a positing and no such positing manages without violence.[113] Law tends towards universality and transcendence; it operates to maintain and is self-preserving, so monopolises violence.[114] The mystical foundation of law is the silence in the violent structure of the founding act. This violence is ungrounded, or grounded only on itself. The foundation of law is mystical because it reiterates and propagates law, despite being a silence. Lawmaking violence is the very condition of violence, so that the ontology of violence is inherent in law as positing. Law-preserving violence is the corollary of this and maintains the hegemony of the dominant and violent juridical order. This violence that founds and conserves law guarantees nothing but power.

Derrida's starting premise is the secularisation of law. His statement that laws maintain their authority because they are law implies Austinian positivism, bearing in mind that according to both Derrida and Austin all law is dependent on a positing. Derrida acknowledges that no such positing is possible without violence or force, implying that at the foundation of law is an ontology of violence through both its establishment and its preservation by the imposition of force. Derrida describes such a foundation as 'mystical', 'theological' and 'transcendent', and associates these theological descriptions with violence. This is seen most explicitly in his statement that at the beginning of justice there was *logos* and force.

Borrowing the first verse of the Gospel According to John, Derrida conflates this Christian mode of expression with violence, secularising it by contending that this force or imposition of law is law's very (immanent) authority, rather than appealing

[109] Derrida, above n 97, 5–6.
[110] ibid 10.
[111] ibid 13.
[112] ibid 33.
[113] P Legrand, 'Introduction (of Derrida's Law)' in P Legrand (ed), *Derrida and Law* (Ashgate, 2009) xxxiv–xxxv.
[114] R Buonamano, 'The Economy of Violence: Derrida on Law and Justice' in Legrand, ibid, 105.

to the divine. Hence, Derrida identifies the secularisation of law, and argues that law has an intrinsic violence in its foundation, structure and practice. He also notes the association of this violence with theological terms and modes of expression borrowed from Christianity. This implies that law possesses pagan elements in the sense that in this secular framework there are 'religious' modes of expression associated with violence.

The theologically distorted or pagan nature of this legal ontology is exacerbated through Derrida's claim that in law reason is seen as irrelevant to the operation of violence, and is ultimately subordinated to 'fate-imposed violence'.[115] In other words, this violence is inevitable and not subject to reason or persuasion—it just is. Indeed, the inability of violence to be rationalised, and the *aporia* or lack of certainty in the very foundation of law, are precisely what gives violence the power to originate, generate and create justice and law, resulting in the recurrent co-implication or involvement of force and violence in the generation of justice and law.[116] Consequently, secular reason in law (which really is blind faith and the rejection of reason, for here we see that reason in law is made redundant by the imposition of violence by fate) is a distorted theology which produces violence in law.

(ii) Benjamin's Critique of Legal Violence

Derrida continues by examining Walter Benjamin's 'Critique of Violence', which distinguishes between the mythic or founding violence of law and the divine or annihilating and destructive violence of law. Derrida notes that any critique of violence 'must find meaning in the fact that violence is not an accident external to the law'.[117] 'That violence which threatens law is inherent in the right to law, the law of law, and the origin of law.'[118] The foundation of all states thus occurs in a way which may be termed revolutionary—it 'inaugurates a new law', and does so 'always in violence'.[119] For example, after a war, a new state is established by law, so it is the violence that causes and establishes law. Another example is the mixing of 'founding and conserving violence in law' through the police.[120]

Benjamin himself defines a critique of violence as 'expounding the relation of violence to law and justice'.[121] The legal system 'tries to erect, in all areas where individual ends could be usefully pursued by violence, legal ends that can only be realised by legal power'.[122] The law sees violence in the hands of individuals as a danger undermining the legal system, and consequently the law employs

115 D LaCapra, 'Violence, Justice and the Force of Law' (1989) 11 *Cardozo Law Review* 1065, 1071.

116 ibid 1067; D Cornell, 'Violence of the Masquerade: Law Dressed up as Justice' (1989) 11 *Cardozo Law Review* 1047, 1049.

117 Derrida, above n 97, 35.

118 ibid.

119 ibid.

120 ibid 42.

121 W Benjamin, 'Critique of Violence' in M Steger and N Lind (eds), *Violence and its Alternatives: An Interdisciplinary Reader* (St Martin's Press, 1999) 57.

122 ibid 59.

systemic violence to prevent individual violence. As such, the law has an 'interest in a monopoly of violence' in order to preserve itself and prohibit any existence of violence outside the law.[123] There is inherent in all military violence, the 'violence that declares peace subsequent to war', a 'lawmaking character'.[124] This is the first function of violence, the lawmaking function. The second function of violence is the 'law-preserving function', a 'threatening violence' which inhibits the criminal based on their ignorance of whether they will be apprehended and suffer the punishment for breaking the law as a 'matter of fate'.[125] As Benjamin notes,

> if violence, violence crowned by fate, is the origin of law, then it may be readily supposed that where the highest violence, that over life and death, occurs in the legal system, the origins of law jut manifestly and fearsomely into existence.[126]

All violence as a means has either of these two functions, and this is implicated in the problematic nature of law itself.

According to Benjamin, in distinguishing mythical violence from divine violence, mythical violence is a 'mere manifestation of the [pagan] gods', for 'God opposes myth' and mythical violence is 'confronted by the divine', which is its 'antithesis'.[127] As argued in the third chapter, Benjamin's mythical violence is fundamentally pagan, given its basis in pagan mythology. Mythical violence is also lawmaking violence, and fate 'in all cases underlies legal violence'.[128] 'Lawmaking is power making, and, to that extent, an immediate manifestation of violence. Justice is the principle of all divine end making, power the principle of all mythical lawmaking.'[129] Fundamentally, according to Benjamin, in mythical violence myth has been 'bastardised with law', and mythical, lawmaking violence is 'pernicious'.[130] Hence, violence alone can guarantee law, and 'the mythical manifestation of immediate violence shows itself fundamentally identical with all legal violence'.[131]

Benjamin echoes Cover and Derrida by diagnosing the indissoluble connection of law with violence, implying a fundamental ontology of violence in law. The language Benjamin uses uniquely links this violence in law with neo-pagan mythology, connoting the operational process of law as a type of supernature. For example, Benjamin refers to the notion of 'fate', or violence crowned with fate, as the origin of law itself, and instrumental in its monopolisation of violence as self-preservation. The notion of fate is irretrievably pagan: for example, in Greek mythology one's destiny is subject to the foibles of the gods. The fact that Benjamin appropriates this language and associates it with violence as the origin and

[123] ibid.
[124] ibid 60.
[125] ibid 61.
[126] ibid 62.
[127] ibid 66–67.
[128] ibid 66.
[129] ibid 67.
[130] ibid 69.
[131] ibid.

foundation of law serves to profoundly demonstrate that both the discourse and social practice of law possess an intrinsic ontology of pagan violence.

In particular, mythical violence is the manifestation of the pagan gods, and Benjamin relates a pagan parable to illustrate its function, and the fact that myth has been 'bastardised' with law renders it 'pernicious'. Moreover, Benjamin's claim that divine violence is antithetical to mythical violence fares no better in terms of evacuating a violent ontology of law, for divine violence, despite its claim to be divine, always inaugurates a new law with violence. It replaces violence with violence. Hence, both Derrida and Benjamin seek to rationalise this notion of bloodless divine violence, which is arguably no less violent than mythic violence.[132]

LaCapra, a commentator on Derrida, law and violence, develops this point further, observing this fixation upon violence and its uncontrolled operation, aiming to stress the desirability of demystifying violence in order to permit control over this image, which can become extremely powerful in conjunction with secular faith and the loss of the sacred, and can lead to violent action independent of knowledge or security regarding the action.[133] LaCapra identifies the fact that Benjamin's binary of mythic and divine violence can therefore be deconstructed as holistically violent, for not only does Benjamin fail to demystify divine violence by explaining how it is bloodless, but he implicates both mythic and divine violence as mutually involved in the sacrifice.[134] Thus, divine violence is no less an ontology of violence than mythic violence, and such an ontology in law is fundamentally non-Christian.

VII. Escaping Legal Violence and the Possibility for Christian Peace

The ontology of violence in law is contingent, and if we wish to redeem our contemporary secular legal system and remove its violence, there is a need to propose a different foundation, the return to and extension of a peaceful Christian theology. This need to redeem law is recognised by Benjamin and Cover. For example, Benjamin poses the question of whether there are 'no other than violent means for regulating conflicting human interests'.[135] In addressing this question, Benjamin argues that there is, and includes 'peaceableness and trust' as two of its subjective preconditions. The 'objective manifestation of these preconditions is determined by the law of unalloyed means and indirect solutions'.[136] In particular,

[132] Cornell, above n 116, 1048; *cf* LaCapra above n 115, 1077.
[133] LaCapra, above n 115, 1065–66.
[134] ibid 1072–73.
[135] Benjamin, above n 121, 62–63.
[136] ibid 63.

Benjamin points to a 'wholly transformed interaction', no longer 'enforced by violence', but more 'consummates than causes' in its effects.[137]

This non-violent means of producing a peaceful legal community is found in Christian theology, which opens up the space for revelation of the truth in the Incarnation, and most particularly in the law of love. This is because Christianity does not advocate the simple abolition of law, which would be replacing violence with violence akin to Benjamin's divine violence, but instead advocates transcending and redeeming the law through the Spirit and love. Christian theology meets Benjamin's preconditions, for Christianity has an ontology of peace and communicates peace between people and God through the Incarnation, and allows unparalleled mutual trust through the law of love, a demonstration of the divine trustworthiness in Christ.

Cover, too, notes that under the secular law of violence, or in the 'civil' or 'imperial' community,

> norms are universal and *enforced* by institutions ... discourse is premised on objectivity—upon that which is external to the discourse itself. Interpersonal commitments are weak, premised only upon a minimalist obligation to refrain from the coercion and violence that would make impossible the objective mode of discourse and the impartial and neutral application of norms.[138]

To this he contrasts Karl Barth, who, writing of Christian community,

> emphasizes the absence from civil community of strong interpersonal bonds, of the common meanings found in shared ritual or prayer, and of a common corpus—Torah, creed, or gospel—that is taught, believed in, and recognized as the moving normative force of the community.[139]

One can either have a secular system of self-interested antagonistic struggle requiring external violence for its mitigation or one can have a peaceful community of strong interpersonal bonds, loving relationships based on the revelation of the divine as the governing principle of the community—a stark contrast between an ontology of violence and an ontology of peace.

Modern law is characterised by its typically proceeding from a sovereign power granted legitimacy through a general popular consent as mediated by representation. If such a procedure is taken to be normative, it can be seen as the embodiment of a Hobbesian natural law for the derivation of legitimate power from conflicts endemic to human life.[140] Ultimately for this reason, life and law are supposed to harmonise, though cannot always or ultimately at all, save negatively and catastrophically. Because the formal framework of law is absolute and is taken to proceed from universal consent, an absolutely sovereign power must be erected to enforce this law, leading to the artificial control of human life. Furthermore, the

[137] ibid 65.
[138] Cover, '*Nomos* and Narrative', above n 100, 13 (original emphasis).
[139] ibid 13–14.
[140] Milbank, 'Paul against Biopolitics', above n 35, 24.

formal system of laws never provides a complete guarantee of order, so the laws must be supplemented and defended through violence, in a way that overrules the principles of the laws themselves. To justify this, an appeal to some transcendent myth is made.

However, 'the immanent secular political sphere is defined by a positivity regulated by formal rules, the aporetic fracture of [which] reveals that the circumscription of the secular is never finally secure'.[141] The secular can never fully regulate, and its attempts to do so exacerbate violence. When the law was ineffective or unjust in medieval modes of governance, an appeal was made to an eternal, divine, transcendent law. To address the violence in our modern mode of governance, the transcendent law required is found through the Incarnation: the law of love, which restores reason to faith and fulfils the need for transcendence while producing a community of peace.

As much as secularised law tends towards antagonism and alienation, and is thus violent since it cannot take account of particularity or difference, so conversely do the law of love and the Trinity take account of difference and the welfare of one's individual neighbour. As much as the emergence of secularised law and justice implies a performative force, by contrast the emergence of the Christian legal ontology of peace is based on the Incarnation and love displayed in Christ, who exposes the violence of the law in his crucifixion by defying death through the letter of the law in his resurrection. In short, it is not necessary to succumb to the constant inauguration of a new law in violence, one governed by the 'fate' of neo-paganism. Rather, like Augustine writing against the violence of original paganism, one can embrace the inauguration of the new law of Christ which governs the City of God: the law of love producing a legal community of peace. The next chapter expands on this law of Christ by examining the trial of Christ.

[141] ibid 28.

5

Violence, Attestation and Revelation: Reading Law and Truth in the Trial of Christ

I. The Trial as a Narrative of Law and Truth

The trial of Christ illustrates the contrast between the theological law of peace revealed by Christ and the secular law of violence. It is the paradigmatic example of secularised law's failure to resolve the tension between attestation and revelation except through violence. Here, attestation refers to a formalistic idea of law as a series of rules exercised by and through power, a secularised law of the letter which lacks spirit. Conversely, revelation refers to the truth of Christ divinely revealed: namely, that law as secular rules of certainty can never comprehend the mystery and faith of the divine, with the result that the secular attempts to suppress the divine through violence. This suppression is displayed in the crucifixion of Christ, yet in this tragic event there is hope—the death of Christ in our place bears the violent curse of the law and his resurrection allows the institution of a new law, one of love and peace.

The first part of the chapter identifies the trial as a repository of law and truth, what is in effect a narrative of a series of events in terms of legal rules which allegedly produce 'truth'. This forms a legal foundation for the subsequent analysis of Christ's trial, which is overviewed with reference to the four gospel accounts. Section II furnishes the theological foundation for this analysis, examining some of the writings of the Apostle Paul regarding his contrast between the law of the letter, the Mosaic *Torah* (which leads to death), and the law of the Spirit, also known as the law of love, enabled and modelled through Christ's sacrifice. The concept of this truth as revelation is also outlined, with particular regard to the notion of truth as divinely instantiated and divinely revealed. The chapter then moves to specifically discuss the Jewish and Roman law forming the legal milieu for the trial of Christ in section III, before analysing the details of the trial itself (as they are related in the four distinct gospel accounts) as the violent clash of rules and power; the prosecution of the trial is therefore characterised by a secularised law which by definition cannot comprehend the divine, but always tries to suppress it. Section IV contends that in the event of Christ, revelation becomes primary, for Christ is firstly a figure that disrupts the idea of law as certain, formal rules through injecting faith and mystery, and secondly an atoning figure who redeems this violent and relentless drive for decision (certainty). With the space opened for a new law in Christ, section V therefore proposes that this is the law of love and faith, and begins to envisage the existence of a community based in mutual trust and self-sacrifice through participating in the divine love—a community with a spirit of life and peace. Section VI notes the Resurrection as key to implementing this law of love and a peaceful community.

There are some aspects of the trial which are universal, transcending times, places and cultures. These common features, stripped of jurisdictional peculiarities, suggest that there is some essence of a trial which is common to the proceedings against Socrates under Athenian law in 399 BC, those brought against Jesus in AD 30 under Jewish and Roman law and the procedure against OJ Simpson in a Los Angeles courtroom approximately 2000 years later.[1]

In particular, the rationale and process of trials are fundamentally an account in the sense that a trial (regardless of differing jurisdictional rules) ideally attempts to discern the backstory or context of a particular factual accusation regarding a person, or a set of ideas or 'facts' about a person which are taken as given. The term 'trial' can then be understood in its 'forensic sense, which, in addition to involving a test of an issue, implies a procedure or ritual to try that issue in a forum whose authority and validity are accepted as binding by the community subject to its jurisdiction'.[2] In particular, it can involve 'the finding out by due examination of the truth of the point in issue or the question between the parties whereupon judgment may be given', and this includes both criminal trials, where the outcome will put the person on trial in jeopardy, and civil trials, where law can be seen as the 'reconciliation of competing interests'.[3] So the trial includes the tracing of alleged ideas and concepts about a person to reveal whether those concepts are in fact substantiated.

The general features of a trial process can be briefly stated as the accusation, the response by the accused, the oral and written argument on the factual and legal issues involving the interrogation of witnesses, the delivery of judgment and, if required, an announcement of sanction.[4] Ultimately, then, the central function of a trial 'is to arrive at a determination, whether that the person charged is guilty or that he is to be absolved from guilt'.[5] A so-called 'fair' trial requires 'rationality' or objectivity, the use of certain canons or rules of evidence to ensure appropriate balance between the competing parties, and that decisions are not made capriciously or with a particular purpose in mind.[6] This idea of rationally matching the

[1] J Jaconelli, 'What is a Trial?' in M Mulholland and B Pullan (eds), *The Trial in History: Volume 1* (Manchester University Press, 2003) 18.

[2] M Mulholland, 'Introduction' in Mulholland and Pullan, ibid, 2–3.

[3] ibid 5.

[4] Jaconelli, above n 1, 24.

[5] ibid 29.

[6] Mulholland, above n 2, 6.

evidence to the question of guilt or innocence is contextualised by the liberal privileging of the individual in the modern context, exemplified by the presumption of innocence and the existence of procedures to exclude evidence which is deemed unfair or unjust to the accused.[7] Hence, both the civil law (inquisitorial) system and the common law (adversarial) system are designed to ascertain the 'true facts so as to come to a just judgment'.[8] Another requirement of a fair or just trial is publicity or openness—justice must be 'seen to be done'.[9] A third requirement is that there must be independence of the judiciary from the government and any of the parties or 'no bias in the tribunal that decides the issue. Freedom from bias is an essential characteristic of the judicial function.'[10]

As this chapter analyses the trial of Christ, I must initially overview the characteristics of his trial and establish firstly whether it is a 'trial' in the sense described above. I can then describe the extent to which I can connect the modern aspects of a Western legal trial to the events described in the gospel accounts pertaining to the trial of Christ. To begin with the account according to Matthew, in Matthew 26:57–68, Jesus is taken before the Sanhedrin at night in secret. The Sanhedrin then seek testimony against Jesus so that they may put him to death, but they find none. Eventually, a witness comes forward telling of Jesus' declaration that he will destroy and rebuild the temple, and Jesus admits that he is the Son of God. The High Priest, Caiaphas, proclaims this as blasphemous and the Sanhedrin decide to put him to death. This is confirmed by another meeting of the Sanhedrin at dawn, and Jesus is then taken before Pilate in Matthew 27:1–2. In verses 11–26 Pilate interrogates Jesus, but Jesus remains silent; Pilate, pressured by the crowd, delivers Jesus over to be crucified despite concluding that he is innocent. Unique to Matthew is the description in verse 19 of Pilate's wife asking Pilate not to become involved in the dispute over the innocent Jesus after being warned in a dream, as well as Pilate symbolically washing his hands of Jesus and the Jewish people, declaring that his blood was on their heads (verses 24–25).

Apart from the details described in Matthew 27:19, 24–25, Mark's account of the trial in 14:53–65; 15:1–15 tells much the same story as Matthew's account. Luke's account in Luke 22:66–70 places the trial before the Sanhedrin in the morning after Jesus' arrest and mocking. Here the Sanhedrin question him in a similar way (though there is no mention of false witnesses), and Jesus implicitly admits that he is the Son of God. The Sanhedrin require no further testimony and take Jesus before Pilate in Luke 23:1–5. They accuse him of claiming kingship in competition with Caesar, and again, Pilate finds no guilt in Jesus. In verses 6–16 Pilate sends Christ to Herod because he is a Galilean within Herod's jurisdiction. Despite questioning from Herod and vehement accusations from the Sanhedrin, Jesus stays silent and Herod returns him to Pilate. Pilate plans to release Jesus since

[7] Jaconelli, above n 1, 26.
[8] Mulholland, above n 2, 9.
[9] ibid 10–11.
[10] ibid 12.

he is innocent (according to verses 18–25), but, due to the protests of the Jews, Pilate eventually accedes to their request.

John's account in John 18:12–14; 19–24; 28–40; 19:1–16 is far more detailed than the synoptics and includes many unique features. In 18:12–14 Jesus is initially led to Annas, rather than Caiaphas, for questioning. Caiaphas had been legally installed as High Priest and leader of the Sanhedrin by Rome in AD 15, but Annas, as his predecessor, would still have been considered the rightful man for the position because the Jews considered the role of High Priest to be until death.[11] Annas questions Jesus in verses 19–24, and Jesus responds by saying that his teachings have always been public. Jesus is then taken to Caiaphas. In verses 28–40 Jesus is taken to Pilate in the early morning. Pilate asks the Jews to resolve this dispute internally, but they respond by saying they do not have authority to put anyone to death. Pilate questions Jesus about the nature of his kingship and Jesus states that he is a king, but that his kingdom is not of this world. His purpose is to bear witness to the truth and everyone who is of the truth listens to him. Pilate responds by asking 'what is truth?', before leaving to tell the Jews that he finds no guilt in Jesus. In John 19:1–16 Pilate appeals to Jesus to contend for his innocence since Pilate has the authority to release or condemn, but Jesus refuses, noting his own authority and the sin of those who delivered him up. Pilate sought to release Jesus, but eventually gave in to the crowd's demands to have him crucified, as the crowd was claiming that Jesus' kingship was in opposition to Caesar.

From these observations, Jesus' trial is in fact a trial in the sense described earlier. There is an accusation or charge, questioning of the accused, testimony and questioning of witnesses, arrival of determination of guilt, delivery of the verdict and sanction by a tribunal. More accurately, there are really two trials—the initial trial before the Sanhedrin, which occurs in a number of phases, and the trial before Pilate. The accounts note that Jesus is questioned by the Sanhedrin and accused of being a blasphemer (Matthew 26:57–68; Mark 14:53–65; Luke 23:66–71; John 18:19–24). Matthew and Mark uniquely record that in the midst of this there is also the testimony of (false) witnesses as evidence for the purpose of establishing the accusations against Jesus (Matthew 26:59–61; Mark 15:55–59). Mark's account states that none of the false witnesses agreed, but the Sanhedrin nevertheless required Jesus to answer the charges; Matthew's account states that two of the witnesses agreed on the charge of destroying and rebuilding the temple and so Jesus was required to answer the charges. Matthew and Mark explicitly record the Sanhedrin's determination that Jesus is guilty of blasphemy and that the penalty deserved is death (Matthew 26:65–66; Mark 14:63–64), while the accounts of Luke and John only imply this verdict and sanction (Luke 22:71–23:1; John 18:24, 28–31). All four accounts record the Sanhedrin taking Jesus to Pilate so that Pilate may question him; though Pilate's inquiry finds no guilt in Jesus, Pilate acquiesces to the verdict of the Sanhedrin and condemns Jesus to death (Matthew 27:1–2, 11–26; Mark 15:1–15; Luke 23:1–5, 13–25; John 18:28–19:16).

[11] C Blomberg, *Jesus and the Gospels* (B&H Publishing Group, 2009) 396.

In these trials, there are connections with the modern Western trial through, for example, the use of witness testimony, arguably a lack of objectivity, and in some situations a lack of publicity (though the trial was very public in other situations). Nevertheless, the unique processes and issues associated with Christ's trial(s) before the Sanhedrin and Pilate are indicative of the legal, political and theological context of the time—and it is precisely that which this chapter analyses in the context of articulating a jurisprudence of peace rather than violence.

For Christ, then, we should bear in mind the various rules and theological ideas which characterise the 'jurisdiction' of his trial, and particularly consider how these are assumed or manipulated to manufacture the desired (violent) outcome. The aim here is not to construct a narrative of the trial in general, but rather to use the trial as a narrative example of how these concepts are incorporated and distorted in the trial of Christ, and how they may be questioned in terms of the violent result. In any case, having considered some of the central characteristics and purposes of the trial in general and Christ's trial in particular, I now proceed to articulate the specific underlying theological concepts and rules.

II. Laws of Sin and Laws of Spirit: Paul, Faith and the *Torah*

A. The Law of Death

The theology undergirding the life, death and resurrection of Jesus Christ (and the interpretation of this event by the early Christians) is contained in the New Testament of the Bible. The New Testament is a collection of 27 writings by various authors shortly after Christ in the first century AD. These writings include the four gospels (historical accounts of Jesus' life and ministry), the Acts of the Apostles (a historical account of the early church and particularly the ministry of the Apostles Peter and Paul), the Pauline epistles (letters written by the Apostle Paul to various churches and individuals), epistles by other prominent members of the early church, such as James, John and Peter, and finally the Revelation, an apocalyptic prophecy experienced by the Apostle John. In particular, the epistles, written by the Apostles and their associates, contain theological reflections on the significance of Jesus' life, death and resurrection, giving advice on how one should live in response to this.

Included among these is the Apostle Paul's Epistle to the Romans. Paul, a self-proclaimed apostle of Jesus Christ, was a missionary sent to preach the good news of salvation by grace through faith to the non-Jewish nations in the mid-first century AD, and to establish churches among these nations. However, Paul had not personally established the church at Rome, nor had he visited there.[12] His desire to travel as an itinerant evangelist, in conjunction with his desire to visit the city of Rome, led him to compose a letter to the church at Rome. In this letter he informed the Romans of his plans and outlined the entirety of the message he had been preaching as an introductory gesture, and to refute prevalent false teaching. As a former Pharisee, and expert in the Jewish law, his doctrine had a natural emphasis on law, both divine and civil.[13] Thus, Paul comprehensively set forth his position on the internal and external functions of the divine and civil law in his Epistle to the Romans.

One of the major themes in Romans is the contrast between the law (of sin), which leads to sin and death, and the (law of the) spirit, which leads to life and peace. When Paul refers to 'the law' in Romans, he usually means the Pentateuch or *Torah*, the first five books of the Old Testament, containing moral, civil and ceremonial laws for the Jewish people. It is this law that Paul sees as leading to violence, sin and death.[14] However, this is not to say Paul's discussion of law exclusively refers to the *Torah*; it could, for example, include reference to the (Roman) civil law. When Paul says that the law kills, he means all of the law—he appears to make no distinction between the ritual law and the moral law.[15] The law of God is the whole law, given by God and connected with sin.[16] One could presume that this also includes the civil law, both that of the Jews, in the *Torah*, and that of the Gentiles, which Romans 13 explicitly discusses. The discussion of law applies to civil and ceremonial, Gentile and Jew.

Sanders goes further, and explicitly connects the *Torah* with the Roman civil law, not making any distinction between the function of the two.[17] This implies that, in Paul's mind and the Jewish context, the question of the authority of law could not be divided with reference to the type of law considered.[18] Paul's contention is that the law should be fulfilled, including ceremonial, moral and civil law, and the method of fulfilling it is by the law of love (Romans 13:8–10).[19] Consequently, admonitions by Paul in regard to the civil law are remarkably in accord with the *Torah* and Jewish tradition.[20] Sanders even goes so far as to state that:

> Since the point is not controversial ... Rom. 13:8–10 makes no obvious distinction between the law that Christians should obey and the Mosaic law. There Paul not only quotes Lev. 19:18, but also itemizes four of the Ten Commandments and adds 'and any other commandment' as being included in Lev. 19:18.[21]

[12] J Murray, *The Epistle to the Romans: The English Text with Introduction, Exposition and Notes* (Wm B Eerdmans, 1997) xiii, xvii.

[13] F Bruce, *The Letter of Paul to the Romans: An Introduction and Commentary* (InterVarsity Press, 1985) 14, 31–32, 50.

[14] R Pfeiffer, *Introduction to the Old Testament* (Adam and Charles Black, 1966) 129.

[15] EP Sanders, *Paul, The Law, and the Jewish People* (Fortress Press, 1983) 83.

[16] ibid 86.

[17] ibid 93.

[18] ibid 96.

[19] ibid.

[20] ibid 94–95.

[21] ibid 99.

It is therefore not inconsistent with Paul's Jewish content and heritage to apply his discussion of the *Torah* in Romans 3–8 to his discussion of the civil law in Romans 13:1–10. Indeed, the general view in Judaism is that God ordained all parts of the law, and rejecting any of the law was tantamount to rejecting God himself.[22]

Returning to the text of Romans specifically, Paul states that:

> If it had not been for the law, I would not have known sin. For I would not have known what it is to covet if the law had not said, 'You shall not covet.' But sin, seizing an opportunity through the commandment, produced in me all kinds of covetousness. For apart from the law, sin lies dead. I was once alive apart from the law, but when the commandment came, sin came alive and I died. The very commandment that promised life proved to be death to me. For sin, seizing an opportunity through the commandment, deceived me and through it killed me.[23]

Here Paul connects the law with sin. Sin may be defined, apart from guilt or moral awareness, as 'all that prevents a person from realising God's purpose and … obeying the commandment'.[24] Though law is not equated with sin, the law makes us aware of sin and produces guilt. The very function of the law itself is not to produce obedience or goodness, but instead to cause moral struggle and inner tension.[25] Therefore, it is the law that empowers sin, for without the law sin lies dormant. When sin is then given the opportunity to manifest through the law, it promises life by holding up the standard for obedience but delivers death due to the impossibility of attaining that standard. Thus, according to Paul, the reason the law fails to give life but instead brings knowledge of sin is because in the law, or the 'old way of the written code', where stringent obedience to a standard is demanded, faith is 'null' because this is irrelevant to striving for obedience, and the law 'brings wrath' since one cannot obey it.[26] The law as written code, as just a series of mandates and prohibitions, renders faith useless and brings violence.

Paul also engages in an extended discussion of the law in his letter to the Galatians. However, in Galatians Paul is not as free to systematically develop his thoughts as he is in the (later) letter to the Romans—here Paul is dealing with the intense controversy of legalism, or the claim by Jewish Christians that Gentiles must keep the *Torah* to be Christians.[27] Therefore, Paul is anxious to expose the destruction that comes from reliance on the law, or the 'works of the flesh' (which may specifically allude to the requirement for physical circumcision to be part of

[22] ibid 103. Milbank too states that Paul's use of 'law' refers to both Roman and Jewish law: see J Milbank, 'Paul against Biopolitics' in J Milbank et al (eds), *Paul's New Moment: Continental Philosophy and the Future of Christian Theology* (Brazos Press, 2010), 44.

[23] Romans 7:7–11.

[24] EC Blackman, 'The Letter of Paul to the Romans' in C Laymon (ed), *The Interpreter's Concise Commentary on Acts and Paul's Letters* (Abingdon, 1983) 137.

[25] ibid 143.

[26] ibid 132; Romans 3:20; 4:14; 7:5–6.

[27] VP Furnish, 'The Letter of Paul to the Galatians' in C Laymon (ed), *The Interpreter's Concise Commentary on Acts and Paul's Letters* (Abingdon, 1983) 272–73.

the church).[28] Paul broadens the problem and describes the way that this type of law leads to violence in Galatians 5:18–21, contrasting it with the Spirit:

> But if you are led by the Spirit, you are not under the law. Now the works of the flesh are evident: sexual immorality, impurity, sensuality, idolatry, sorcery, enmity, strife, jealousy, fits of anger, rivalries, dissensions, divisions, envy, drunkenness, orgies, and things like these. I warn you, as I warned you before, that those who do such things will not inherit the kingdom of God.

In other words, Paul argues that under the law sin dominates and manifests in all manner of violent acts, with the result that those who engage in such conduct will not inherit the kingdom of God. This is why Paul describes the law as a 'curse' which 'imprisons' us and inevitably leads to violence, sin and death, 'for if a law had been given that could give life, then righteousness would indeed be by the law'.[29] The law 'demands doing, in a formal, legalistic sense'.[30] Elsewhere Paul refers to the law, the written code devoid of spirit, as 'the ministry of death', for 'the letter kills'.[31] It is finally worth noting that Paul is here primarily referring to 'internal' spiritual death, but his position also encompasses an 'external' physical death through legal violence, specifically displayed through the crucifixion of Christ. Paul appears to refer to this in Romans 5 in explaining how death entered the world through sin in relation to Adam.

B. The Law of Life

(i) Paul For and Against Law

The astute Pauline scholar may recognise a difficulty here. I (allegedly following Paul) have so far been quite critical of the (Mosaic) law, claiming that it leads to violence and death, and in some sense annuls faith. However, this does not mean that Paul is intrinsically against the law. Indeed, he says 'What then shall we say? That the law is sin? By no means! ... the law is holy, and the commandment is holy and righteous and good.'[32] So the problem is apparently not with the inherent notion of 'the law'. Nor is it an issue of the law's 'secular' origin, for the Mosaic law was revealed to Moses by God (see, eg, Exodus 19–20). Instead, the problem is the legalistic, codified, formal nature of law—not that it lacks faith in the broad sense of being from the secular, but that it lacks faith and spirit in the more specific sense of lacking the revelation of Christ and our participation in this revelation. It is not that the law is intrinsically evil, but that it has been distorted (secularised) and superseded, so that continuing to impose its application results in violence—the

[28] ibid 288, 298–99.
[29] Galatians 3:10, 21, 23.
[30] Furnish, above n 27, 289.
[31] 2 Corinthians 3:3, 6.
[32] Romans 7:7a; 12.

circumscription and limitation (alienation) of interactions between persons and the divine.

> Summarizing, we can state that for Paul the law is still holy and of divine origin—this is denied nowhere in his texts. Yet the law is no longer valid for the Christians who should not even attempt to comply with it: it expired when Christ appeared.[33]

Paul explains why in Romans:

> For the law of the Spirit of life has set you free in Christ Jesus from the law of sin and death. For God has done what the law, weakened by the flesh, could not do. By sending his own Son in the likeness of sinful flesh and for sin, he condemned sin in the flesh, in order that the righteous requirement of the law might be fulfilled in us, who walk not according to the flesh but according to the Spirit. For those who live according to the flesh set their minds on the things of the flesh, but those who live according to the Spirit set their minds on the things of the Spirit. For to set the mind on the flesh is death, but to set the mind on the Spirit is life and peace.[34]

For Paul, the life, death and resurrection of Christ is foundational for breaking the curse of the secularised letter of the law, since the same Spirit which raised Christ from the dead gives life to the law and redeems it, transforming it by faith. In this passage Paul uses law 'in the sense of "authority" or "principle". The new regime is inaugurated by the Spirit … which is, or creates, life. It cancels out the results of that other regime which spread sin and death.'[35] Though the law is still in place, it is a fundamentally different system—one which produces life rather than death.

In the similar context of refuting the claim that adherence to legalistic ordinances is necessary for salvation, Paul states in Colossians that, through faith in the powerful working of God, those who believe in Christ were 'raised to life together with Christ' by his 'cancelling of the demands of the letter of the law'.[36] Christ, in his death and resurrection, 'brought freedom from this enslavement to an external code'.[37] In this way, with Christ, the Christian has died to the old law and is consequently released from its imprisonment constraining us to endless and impossible adherence, and is raised from the dead with him 'so that we serve in the new way of the Spirit and not in the old way of the written code'.[38] Through the resurrection of Christ, law has been redeemed in the sense that the old law is gone and the new has come, so that we may obey this law in the new way of the Spirit of life, and not the old way of the written code, which leads to sin and death.

In Romans, Paul argues that such obedience is found in the type of faith of Abraham, who obeyed the commands of God through a spirit of trust in the

[33] L Thuren, *Derhetorising Paul: A Dynamic Perspective on Pauline Theology and the Law* (Mohr Siebeck, 2000) 181.

[34] Romans 8:2–6.

[35] Blackman, above n 559, 147.

[36] Colossians 2:12–15; Furnish, above n 27, 382.

[37] Victor Paul Furnish, 'The Letter of Paul to the Colossians' in Charles Laymon (ed), *The Interpreter's Concise Commentary on Acts and Paul's Letters* (Abingdon, 1983) 382.

[38] Romans 7:4–6.

faithfulness and truth of God. Hence, if we have the same faith as Abraham, the same righteousness will be accounted to us who believe that the dead Jesus Christ was raised for our justification. This Pauline notion of justification by faith is the essence of Christian peace, for Paul contends that 'since we have been justified by faith, we have peace with God through our Lord Jesus Christ'.[39] The specific importance of faith will be explained later, but for now it should be noted that faith in the resurrection of Christ is fundamental in Paul's explanation of how the law is redeemed in the Spirit from the old written code which leads to death. It is on this basis that Paul can argue in Romans 8:2–6 that the law of the Spirit of life in Christ Jesus has set us free from the law of sin, violence and death, instituting a new law so that the law of the Spirit consequently produces peace.

Paul expands on some implications of this new covenant, the law of the Spirit which gives life rather than the law of the letter which kills, in 2 Corinthians 3. 2 Corinthians was written to the church at Corinth at a time when it was rife with sin and false teachers. In particular, these false teachers claimed that Paul was a false Apostle. Paul responds by arguing that his authority as an Apostle is grounded in the fact that God has made him competent as a minister of the new covenant in the Spirit, which in turn forms the foundation for the establishment of the church itself.[40] In particular, Paul notes that, since the former 'ministry of death' came with a degree of glory such that the Israelites could not even gaze upon it, the new ministry of life through the Spirit comes with 'even more glory'—the glory of the Lord Jesus Christ.[41] John Milbank's notion of Christ as Incarnational Paradox, where paradox is etymologically divided into para-doxa, or double/overwhelming glory, would seem to allude to this.

Those who are captive to the old law of the letter are 'veiled' in their perception of the glory of Christ Incarnate, and so what is required is the true glory of Christ to be revealed. Such occurs through the Spirit, which brings freedom.[42]

This revelation of the glory of Christ is also discussed in the opening chapter of the Gospel According to John. John is fundamentally writing to demonstrate to his audience of fledgling churches that Jesus Christ is the Son of God so that they may believe; Jesus is viewed as the revelatory Word of God, revealing the truth of the ultimate reality of God's person and character.[43] The light of Christ's glory illuminates those who believe and is the full display of God's magnificence to the world.[44] So John states that we have 'seen the glory of Christ as the only Son of the Father, full of grace and truth'.[45] The glory of Christ bringing grace

[39] Romans 4:20–5:1.

[40] J Price, 'The Second Letter of Paul to the Corinthians' in C Laymon (ed), *The Interpreter's Concise Commentary on Acts and Paul's Letters* (Abingdon, 1983) 245.

[41] 2 Corinthians 3:7–8.

[42] See 2 Corinthians 3:6–17.

[43] R Gundry, *A Survey of the New Testament* (Zondervan, 1970) 104–05.

[44] ibid 118.

[45] John 1:14.

and truth is then explicitly contrasted with the Old Testament law, 'for the law was given through Moses; grace and truth came through Jesus Christ'.[46] With this contrast John aims to transform the prevailing paradigm that the law is the Word or *logos* of God, the ultimate communication of God to humanity.[47] Instead, the way to know God, to participate in his being, is through Jesus Christ, not through the law.[48]

The ministry of the Spirit is central to revealing the glory (and thus the divinity) of Christ, and revealing the glory of Christ is equivalent to grace and truth. Indeed, the connection between revelation and truth is key, and may be explained through linguistic analysis of the New Testament in conjunction with the above textual considerations. As such, in contrast to the attestation of the truth of the glory (or divinity) of Christ according to the Old Testament law, which actually veils the glory of Christ and leads to death, the new way of the Spirit which leads to life and peace involves divine revelation of the glory of Christ, and this is truth—as the Gospel According to John states, God in this way has made Christ known.[49] I consequently turn to consider the linguistic context of this argument that New Testament truth is divine revelation.

(ii) The New Law: Truth, Revelation, Participation

The New Testament was written in a particular dialect of Greek known as *koine*, or 'common' Greek (as opposed to the classical Greek used by the philosophers), since it was the standard language of routine commerce and communication. This language originated from the ancient Hellenes, who settled in the Greek peninsula in the thirteenth century BC, and was spoken by both the cultured and the laity. Therefore, it was a language uniquely suited to the effective propagation of the good news of Christ to the nations of the world.[50] Uniquely, the primarily Jewish background and consequent Semitic influence on the New Testament writers often resulted in a nuanced use of common Greek, blending the wisdom of Hebrew with the dialectic philosophy of Greek, and the candour of Hebrew thought with the precision of Greek expression. As such, New Testament Greek frequently created its own idiom.[51] It is particularly necessary in this context that an analysis of the New Testament linguistic concept of truth reflects an understanding of the relevant New Testament Greek.

There are eight words in the New Testament which are consistently translated as truth, or some derivative or equivalent.[52] The most common of these is *aletheia*,

[46] John 1:17.

[47] J Painter, 'John the Evangelist as Theologian' in D Peterson and J Pryor (eds), *In the Fullness of Time* (Anzea, 1992) 99.

[48] ibid 102.

[49] John 1:18.

[50] D Black, *Learn to Read New Testament Greek* (Broadman and Holman Publishers, 1994) 1.

[51] L Walker, 'Biblical Languages' in D Horton (ed), *The Portable Seminary* (Bethany House, 2006) 60–65.

[52] R Young, *Analytical Concordance to the Bible* (Wm B Eerdmans, 1977) 1005.

and its translation is multifaceted not because of its ambiguity, but because of how its meaning alters according to the context in which it is used. *Aletheia* is derived from *alethes*, which has its root in the combination of *a*, the first letter of the Greek alphabet and a particle used as a prefix to express a negation, with *lanthano*, a prolonged form of a primitive verb which means to be hidden, concealed, or secret. Thus, the root form of *aletheia* expresses a meaning equivalent to the notion of negating a secret, revealing a thing that has been concealed or exposing something hidden.[53] This equivalence of *revelation* (revealing) with *truth* (and therefore *concealing* with *lies/falsehood*) provides the framework for considering the New Testament use of *aletheia*.

A major way that *aletheia* is used in the New Testament is to express the truth of the Christian Religion, or that which is revealed by God about himself and humanity through the Scriptures. For example, in John 17:17 Jesus prays to God the Father, asking him to sanctify believers in the truth (*aletheia*) and stating that his word is truth (*aletheia*). Specifically, the truth of God, which is able to sanctify (make believers holy), is the good news that Jesus died on the cross and rose again from the dead, so that sinners who repent and trust in him may have their punishment forgiven, being reconciled with God and inheriting everlasting life. In the New Testament, this expresses an objective reality, such as when the Apostle Paul states that the truth (*aletheia*) of the gospel was preserved for the Galatian church in Galatians 2:5.[54] This truth is opposed to and contrasted with the sinful 'lies' of the pagans, Jews and false teachers claiming to be Christian. Similarly, Jesus states in John 8:31–32 that if people obey his word, they will know the truth of the gospel, and this truth will set them free from their sin. Finally, *aletheia* also has a subjective meaning, referring to truth as a personal excellence where a person is free to speak forthrightly without adverse affection, falsehood, simulation or deceit, such as in Ephesians 4:25 when Paul encourages believers to speak truth to one another, for we are all of one body.

So, even though truth or revelation is required for life and peace, this is not due to the law being intrinsically evil. Rather, 'secularised' law—law as a pure series of technical, formal and legalistic rules—is incompatible with the Christian life of the Spirit, the truth of giving and receiving love revealed from and through the divine. The modern Western legal system is incompatible with *aletheia* and the participatory life of the Spirit, for its attempt to categorise, prohibit, mandate, contract and so forth can ultimately be seen as an act of exclusion and communal alienation, or violence. With this context in mind, we may now move on to consider how this paradigmatically occurs in the trial of Christ.

[53] Thayer and Smith, 'Greek Lexicon Entry for Aletheia' (15 February 2012) *The New Testament Greek Lexicon*, available at www.studylight.org/lex/grk/view.cgi?number=225.

[54] A Kostenberger, *Exegetical Commentary on John* (Baker, 2004) 496.

III. Christ Crucified: Conviction by the Law of Death

A. Law as Rules

(i) Old Testament Context and Rules

The first relevant element of Christ's trial is the use of and emphasis on law as a series of rules—particularly the laws contained in the Old Testament. This can be seen in John's account, where Pilate tells the Sanhedrin to judge Christ according to their own law and the Sanhedrin respond by saying that it is not lawful for them to put anyone to death.[55] It is implied that the Sanhedrin have already judged Jesus according to their law and that the verdict reached was death. Since Christ was tried under this law, it is instructive to initially outline the governing legal framework of the Old Testament. All four gospel accounts agree that Jesus was accused of blasphemy (Matthew 26:65; Mark 14:64; Luke 22:70–71; John 5:18), or claiming equality and identity with God—a crime punishable by death according to Leviticus 24:16: 'Whoever blasphemes the name of the Lord shall surely be put to death.' The Sanhedrin explicitly confirm this in John 19:7: 'We have a law, and according to that law he ought to die because he has made himself the Son of God.' This is contained in the Pentateuch and is part of the Old Testament corpus referenced by Paul as 'the law'. The Old Testament is the collection of Hebrew Scriptures which record the history of the world and particularly the Jewish nation, from the creation of humanity to God's inception of the Abrahamic Covenant of reconciliation through to the establishment of the nation of Israel. It includes genres such as historical narrative, wisdom literature, prophecy and, most significantly, law. Its major theme is the problem of disobedience to the law and human rebellion against God, and God's plan to forgive this and to reconcile humanity with himself through the sacrifice of a promised Messiah.

The Old Testament was originally written in Hebrew, though a few passages are in Aramaic.[56] Biblical Hebrew is part of a family of languages known as Semitic. The similarities in the grammar, syntax and vocabulary of the Semitic languages have caused historical linguists to infer a common origin, and the study of Biblical Hebrew in particular is important for understanding the origin and character of the Old Testament, as well as the many Hebraisms and Semitisms found in the New Testament.[57] Lexicographically, Biblical Hebrew is essentially distinct from Indo-European languages and Germanic languages, such as English.[58] It is

[55] John 18:31.
[56] Walker, above n 51, 49.
[57] A Ross, *Introducing Biblical Hebrew* (Baker, 2001) 11, 16.
[58] E Kautzsch (ed), *Gesenius' Hebrew Grammar* (Clarendon Press, 1898) 4.

concrete, emotional and vivid, and of a picturesque quality so that abstract intellectual or theological terms like truth, sin or thought are expressed visually by physical actions or natural objects.[59]

There are approximately ten Hebrew words in the Old Testament which are consistently translated as 'truth', or some derivative or equivalent thereof.[60] The most common of these is *emeth*, which can be variously translated as firmness, reliability and solidity, and is used in the context of the spoken and written word, testimony, doctrine and divine instruction. The primary sense in which *emeth* is used is to express certainty and reliability that particular events have transpired, which is confirmed through eyewitness testimony or attestation.[61] As a general example, in Deuteronomy 17:4 the people of Israel are commanded to inquire as to whether idolatry has occurred amongst them and, if that event is found to be *true* (ie it is established that the event has certainly and reliably occurred), particular consequences follow.

In the Pentateuch there is a major relationship between law and truth, and correspondingly it has numerous references to witnesses and testimony. The first and most important of these is the ninth of the Ten Commandments, the injunction to 'not bear false witness against your neighbour'.[62] This commandment is essential to the effective functioning of the Jewish legal system, for faithful witness testimony was central to the determination of guilt or innocence, and ultimately to the reputation and even life of the accused person. Thus, the Hebrew law compelled truthful and faithful testimony: that the account of events would be *emeth*: sincere, reliable and conform to the facts of reality. According to Exodus 23:2, bearing false witness through siding with a majority would pervert the course of justice, since it would be unjust for the person to be convicted and punished for a crime they had not committed due to the testimony of a false witness.

In Numbers 35:30, in the particular context of murder, safeguards are implemented to ensure that justice is done: 'If anyone kills a person, the murderer shall be put to death on the evidence of witnesses. But no person shall be put to death on the testimony of one witness.' Deuteronomy 19:15–21 expands:

> A single witness shall not suffice against a person for any crime or for any wrong in connection with any offense that he has committed. Only on the evidence of two witnesses or of three witnesses shall a charge be established. If a malicious witness arises to accuse a person of wrongdoing, then both parties to the dispute shall appear before the Lord, before the priests and the judges who are in office in those days. The judges shall inquire diligently, and if the witness is a false witness and has accused his brother falsely, then you shall do to him as he had meant to do to his brother. So you shall purge the evil from your midst. And the rest shall hear and fear, and shall never again commit any such evil among you. Your eye shall not pity. It shall be life for life, eye for eye, tooth for tooth, hand for hand, foot for foot.

[59] Pfeiffer, above n 14, 15.
[60] Young, above n 52, 1004–05.
[61] ibid.
[62] Exodus 20:16.

There is much here that is similar to our earlier summary of the trial. The laws of witness testimony are a complex series of stringent rules designed to uncover the facts and dispense pure justice as retribution. No one shall be convicted on the evidence of one witness; there must be at least two or three corroborating testimonies, in conjunction with a detailed inquiry by the judges to see whether the testimonies correspond to the reality of the events. Guilt or innocence was fundamentally established through the multiple attestations of personally veracious and characteristically reliable witnesses who described events according to the reality of their transpiration.

The probability of true witness testimony was increased by the corroboration of accounts and severe punishment in the event of false witness. Where witness testimony was contradictory, the sitting judges would inquire diligently into the truth of the events (ie what actually occurred), and the true testimony would be discovered. In this way, the ancient Hebrews dispensed justice (punishment of the rule-breaker) by establishing the guilt or innocence of the relevant parties according to the reality of the facts through witness testimony and detailed inquiry: in other words, by discerning the truth of the events. Therefore, establishing truth through attestation was a major theme of the Hebrew legal system expressed by the Pentateuch.

(ii) Roman and Jewish Rules

Having established the Jewish legal context of Jesus' trial, I can now turn to specifically consider the trial itself in the Roman context. The Roman law in operation at the time of Christ had numerous sources, including vote by people's assembly, resolutions of the senate, decrees from the emperor and judicial decisions. In particular, the provincial governors (including Pilate) held the *imperium*, which gave them almost complete power over the life and death of the people under their control—only the governor could impose the death sentence, and this power was non-delegable.[63] This is the reason why the Sanhedrin needed to deliver Jesus to Pilate as recorded in all four accounts, and why John explicitly records that it was 'not lawful' for the Sanhedrin to put anyone to death.[64] Though the Sanhedrin could deliver guilty verdicts and sanction death, they needed Pilate's permission to do this. The normal judicial procedure involved the drawing up of charges and penalties and the formal act of accusation by an interested party (as there was no public prosecutor). The Jewish officials illustrate this in regard to Jesus' trial; their meetings or 'Jewish trial' would have been to settle on what charges could be sustained before Pilate, and after the trial process, where the accused and accuser would meet together and lay out their case before the governor, the governor would make whatever decision he deemed to be just and proper.[65]

[63] E Ferguson, *Backgrounds of Early Christianity* (Wm B Eerdmans, 2003) 64.
[64] John 18:31.
[65] Ferguson, above n 63, 65.

The legal status of first-century Jews under the occupation of the Roman Empire was determined by three systems of law: the Roman civic law, or 'Common law'; the 'Jewry law' or 'privileges based on custom and on legal dispositions enacted by Hellenistic and Roman magistrates'; and the laws of traditional Judaism, or *halachah*.[66] This tiered structure was hierarchical, with Roman law at the apex, followed by Jewry law and the *halachah* at the bottom. As such, there was much flexibility and compromise between the different systems, which occasionally resulted in conflict.[67] However,

> Roman policy ... generally affirmed the right of people to live according to their ancestral laws. This right was granted to Greek cities as well as to Jewish communities ... the reason for this was simply that it was the easiest way to keep peace.[68]

In particular, the first-century Jewish judicial system comprised five different courts, with the Sanhedrin as the supreme court.[69] Christ's trial occurred before the Sanhedrin, which was constituted of Sadducees (the priestly aristocracy), Pharisees (the moral and religious leaders) and Scribes (the experts in Jewish law and legal procedure).[70] This body exercised both civil and criminal jurisdiction according to Jewish law, and had administrative authority and its own officers of justice to perform arrests.[71] With the Roman occupancy at the time of Christ, the Sanhedrin was empowered to judge cases not involving capital punishment, but could only make recommendations of its findings to the Roman procurator in cases of capital punishment, who then had the power to affirm or deny the finding. However, in Jewish law the Sanhedrin also had the power over life and death, so that the procurator's judgment was usually in accordance with the demands of the Sanhedrin. The Sanhedrin had two main areas of responsibility where it rendered judgments: the political (administrative and judicial) and the religious.[72]

In terms of Christ's trial specifically, he is brought before the Sanhedrin in three phases: an informal hearing before Annas, uniquely recorded in John 18:13, 19–24; a more formal trial before Caiaphas and the rest of the council while it is still dark (recorded only in Matthew 26:57–68 and Mark 14:53–65, though alluded to in John 18:24); and finally a brief formal verdict by the same court in the morning (recorded with detail in Luke 23:66–71, and referred to in Matthew 27:1; Mark 15:1; John 18:28), which New Testament scholar Craig Blomberg surmises

[66] A Linder, 'The Legal Status of the Jews in the Roman Empire' in S Katz et al (eds), *The Cambridge History of Judaism. Volume 4. The Late Roman-Rabbinic Period* (Cambridge University Press, 2006) 131.

[67] ibid 128–29, 131.

[68] J Collins, *Jewish Cult and Hellenistic Culture: Essays on the Jewish Encounter with Hellenism and Roman Rule* (Brill, 2005) 209.

[69] Linder, above n 66, 136.

[70] See Matthew 26:57–59; Mark 14:53; Luke 22:66 ('chief priests', 'elders', 'scribes'); John 19:6 ('chief priests', 'officers').

[71] J Thompson, 'Sanhedrin' in J Douglas (ed), *The Illustrated Bible Dictionary Part 3* (InterVarsity Press, 1980) 1390–91.

[72] ibid.

was to create an 'aura of legality'.[73] In terms of court procedure, the Sanhedrin had specified times and places to meet. There was no 'jury of peers', but instead the Sanhedrin themselves were both judge and jury. Twenty-three judges were required for a quorum, and for acquittal an absolute majority judgment sufficed, whereas for condemnation a two-thirds majority was required.[74] If more than half but less than two-thirds of the judges voted for condemnation, two judges were added and the process repeated until a verdict was reached, up to a total of 71 judges. The entire process was designed so that the benefit of the doubt always lay with the accused.[75]

B. Law as Power

(i) *The Political Sanhedrin*

Despite the existence of these rules and procedures, many were not followed by the Sanhedrin in regard to the trial of Christ in the gospel accounts. Blomberg observes that the law can be manipulated by people in the name of a higher political cause, and this was displayed through an instrumental breach of the rules in regard to the trial of Christ.[76] The Sanhedrin, as represented by the gospels, was not interested in seeking the truth, only in silencing Christ. For example, Matthew records that the Pharisees 'conspired against him, how to destroy him' (12:14), that they 'were seeking to arrest him' (21:46) and that they 'plotted together in order to arrest Jesus by stealth and kill him' (26:3–4).[77] They had already determined Christ's guilt before the questioning and deliberation occurred, so that the trial was a sham for their political rationale of silencing Christ and concealing truth, and therefore it was ultimately a 'miscarriage of justice'—even though they still needed to implement the death penalty through Pilate.[78] The Sanhedrin had not received *aletheia* or divine revelation regarding the truth of Christ, so did not have faith in him. Since the discourses of Christ apparently threatened their power and position, it was their purely secular or pagan reason, or selfish desires in the sense of seeking to protect their sovereign authority and their own political power, that precluded the operation of true, divine law which would have exonerated Christ as the divine truth. Instead, a miscarriage of justice occurred, divine law was not applied and Christ was condemned.

To facilitate this condemnation of Jesus, the Sanhedrin manipulated the rules by constructing false testimony and adducing false witnesses. Matthew records that initially none of the false witness testimony was able to stand, for the testimony

[73] Blomberg, above n 11, 396.
[74] Thompson, above n 71, 1391.
[75] ibid.
[76] Blomberg, above n 11, 399.
[77] See also Mark 14:1–2; Luke 22:2; John 11:45–57.
[78] Blomberg, above n 11, 399.

did not agree and could not be corroborated. However, two witnesses then came forward and charged that Jesus claimed he would destroy the temple and rebuild it in three days. Mark also records that the false witnesses disagreed, including on the matter of the temple's destruction. Since the Jewish law requires witnesses to agree, Jesus was not declared guilty on the basis of this testimony and he refused to answer the charge.[79] It was Jesus' tacit admissions during the trial which secured the charges, in conjunction with his more explicit statements during his public ministry pertaining to his claims to be God and equal with God.[80] The relevant question, then, is whether the evidence adduced by Jesus establishes the truth of his claims, for if Jesus was in fact not God or equal with God, contrary to what he claimed, he was guilty of blasphemy according to the Jewish law and deserved the punishment of death so that 'justice' was done. If Jesus was in fact God as he claimed, he was not guilty of blasphemy since he was merely attesting to the truth.

First, Jesus states that, according to the Jewish law, if he bears witness of himself, his testimony is not true (reliable), for there is only one witness.[81] He proceeds to argue, however, that *his* testimony alone is sufficient to prove true in the sense of being reliable because he comes from God the Father and will return to God the Father.[82] Hence, in this circumstance the character of the witness directly impacts the reliability of the testimony, for God himself requires no corroborator as one that is eminently reliable. The problem here is that this would seem to beg the question, for the divine veracity of Jesus as a witness is assumed when his divinity is precisely what is being investigated through witness testimony. So, for the moment, the conclusion must be that Jesus' solitary witness cannot assist in establishing his divinity. Jesus subsequently argues that in the case of concurring multiple (two or more) witnesses, the testimony is true. Not only does Jesus bear witness of himself, but so does John the Baptist, the works Jesus performs and the Father through the Scriptures.[83] These witnesses combine to give concurring testimony regarding the divinity of Christ, and therefore, according to the Jewish law, the testimony is reliable. It follows that Jesus' personal testimony regarding himself is also reliable, strengthening the truth of the witness. Therefore, since, according to the Jewish standard, it is true that Jesus actually is God, according to the Jewish law he is not guilty of blasphemy, and the Sanhedrin was unjust and false to condemn him.

[79] C Laymon (ed), *The Interpreter's Concise Commentary on Acts and Paul's Letters* (Abingdon, 1983) 18; Mark 14:55–59.

[80] Matthew 26:57–58; Luke 22:66–71; John 5:18; John 8:58–59.

[81] John 5:31.

[82] John 8:14–16.

[83] John 5:30–46. These witnesses, however, are not adduced at Jesus' trial. At this point John the Baptist is dead (see Mark 6:14–29; Matthew 14:1–12), and the Jews rejected the other two witnesses a priori as they were already convinced of Jesus' guilt.

(ii) The Truth of Pilate

However, it is not merely the Jewish *Torah* and Jewish politics which contributed to Christ's crucifixion, so that the argument may not succumb to the charge of anti-Semitism. We have seen in each of the four gospel accounts that there is an emphasis on condemning the Jews as rebelling against God's will and rejecting the promised Messiah, while Pilate is exonerated as essentially being coerced by the political climate; he is unable to declare Jesus innocent and release him even though he desires to. This is most apparent in Matthew's account, which includes the two unique elements of Pilate's wife being warned in a dream that Jesus is innocent and that Pilate should not become involved, and Pilate washing his hands of Jesus' fate with the Jews, declaring that Jesus' blood will be on them and their children. The warning is additional divine evidence of Jesus' innocence and the corresponding guilt of the Jews, emphasised by their taking full responsibility for the shedding of Jesus' blood.[84] These aspects may be explained by the fact that Matthew was writing primarily to Jewish Christians who were living in tension with the traditional synagogues; Matthew sought to establish that Jesus was the true Messiah and to contrast this faithfulness to divine revelation with the guilt and blindness of those Jews who rejected Christ.[85] It is from these considerations that blame for Jesus' execution has been placed on the Jewish people as a whole, resulting in bitterness and anti-Jewish sentiment.[86] It may also have been the case that the early Christians, living under the rule of the Roman Empire, wished to show their loyalty to Roman authority and minimise the perception of threat.[87]

However, Pontius Pilate and the Romans are equally culpable, because their secular reason and pagan politics of power condoned and effectively allowed Christ's death.[88] At the time, Pilate was the procurator of Judaea in Israel, which meant he had full control of the province.[89] He was in charge of the occupying army and had power over life and death, being able to reverse capital sentences passed by the Sanhedrin as they had to be ratified by him.[90] Importantly, he also appointed the High Priests and controlled the temple as well as its funds and contents, including the High Priest's vestments.[91] Pilate presided over a tumultuous period in Judaea, with numerous rebellions and slaughters occurring under his rule. Consequently, in the context of the trial of Christ, Pilate was wary of imperial displeasure if the (contemporary) Roman Emperor Tiberius heard of further unrest in the area.[92]

[84] HC Kee, 'The Gospel According to Matthew' in C Laymon (ed), *Interpreter's Concise Commentary* (Abingdon Press, 1983) 92–93.

[85] Blomberg, above n 11, 150–151.

[86] Kee, above n 84, 93.

[87] M Shepherd, 'The Gospel According to John' in C Laymon (ed), *Interpreter's Concise Commentary* (Abingdon Press, 1983) 329.

[88] Blomberg, above n 11, 400.

[89] D Wheaton, 'Pilate' in Douglas, above n 71, 1229–30.

[90] ibid.

[91] ibid.

[92] ibid.

In other words, it was Pilate's power relations with Rome which resulted in his ultimate approval of the violence.

When the Sanhedrin took Jesus to Pilate to obtain his permission for crucifixion, even though Pilate believed Christ was innocent of anything deserving death, he dared not alienate the Jews and risk a rebellion, instead affirming their testimony for fear of losing his power as procurator of Judaea.[93] The Sanhedrin emphasised the claims of Jesus' kingship and set this against the Roman kingship of Caesar: 'if you release this man, you are not Caesar's friend. Everyone who makes himself a king opposes Caesar'.[94] This crafty approach constructed a dangerous dilemma for Pilate: condemn an innocent man to death or risk politically destabilising claims that he was acknowledging Jesus as king in competition with Caesar. Pilate 'yields to the fear of his own political position' and takes the former option.[95] In essence, while himself being manipulated, Pilate selfishly manipulates the legal situation in order to maintain his own power. Therefore, for both Jew and Gentile, the law is a secularised, formal set of rules which can be manipulated in a Machiavellian (pagan) sense to achieve political outcomes: in this situation, the crucifixion of Christ.

This is particularly exposed in the Gospel According to John, when Pilate and Christ converse about truth or *aletheia*—divine revelation:

> So Pilate entered his headquarters again and called Jesus and said to him, 'Are you the King of the Jews?' Jesus answered, 'Do you say this of your own accord, or did others say it to you about me?' Pilate answered, 'Am I a Jew? Your own nation and the chief priests have delivered you over to me. What have you done?' Jesus answered, 'My kingdom is not of this world. If my kingdom were of this world, my servants would have been fighting, that I might not be delivered over to the Jews. But my kingdom is not from the world.' Then Pilate said to him, 'So you are a king?' Jesus answered, 'You say that I am a king. For this purpose I was born and for this purpose I have come into the world—to bear witness to the truth. Everyone who is of the truth listens to my voice.' Pilate said to him, 'What is truth?'[96]

Here, Pilate, despite later affirming the innocence of Jesus in John 19:4, in response asks what truth is in an apparently rhetorical way. It is apparently rhetorical because Pilate does not stay to hear the answer or discuss it; instead, he walks back out to the Jews. If this was a genuine inquiry by Pilate, rather than a haphazard statement, he would have remained to discuss the matter with Jesus. John Milbank agrees with this interpretation. In order to justify his claim of theology critiquing philosophy, Milbank approvingly cites Johann Georg Hamann, an eighteenth-century German philosopher, deploying a critique of the figure of Pontius Pilate during the trial of Christ. 'Pilate represents the Enlightenment, which rules and inquires after truth. But, notoriously, he only jests and does not stay for an answer'—if he

[93] Blomberg, above n 11, 401.
[94] John 19:12.
[95] Shepherd, above n 87, 328.
[96] John 18:33–38.

had, he would have seen the truth as the suffering Christ before him.[97] The apparent rejection of this sight or spectacle of Christ indicates that pure philosophical reason has a fundamentally non-realist impulse which leaves common-sense perception behind. By contrast, a kind of faith is involved in everyday life when we recognise the real, particularly a faith or trust in perception, which is ultimately faith in God who creates out of nothing and sustains everything in being.[98]

The fact that this is the Old Testament law, which Paul understands as formalistic rules devoid of faith and life, implies that the faith of pure philosophical reason cannot be trust, and particularly cannot be trust in God. Instead, the operation of secular reason results not in a trust or faith in perception in the theological sense, but rather an indeterminacy or barrier—a blind faith, operating without reason. This is the ultimate end of secular reason. Pilate, in Hamann's depiction, representing this secular reason of the Enlightenment, scoffs at the notion of defining truth, exposing nihilistic uncertainty and indeterminacy as the fundamental limit and impasse of secular reason. And this reason without revelation cannot yield truth.

Hence, Jesus' contentions to demonstrate the truth of his claims that he is the truth or that he is God according to the laws of witness testimony under the Old Testament are fruitless. Despite his perfect adherence to the system of rules, the nihilistic uncertainty remains and produces a violent drive for decision in regard to Christ; the crowd, the Sanhedrin and even Pilate himself do not believe that Jesus is God and his attestation is true. So they decide to crucify him, and Pilate washes his hands of the matter. As explained by Paul in Romans 7:10, 'the very commandment that promised life proved to be death' for Christ. The promise of the Old Testament laws of witness testimony to yield truth and consequently life only produced death. Therefore, the (secular) formalism of the rules in conjunction with the pagan power relations within the law ultimately lead to violence and death.

For Christ, this violence and death occurred through him being beaten, mocked, whipped and finally crucified.[99] According to Paul in Galatians, Christ in this way 'becomes a curse' as a result of the law being 'not of faith'—for 'cursed is everyone who is hanged on a tree'.[100] Christ suffers the law's curse by manifesting the way in which the law demands a formalistic adherence which can never be satisfied, as well as displaying the violence and death that comes as a result. Hence the law simultaneously curses Christ by causing him to suffer its violence and death through its condemnation and endorses this violence and death by affirming the curse through the given method of violence and death—that is, crucifixion is hanging on a tree and consequently Christ is cursed by virtue of his crucifixion.

[97] J Milbank, 'Knowledge: The Theological Critique of Philosophy in Hamann and Jacobi' in J Milbank et al (eds), *Radical Orthodoxy: A New Theology* (Routledge, 1999) 25.

[98] ibid 25–27.

[99] See, eg, Mark 15:15–37.

[100] Galatians 3:10–14.

C. Law as Secular and Pagan?

Both the Jewish law and the Roman law fail to exonerate Christ. The secular, formal, codified, legalistic nature of these laws cannot confront *aletheia*, the truth or revelation of Christ's divinity, and so attempt to suppress it through violence. Exacerbating this is the pagan ontology represented through the actions of the legal actors involved. Pilate, as a Roman governor, is intimately involved with this pagan toleration of difference and regulation of violence by violence—an instrument in the so-called 'Roman peace'. In addition, both Pilate and the Sanhedrin adopt a Machiavellian attitude in their dealings with Christ. They are centrally concerned with maintaining their own power, and they engage in deception and tricks to achieve this. The Sanhedrin manipulates the rules in an attempt to convict Christ, and also manipulate Pilate by implicitly threatening to cause a riot if he does not accede to their wishes—aware that Pilate could not politically afford more unrest. Pilate, too, despite protesting the innocence of Christ (that he has done nothing deserving of death), cared more for retaining his position as governor, and was willing to condemn an innocent man in order to achieve this. Such actions exemplify law as secular and pagan, and the result is violence and death. Milbank ultimately states that 'one could argue that the Cross exposed the structure of arbitrary sovereign power in its ultimate exceptional yet typical instance ... This is its act of discernment of the worst human violence.'[101]

However, even if we assume a 'good faith' trial of Christ—possibly in our modern context of the trial—it is entirely conceivable that he still would not have been acquitted. When one considers the complex system of rules that govern the admissibility and weight of evidence, Christ's 'witness' of miracles may not have sufficed. Not only this, but the testimonial evidence from Christ and others may well be called into question in terms of its reliability. For example, according to these rules there would seem to be nothing (in principle) to distinguish Jesus from other Messianic claimants of the time.[102] Perhaps it is an inevitable legal truth that Jesus is not really the Christ.

The problem with this approach is that it is already operating under secular assumptions and a focus on rules. These issues involve questions that assume a formal certainty and exclude faith with divine revelation. The really critical point is that 'the Sanhedrin is implicitly told [by Christ] that their problem is not lack of evidence for his Messiahship but lack of openness to the possibility of belief'.[103] So Milbank argues that 'God himself had pronounced the ultimate verdict on the Christological claim which is now on trial ... and the evidence for this verdict is *already* available in the event of Jesus' resurrection-exaltation'.[104] The revelation of

[101] J Milbank, *Being Reconciled: Ontology and Pardon* (Routledge, 2003) 93.

[102] See, eg, Acts 5:27–42.

[103] A Neagoe, *Trial of the Gospels* (Cambridge University Press, 2002) 65.

[104] J Milbank, *The Word Made Strange: Theology, Language, Culture* (Blackwell, 1997) 66 (original emphasis).

Christ as gloriously raised and exalted testifies to and ultimately verifies his claim to divinity.[105] It is not verified according to a secular canon of rules or reason, but by the nature of the work. As Milbank notes, the Gospel According to John in particular

> suggests that Jesus realises in his own person the Father's work because he is the Father's proper work, the radiance of glory which is not dissoluble from the Father's very being. Both witnesses cohere together. Nothing can *prove* or establish the perfection of Jesus's human work, for if it *is* perfect, then the work must itself define the character of perfection.[106]

In other words, 'Jesus is not recognised as the … Christ, before being recognised as the divine *Logos*, which realises and establishes, without thereby displacing, the Father's infinite power of origination'.[107] Only divine revelation, the Father revealing the Son, can actually establish that Jesus is the Christ as *aletheia*, or theological truth. This occurs through a faith enlightened by grace—recognition of Christ as the divine *logos* or reason.

Milbank claims that there were only two possibilities for representing the various images of God: Judaism, which focused around the Law, on 'one figure at the expense of the others', or an 'abstract synthesis' which

> can only be a betrayal of the plenitude of meaning of the individual figures … by contrast, the poetic synthesis in Christ *returns* us to the figures, because he establishes them for the first time in total interrelation as the true human representation, the true human text.[108]

This indicates why law as a series of formal, exclusive, alienating rules fails—it does not and cannot recognise Christ as the *logos*, so it cannot linguistically represent him (nor can it represent the 'total human intent').[109] Instead, it focuses on one figure at the expense of the others (for example, Christ claims to be God so he must necessarily be a blasphemer, rather than God) or abstractly synthesises (for example, Christ performs so-called miracles so he must be demonic, like other so-called miracle workers).[110] Since Christ cannot be categorised according to the legal rules, he is rejected. This rejection not only is violent in terms of its theological distortion of Christ's identity, but also ultimately leads to the physical violence of crucifixion. The legal truth which then emerges through a secular series of rules is not only false, but violent. If this is accepted, the key to establishing a peaceful legal community conceivably lies not in attestation, but in revelation of theological truth.

[105] See, eg, Acts 2:22–33.
[106] Milbank, *Word Made Strange*, above n 104, 135. See John 1:1–18 (original emphasis).
[107] ibid. See John 5:17–47.
[108] ibid 136 (original emphasis).
[109] ibid.
[110] John 10:33; Matthew 12:24.

IV. The Revelation of Christ: Faith, Mystery, Atonement

A. Christ as Disrupting Secular Formalism

In Christ we see a figure of indeterminacy and ambiguity, the exemplary figure of paradox. He is both God and man, dead yet raised, present and absent. The claim that only the divine revelation of Christ can yield truth, apart from the secular rules of pure reason, anticipates the mystery that shrouds comprehension of Christ's identity and disrupts the certainty and formalism of the secular law, exposing only its violence in the face of such mystery. With the deconstruction of secular reason and rule systems, this opens the space for faith based on *aletheia*, divine truth or revelation.

(i) Christ, Faith and Aletheia

In such a context, it is instructive to consider how Jesus Christ establishes the relationship between himself and *aletheia* in the gospels, particularly in John's account, which seeks to identify Jesus as the Son of God, co-equal with the Father. Jesus unambiguously identifies himself as the truth (*aletheia*) in John 14:6 when he states 'I am the truth'. Bearing in mind the prior analysis of *aletheia*, as well as the Bible's position on Jesus Christ himself, the profundity of this assertion cannot be overestimated. First, as *aletheia* refers to the revelation of God, Jesus is saying that he is the divine reality, equating himself with God and his revealed truth in the Bible.[111] Indeed, Jesus confirms that 'whoever has seen me has seen the Father'.[112] Jesus is the revelation or *aletheia* of the Father, and therefore Jesus is the truth. This is the sense in which the Gospel According to John describes Christ as bringing grace and truth, as compared with the Law of Moses—Christ is the divine reality and fulfilment of the Mosaic Law since he perfectly adheres to it and is the material to which it points, the substance comprising God's complete revelation of his plan, and therefore the truth of it.[113]

Furthermore, there are numerous ways in which God himself has revealed, or made known, the glory of Christ. The first such occasion was when Christ was baptised by John, and 'the Spirit descend[ed] from heaven like a dove, and it remained on him'.[114] The Spirit by revelation affirmed the glory of Christ, and it is surely no coincidence that the Spirit appeared in the form of a dove, a symbol of peace. As Christ said to his disciples, 'the Spirit of truth will lead you into all the

[111] John 1:1—Jesus is the Word of God and is God.
[112] John 14:9.
[113] W Hendrickson, *Exposition of the Gospel According to John* (Baker, 2004) 89; John 1:17; Colossians 2:16–17.
[114] John 1:32.

truth … he will glorify me'.[115] So through *aletheia* or revelation the truth of the glory of Christ was displayed, and the dove signifies that this truth is peace.

There are further examples of God revealing the divinity of Christ, particularly in Matthew's account, which seeks to demonstrate that Jesus is the true, divine Messiah or Christ. There is the Transfiguration, where Christ is transfigured before his disciples, with his face shining like the sun and his clothes as white as light. At this point, God the Father says that Jesus is his beloved Son, with whom he is well pleased.[116] Thus, the glory of Christ is explicitly or physically revealed by the Father. Still, possibly the clearest instance of the *aletheia* of Christ is where the Apostle Peter affirms the deity of Christ. In response to this, Jesus says 'Blessed are you, Simon Bar-Jonah! For flesh and blood has not revealed this to you, but my Father who is in heaven.'[117] Here, according to Christ's assertion, the Father reveals the nature of Christ to Peter, so that by revelation he comes to the knowledge of the truth. Jesus explicitly contrasts this divine revelation with 'revelation by flesh and blood', or what is effectively secular, human attestation.

However, this is not to say that attestation is completely excluded. To the extent that attestation is combined with divine revelation and jettisoned of its secular, violent aspects, attestation remains an effective means of revealing truth. An example of this is found in the attestation of the prophet Malachi in the Old Testament, where God is revealed as testifying that 'my covenant with him was one of life and peace … true law was in his mouth, and no wrong was found on his lips. He walked with me in peace and uprightness, and he turned away many from sin.'[118] In addition, Isaiah the prophet testifies that 'out of Zion shall go the law, and the word of the Lord from Jerusalem'.[119] There are a number of valuable insights to be observed about these verses: first, the Septuagint, the Greek translation of the Hebrew Old Testament, uses the terms *aletheia*, *nomos* and *logos*, which are translated as truth, law and word, respectively.[120] Secondly, Augustine confirms that both these passages speak prophetically of Christ, and the covenant mentioned refers to the new covenant.[121] Finally, Isaiah 2:3 is an example of synonymous parallelism, a Hebrew literary device where the first part of a thought is repeated or clarified by the second part of the thought.[122] So Zion is clarified to mean Jerusalem; the word of the Lord, whom we know to be Christ from John 1:1, is equated to the law. Combining the passages, from this attestation with

[115] John 16:13–14.

[116] Matthew 17:2, 5.

[117] Matthew 16:16–17.

[118] Malachi 2:5–6.

[119] Isaiah 2:3.

[120] Strong, 'Malachi 2:5–6' (7 October 2013) *Strong's Interlinear Bible*, available at www.studylight.org/desk/interlinear.cgi?search_form_type=interlinear&q1=Malachi+2%3A5-6&ot=lxx&nt=wh&s=0&t3=str_nas&ns=0; Strong, 'Isaiah 2:3' (7 October 2013) *Strong's Interlinear Bible*, available at www.studylight.org/desk/interlinear.cgi?search_form_type=interlinear&q1=Isaiah+2%3A3&ot=lxx&nt=wh&s=0&t3=str_nas&ns=0.

[121] Augustine, *Concerning the City of God Against the Pagans* (Penguin, 2008) 808–09, 840.

[122] R Kaplan, 'Cultural Thought Patterns in Inter-Cultural Education' (2006) 16(1) *Language Learning* 1, 7.

revelation we see that in Christ is the unity and symbiosis of truth and law, and that his covenant brings life and peace, which is the new covenant of the Spirit: the law of love. Hence, testimony combined with divine revelation points to a redeemed attestation, one which brings life and peace through the law of love.

This can be further observed in the fact that the root form of *aletheia* is *alethes*, which literally means to reveal or uncover. However, in the New Testament *alethes* is typically used in the sense of some particular witness or testimony being genuine, honest, sincere and trustworthy—and therefore true. It is also used in the sense of loving and speaking the truth.[123] For example, in Titus 1:13 a person from a certain people group gives testimony regarding the negative character of that group, and that witness is said to be true (*alethes*). This is the case for any faithful witness, especially including God himself as the divine revealer, who loves truth and is honest and trustworthy.[124] However, in Christ this truth is not expressed in propositions, but is instead personal, knowable and reliable due to the stability and integrity of the truth-bearer. Jesus as the truth embodies and materially personifies God and his word as truth, allowing the reality of the divine relationship to be conceptually apprehended and expressed, and thus truth divinely revealed is to be understood, trusted and personally committed to.[125] Here we begin to see hints of how the Old Testament law of secular attestation is not abolished, but redeemed and transformed, for Christ is revealed as truth and divine peace through the Resurrection and his consequent bringing of life and peace. As Jesus says in John 8:31–32, knowledge of the truth brings freedom, for divine revelation or *aletheia* is a law of the Spirit, the new way which leads to life and peace by the same Spirit which raised Christ from the dead, the same Spirit which brings freedom.

In addition, it follows from Christ's equating himself with *aletheia* that he personally possesses (or even 'is') the subjective aspect of *aletheia*, namely excellence of veracious character to speak the facts of reality unencumbered by falsehood or deceit. This observation returns us to the situation of Christ appearing before Pontius Pilate and stating that his purpose is to bear witness to the truth and that all who are of the truth listen to his voice, and Pilate's response inquiring as to the definition of truth. In each instance, the relevant Greek word translated as truth is *aletheia*. Jesus declaring himself to be 'of the truth' and a witness to the truth implies that he alone is the one who reveals the divine, who can reliably speak and show the truth that displays the reality of God and his interactions with humanity. As such, he is to be believed and followed.

However, Pilate's response is not a genuine philosophical query, but represents a sceptical refusal to accept Jesus as the truth and demonstrates that Pilate is not of the truth, for he has not listened to Jesus' voice. Though Jesus' witness is true according to the rules of the formal state, this attestation to the divine reality (with its focus on conforming to the rules) is a merely secular one. The testimony was

[123] Young, above n 52, 1005.
[124] Romans 3:4.
[125] R Brown, *The Gospel According to John* (Geoffrey Chapman, 1984) 621, 628–31.

certain in the formal sense and so excluded trust or belief, and this paradoxically meant the testimony was nihilistically uncertain because it lacked the crucial aspect of divine revelation, and it was therefore rejected by Pilate—it did not result in faith. Where the truth of the divine reality is revealed, it does produce faith (*pistis*, or strong trust and persuasion by the divine) and trust in the mystery of the divine. Thus, if Jesus' testimony had been divinely revealed to Pilate, he would have believed, instead of 'delivering [Christ] over to them to be crucified' because he was motivated by the secular or pagan desire for political power.[126] Even Christ implicitly acknowledges that political power is a secular or pagan desire. It is a secular desire because it is a violent distortion of Christ's view of his kingdom, a community instantiated through peace; it is a pagan desire because the pagans seek to maintain their power through manipulation and dominance in a Machiavellian sense. Ultimately, Christ argues that struggle and violence for the purpose of obtaining political power is antithetical to his idea of the kingdom: 'My kingdom is not of this world. If my kingdom were of this world, my servants would have been fighting, that I might not be delivered over to the Jews. But my kingdom is not from the world.'[127]

The interaction between Jesus and Pilate exemplifies the Christian notion that truth is not merely abstract propositional knowledge requiring intellectual assent, but has an indispensable element of personal trustworthiness or faith produced through *aletheia*. This trust ultimately stems from the fact that the relation which is *aletheia* has its basis and participation in ultimate being: the love and peace existing in the divine Trinity.[128] Hence, where attestation according to the formal rules system of the secular state ultimately leads to an inability to comprehend the mystery of the divine, which produces an ontological violence of alienation and suppression, divine revelation through Christ disrupts the formalism of the secular and embraces the mystery, trusting in the divine. This results in life and peace—the end of secular state violence.

(ii) Against Christ: The Violent Drive for Decision

Legal formalism results in violence due to its need for certainty and finality in decision-making. The secular, formalistic desire for certainty according to the rules dictates that a decision must always be made, even in the face of mystery or something which does not accord with the established canon of rules. Derrida insightfully exposes this in his contrast between justice and law, already discussed in Chapter 3. At the moment of justice there is a paradoxical or aporetic place of undecidability or mystery where a decision must be made. In the arrival of this space, there is an incalculable spirit of decision, unbound by rules and outside of statutory categories, yet also within the letter or regulated system of law itself. However, in the context of the trial of Christ, the mystery is Christ himself, and a

[126] John 19:16.
[127] John 18:36.
[128] Kostenberger, above n 54, 529.

decision must be made on whether he is truly divine—and since the secular rules cannot comprehend this mystery, the decision is made to condemn and crucify.

This violent drive for decision specifically in regard to Christ is effectively portrayed and illustrated through Fyodor Dostoyevsky's celebrated story of the Grand Inquisitor in *The Brothers Karamazov*.[129] In this fictional account set during the height of the Inquisition, the Inquisitor confronts a man who appears to be Christ, and is accepted by the people as such. He takes the man in and states:

> 'Is it you? You?' But receiving no answer, he quickly adds: 'Do not answer, be silent. After all, what could you say? I know too well what you would say ... I do not know who you are, and I do not want to know: whether it is you, or only his likeness; but tomorrow I shall condemn you and burn you at the stake as the most evil of heretics ...'[130]

The Inquisitor is so motivated by decision that he ultimately does not care whether it is Christ or not, and will not listen. Instead, he is driven to simply condemn. What is most fascinating about this account is that Alyosha, who is being told the story by Ivan, responds by saying 'Your Inquisitor doesn't believe in God, that's his whole secret!'—and this is affirmed by Ivan.[131] The point is that this violent drive to decision, this enthusiasm to condemn and crucify Christ, is fundamentally based in the *secular*, in the sense of lacking belief in Christ the God-man. Pilate may well have believed in the pagan gods of Rome and the Sanhedrin believed in the God of Israel, but what they both had in common was their lack of faith in Christ—and it was this lack of divine revelation (which would have enabled faith), in conjunction with the secular emphasis on rules and pagan power plays, that led to the violence committed against Christ.

B. Redeeming the Drive for Decision

How, then, do we avoid the drive for decision against the undecidable, the pursuit of certainty in the face of mystery? As we have seen with Christ, to simply succumb and decide produces violence. More importantly, the trial and atonement of Christ is not unique in the sense that it can be compartmentalised into a singular instance with no purchase on contemporary legal ontology. Any attempt to limit the universality of Christ's condemnation is yet another example of a secular attempt to bound and alienate the divine. For through creaturely participation in the divine, the atonement continues. It cannot be categorised, but is forever and again displayed in all human relationships:

> In his death, Jesus entered into absolute solidarity with each and every one of us. He died the death which any of us, under sovereign authority, in exceptional circumstances which always prove the rule, may possibly die. He died as three times excluded: by the

[129] F Dostoevsky, *The Brothers Karamazov* (Vintage, 2004) 246–64.
[130] ibid 250.
[131] ibid 261.

> Jewish law of its tribal nation; by the Roman universal law of empire; by the democratic will of the mob. In the whole summed-up history of human polity—the tribe, the universal absolute state, the democratic consensus—God found no place ... He died the death of all of us—since he died the death that proves and exemplifies sovereignty in its arbitrariness.[132]

So we cannot simply attempt to legally distinguish issues of (theological) revelation and issues of (secular) attestation—by having respective parallel courts, for example. The effort to subsume *aletheia* into the secular legal institution, to have revelation and attestation coexist, simply will not do—it will reproduce the violence displayed in the trial of Christ and in innumerable other situations involving the arbitrary application of sovereign power. If we use something other than revelation to judge and distinguish revelation, then we have already reinscribed the secular as the dominant rule once again.

Instead of the drive for decision and secular categorisation, there is another type of will which can redeem the community, producing peace rather than violence. Milbank explains:

> Instead there is created will which participates in God, wherein life and *Logos* (Spirit and Son) communicate as one. Such a will is never the presupposed 'pure nature' of sovereignty and liberal rights theory. Instead it is already a will to reciprocity and to harmony with others according to an ineffable order and measure, which is yet not the measure of law. Such a will does not consist sovereignly in itself, and so cannot be betrayed by any executive—instead it only *is* in its always-already othering as execution: always for furtherance and not termination of life. Therefore by offering ourselves in and with Christ, we do not really lose ourselves, but live the genuine and eternal absolute life that returns as it proceeds outward.[133]

So 'the New Testament incarnates a new divine polity' which abolishes the violence of alienation without causing antagonism through conflation, 'because it reconceives "unity" beyond "singularity"' according to the perfect relationship of the Trinity, revealed in Christ.[134] By participating in the divine nature through a will of love and peace, an offering of ourselves in and with Christ, we may bring into existence a supernatural society—one that gives life rather than takes it.

V. Light in the Darkness: The Law of Love, Faith and Participation

A codified, formal, legalistic law instrumentalised through the exercise of arbitrary sovereignty can never overcome or comprehend the divine, which includes both

[132] Milbank, *Being Reconciled*, above n 101, 96–97.
[133] ibid 102 (original emphasis).
[134] ibid 101–02.

Christ as the source of the divine nature and us as participants in the divine nature. Such a secular approach will always try to categorise, to exclude, to rule, to decide and to make certain, excluding faith and producing violence. So perhaps the key to establishing a community or law of peace is to allow faith—a law embracing the mystery of Creator and created, the enchantment of human relationship based in trust and love and giving of self to neighbour, which actually and paradoxically increases subjectivity. This is not a law which leads to death, but a law which gives life.

A. A New Law: Mutual Trust as Communal Good

Hence, faith and truth are indissolubly linked in Christian theology as providing an alternative legal community. The new law of the Spirit reveals the truth of the divinely revealed Christ and both produces and is apprehended by faith, so that faith supplements reason and allows true participation in the divine relations. Paul promotes a polity governed by faith or trust, persuasion by *aletheia*, or the divine revelation of truth. He also stresses that this rule of trust constitutes a more fundamental mode of eternal law.[135] Such trust is a 'vertical' trust that God is just to an eminent and infinite extent that we cannot begin to fathom and a trust that this justice will eventually triumph so that a harmony of peace and order will embrace humanity.[136] It is also a 'horizontal' trust and mutual dependence between each member of the community. It may appear that trust is a weak recourse compared to the safeguards and balances provided by the parliament, the judiciary and the executive, but even these institutions are administered by humans capable of treachery and error. Thus, a suspension of mistrust and a positive working to increase bonds of solidarity are the only reliable foundation for a community. To trust or depend on others, standing on the shoulders of giants, is the only way to extend one's own reach and obtain a collective strength.[137]

So the new law of the Spirit constituted by faith relies on the divine revelation of the glory and sacrificial love of Christ, which eventually leads to freedom, an ontology of life and peace. Another important component of this new law of the Spirit that truth is divine revelation leading to peace is that it does not abolish the old law of truth as secular rules of attestation, but transforms and redeems this law. For example, in Galatians 3:19–25 Paul explains that the old law cannot 'give life', but instead 'imprisoned everything under sin', leading to death. However, with the arrival of Christ, the imprisonment of the old law is removed so that the promise of faith may be given to those who believe, those who behold his glory. As Paul says elsewhere, 'now we are released from the law, having died to that which held us captive, so that we serve in the new way of the Spirit and not in the old

[135] Milbank, 'Paul against Biopolitics', above n 22, 49–50.
[136] ibid 53.
[137] ibid.

way of the written code'.[138] This new way of the Spirit is 'love, joy, peace, patience, kindness, goodness, faithfulness, gentleness, self-control'.[139]

Significantly, Paul proceeds to say that against such things there is no law, for the old law of sin and death has been removed and the new law is based on this fruit of the Spirit, so that there is no law against it. Indeed, there is no need for a law to be against it. But this removal of the old law is not its being abolished. Rather, as stated in Matthew's account, which possesses the Jewish emphasis on the enduring nature of the law, Christ says he came 'not to abolish' the law, but to 'fulfil' it, and nothing will pass from the law until 'all is accomplished'.[140] Jesus further explains what this means in Matthew 22:37–40, where he argues that to 'love God' and to 'love your neighbour' form the basis of the Old Testament law. The law of love, to love your neighbour as yourself, fulfils the law. Therefore, the old law of the letter is redeemed, transformed and ultimately fulfilled by the new law of the Spirit, which promotes the desire for peace, love and harmony. Since the law of love fulfils the old law, it follows that the law of love and the new way of the Spirit are equivalent.

Bearing in mind that 'law' may refer to both the Jewish *Torah* and the Roman civil law, Paul explicitly adopts the theme of love fulfilling the law in the specific context of civil law in Romans 13:1–10, explaining in verses 8–10 that 'love fulfils the law' because 'it does no wrong to a neighbour'. If one loves their neighbour, they will not murder them or steal from them and so forth according to the commandments of the old law, and therefore love fulfils the law. Paul both explicitly and implicitly justifies obedience to the civil authorities through the law of love, thus redeeming and transforming the old law by the new law, and applying this principle to the civil law. In verses 7 and 8, he explicitly provides the foundation for obedience to the civil law by stating that one should render to all what is owed to them, particularly taxes, revenue, respect and honour. This is specifically addressing the issue of paying taxes to the civil authorities who make and enforce the civil laws. So the argument is that, since the civil authorities will fulfil the law by ensuring it is obeyed, according to verse 8 (owe no one anything except to love one another, for love fulfils the law) we should obey the law as a function of love by giving the civil authorities the taxes they are owed in order to fulfil the law. Thus, the fulfilling (which refers to obedience) of the law has its basis in the law of love.

Secondly, the law of love is implicitly invoked in verse 2, where obedience of the civil law is premised on the fact that the civil law is ultimately instituted by God, so that disobeying the civil law is equivalent to disobeying God. Since the law of love includes obeying God as a function of that love, Paul is essentially saying that when one is fulfilling or obeying the civil law, one is effectively loving God by being obedient to him. Hence, the law of love fulfils and redeems the civil law. Finally, the law of love is the contextual precondition of obedience to the civil authorities in the passage immediately preceding Romans 13:1–10. In Romans 12:17–21, Paul

[138] Romans 7:6.
[139] Galatians 5:22–23.
[140] Matthew 5:17–18; Kee, above n 619, 19.

states that one should not repay evil with evil, but overcome evil with good, doing good to one's enemies and loving them. This is the essence of the law of love, and its most extreme application: in the context of the law of love—to love your neighbour as yourself—Jesus explains in the Parable of the Good Samaritan that one's neighbour can be even their most bitter enemy, for the Jews and Samaritans were enemies. Thus, to avenge one's enemy is contrary to the law of love, so Paul implies that, instead of taking personal revenge, one should be subject to the civil authorities. Since the law of love is Paul's argument for not taking personal revenge, it follows that the law of love is the foundation for the fulfilling of the civil law in Romans 13. Therefore, the new way of the Spirit, the law of love, not only transforms and redeems the secularised Old Testament law, but also opens the space for a redeemed legal community, a Christian ontology of peace and truth as *aletheia*—revelation of and participation in the divine.

B. The Perpetual Atonement

It could be objected that, rather than law itself being secular and leading to violence, it is our human failure to properly implement divine truth in the legal system that results in violence. Put in somewhat stronger terms, it is the human appropriation of divine truth for nefarious purposes that results in violence—not the secular. One thinks, for example, of the Crusades, the Inquisition and the like. It is certainly not disputed that such an appropriation of theology produces violence, but the precise point here is that it is a *mis*appropriation; any variation of Christian theology which possesses a violent ontology is a distortion, a failure to properly participate in the ontological peace of the divine relations. Sometimes, even when law is properly applied, there is violence and death. In this sense, the atonement is inevitable; Christ always has to die.

But it is in the paradoxically unique exemplar of Christ's death in law, the law of love divinely revealed through the Incarnation, that we see the possibility for peace through the refusal of violence in law. For Christ's crucifixion 'restores the Good' and 'restores peace', enabling the 'possibility of mutual reconciliation'.[141] This is because in Christ is displayed the one who 'endures and compensates for evil … suffers violence without violent opposition, and yet at the same time positively opposes violence with a counter-violence to violence as such, which positively reasserts peace'.[142] This also provides a new perspective for considering Cover's example of martyrdom as the foundation for law. Through the Incarnation, rather than martyrdom indicating the establishment of law by dominance, law is established through love, the peaceful resistance against violence. The curse demonstrated by the application of secularised law and manifested in the violent

[141] Milbank, *Being Reconciled*, above n 101, 79.
[142] ibid. See also ibid 26–43.

punishment of Christ does not kill all hope, for the example of Christ is paradigmatic for observing the need to and possibility of avoiding punishment and pursuing peace. Indeed, the trial and punishment of Jesus condemns all other trials and punishments and forms of alien discipline.[143] The only finally tolerable and non-sinful punishment for Christians must be the self-punishment inherent in sin. When a person commits an evil act, they are cut off from the social peace and this means they are visited with social anger. But the aim should be to reduce this anger to a calm fury against the sin, and to offer the sinner nothing but goodwill, so bringing them to the point of realising that their isolation is self-imposed. Thus, this instance of punishment is paradoxically its instance of immediate cancellation.[144]

Rather than encouraging the violence of legal punishment through secularised sovereign power, Christianity advocates showing kindness to the sinner with the hope that they will see their communal isolation is through their own action, and that forgiveness from the community and reconciliation to the community is possible because of Christ. Indeed, the ultimate instance of punishment paradoxically being its immediate cancellation is the crucifixion of Christ, for in Christian theology the violence and punishment of the Crucifixion cannot be considered in isolation from the peace and reconciliation of the Resurrection. It is the resurrection of Christ, presupposing his crucifixion and condemnation under the law, which cancels the curse of the secularised law as arbitrary sovereign power that leads to violence and death, transforming it, redeeming it and revealing truth that leads to the law of the Spirit, which is life and social peace. For in Christ's refusal to respond to violence with violence, and in his relinquishing of himself, he is immediately returned through resurrection.[145]

C. Resurrection: Christ our Peace

Paul, in emphasising the unity of Jews and Gentiles in Christ, writes:

> But now in Christ Jesus you who once were far off have been brought near by the blood of Christ. For he himself is our peace, who has made us both one and has broken down in his flesh the dividing wall of hostility by abolishing the law of commandments expressed in ordinances, that he might create in himself one new man in place of the two, so making peace, and might reconcile us both to God in one body through the cross, thereby killing the hostility. And he came and preached peace to you who were far off and peace to those who were near. For through him we both have access in one Spirit to the Father.[146]

[143] J Milbank, *Theology and Social Theory: Beyond Secular Reason* (Blackwell, 1990) 427.
[144] ibid 428.
[145] Milbank, *Being Reconciled*, above n 101, 100.
[146] Ephesians 2:13–18.

In Christ, the old law of alienation and antagonism is abolished. Rather than law as a secular series of mandates and prohibitions, which separate and categorise (causing hostility and conflict between the divided members of society), the death of Christ unites and harmonises. In Christ, there is the refusal of violence and the sacrifice of love to all. Since, in Christ, all Jews and Gentiles have been reconciled to God, all Jews and Gentiles have been reconciled to each other. It is not that the differences between peoples have been excluded or devalued. It is not that Jews and Gentiles have their distinctive identity erased. Rather, for those in Christ, the differences that exist no longer alienate them from one another. This peace uniquely comes through Christ—'in Christ' you have been 'brought near by the blood of Christ', and 'he himself is our peace'. It follows that it is only through the revelation of truth, the Christ Event displayed through the Incarnation, Crucifixion and Resurrection, that we can shape our social existence to promote peace and reconciliation, removing the violence of alienation.

A society of peace through mutual love as self-sacrifice and the removal of arbitrary categories is both enabled and modelled by Christ. This is an intrinsically supernatural society, one that cannot be comprehended, constrained or codified by a secular, legalistic law. It is opposed to the natural society or, as Hobbes termed it, the state of nature. The society of secular liberalism or Hobbesian nature is the life which pursues death. It is the life which seeks the assertion of oneself over another, a life that is overlaid with alienating formal divisions. However, with the vision of Christ who gives life through resurrection, death is no longer authoritative.[147] Rather than the Hobbesian need for law to restrict the violent outworking of intrinsic self-interest, in Christ we are no longer bounded by law and death, since we have died with Christ, and are also risen with him so that we can continuously promote peace and the good through our (super)natural communal life—and consequently the law is no longer needed.[148]

However, given the suffering and death that has contingently entered this world—'Christ on the cross suffered death, the ravages of human malice, and the attempt by *nomos* (Roman and Jewish) to control and economise this malice for the sake of the seemingly best achievable welfare of the political community'—we are also called to suffer like Christ. We can suffer because 'there has been disclosed by the passage through the cross another, more-living, actively receptive, and participatory life that knows no death'—through Christ's resurrection and the spiritual life of mutual community.[149] Beyond a secular law and by the law of love, through Christ's death and resurrection we can once more instantiate a legal community of flourishing and giving life.

[147] Milbank, 'Paul against Biopolitics', above n 22, 42–43.
[148] ibid 43.
[149] ibid 44–45.

VI. Resurrecting the Peaceful Legal Community

So Christ's incarnation, crucifixion and resurrection point to the beyond of the mystery of the Trinitarian relations, revealing the glory and love that subsists between Father and Son by the Spirit, and allowing participation in that love and glory by faith. This truth as *aletheia*, or divine revelation, removes the violence and death of the law of sin and secular attestation, transforming and redeeming the law by the new way of the Spirit, the law of love. This law comes by the same Spirit that raised Christ from the dead and removes the former hostility and enmity of the old secular way of alienation and antagonism, and therefore leads to life and peace. In traditional modes of violence there is a dualism of the included and the excluded, and the old secular law remains trapped by this dualism, as alluded to by Paul in the Ephesians passage. Conversely, the Christian idea of law aspires to a law that is at one with life—with Being.[150] This law is the law of love, which reveals and reproduces the divine being, producing life and peace. Hence Christ, the *logos* and *aletheia* of God, in whom faith and reason unite and truth is revealed, redeems and transforms law, uniquely bringing to it a Christian ontology of peace through the law of love.

This vision is ideally a blueprint for society, but it also provides the means to live in our current society. It is not advocating theocracy, but a Christian polity within what may be a secular state—a Christian approach which may redeem and transform conceptions of the state. The fact that one can redeem the other implies that there is still a distinction between the two—Jesus' kingdom is not of this world, it is a heavenly peace which may be brought to earth to the extent that we participate in the divine being. As such, there is no need to finally alienate the secular in articulating the theological. The material love craved by the secular is not to be ignored. Secular materiality may be redeemed through this same law of life by the Resurrection. For in the Resurrection, paradoxically, true materialism may be found in the most spiritual of events, and life is achieved through death. Furthermore, as the material practice of the secular is continued (but redeemed) through faith, belief itself may come.

[150] J Milbank, 'Postmodern Critical Augustinianism: A Short *Summa* in Forty-Two Responses to Unasked Questions' in G Ward (ed), *The Postmodern God: A Theological Reader* (Blackwell Publishers, 1997) 270.

6

The Paradox of Law and Truth in Christianity: On Materialism, the Sublime and Reading the Pauline Law of Love

I. Žižek, Materialism and the Christian Legacy

A. A Paradoxical Position

In essence, I have proposed the Christian or Pauline law of love as the foundation for a redeemed system of peaceful human community. What is interesting is that even an atheist like Slovenian Lacanian-Marxist philosopher, Slavoj Žižek, views this Christian legacy as worth fighting for. Žižek frankly acknowledges his atheistic position:

> For me, there is no transcendent God-Father who discloses himself to us, humans, only in a limited way. The reason God can only appear incognito is that there is nothing to take cognisance of here: God is hidden not to hide some transcendent truth, but to hide the fact there is nothing to hide.[1]

Why is the 'Christian legacy worth fighting for?'[2] Žižek apparently sees something in Christianity that ought to be recovered, something that Milbank has also identified (though their understandings are different)—materialism and the sublime. So through Žižek and his discussion of Christian material sublimity we can clarify and deepen our understanding of the structure of Christian truth in the form of Incarnational Paradox, the Resurrection and the law of love, for the purpose of articulating the foundation for a human community of peace. His direct interactions with Milbank also make Žižek a productive counterpoint, so that we can work with Žižek in order to shape this structure of truth. Through this process we can also indicate a way in which those who engage in a secular approach may be

[1] S Žižek, 'Dialectical Clarity Versus the Misty Conceit of Paradox' in C Davis (ed), *The Monstrosity of Christ: Paradox or Dialectic* (MIT Press, 2009) 235–36.

[2] S Žižek, *The Fragile Absolute: Or, why is the Christian Legacy Worth Fighting For?* (Verso, 2000) 2.

equally loved in a Christian community of peace, rather than existing in a space of alienation from this community or antagonism within this community, which would perpetuate the violence we are attempting to avoid.

This chapter proposes that the key to restoring reason to faith, and providing a sublime Christian materialism which resolves the problem of alienation and antagonism, is the Incarnational Paradox, incorporating the Resurrection as well as the Crucifixion, which assumes and instantiates the Pauline law of love: that one should love their neighbours as themselves. Section I of the chapter introduces the secular position of Slavoj Žižek, describing his atheistic Christian materialism and adjusting it to arrive at a theological Christian materialism which properly incorporates resurrection. In section II, Žižek's terminology of the 'Sublime Object' is adopted and paradigmatically applied to Christ's defeat of death through resurrection.

Section III contends that we may participate in this sublimity through faith in the paradox of Christ's incarnation, crucifixion and resurrection—that in order to have true and flourishing life, we must first die. This unites reason and faith, reveals the law of love, and enables its replication in the community. According to this reading of Paul, it is the uniting of humanity through the Resurrection which institutes the law of love, and makes a community grounded in the truth of loving the individual possible; it follows that law and truth are paradoxical yet symbiotic in Christian theology as they form the foundation for a peaceful legal community. Section IV notes there is one further paradox which can allow final peace in the community, even between the secular and the faithful—that just as the practice of love follows faith, so faith follows the practice of love.

B. Structuring the Christian Material

Žižek states that:

> My claim is not merely that I am a materialist through and through, and that the subversive kernel of Christianity is accessible also to a materialist approach; my thesis is much stronger: this kernel is accessible *only* to a materialist approach—and vice versa: to become a true dialectical materialist, one should go through the Christian experience.[3]

His focus on the material here is central. It indicates that Žižek is not advocating some sort of secular ethic, or embracing some sentimental understanding of Jesus as merely a good moral teacher. The question is not one pertaining to the content of Christianity, but rather its structure. This is because, for Žižek, the Christian experience is uniquely associated with absence or void through the death of God. The idea stems from his understanding of materialism itself: it

> is not the assertion of inert material density in its humid heaviness—such a 'materialism' can always serve as a support for gnostic spiritualist obscurantism. In contrast, a true

[3] S Žižek, *The Puppet and the Dwarf* (MIT, 2003) 6 (original emphasis).

> materialism joyously assumes the 'disappearance of matter', the fact that there is only void.[4]

Materialism is not that which is earthy, but focuses on the nothing, the void; true materialism emphasises the contingency and finality of matter which will be no more.

Žižek argues that Christianity is necessary in order to articulate a genuine materialism, because it alone points to the void, the 'ontological incompleteness of reality', through its description of the death of God. And the term 'God' does not literally refer to some personal, all-powerful, benevolent being as in the Christian tradition (for such a being does not exist for the pure materialist), nor to a metaphor for human attitudes, but to that in humanity which is not human yet sustains human being.[5] The emphasis here is on the material practices of Christianity which stem from the absence of its God or, as Lacan understands it, the Big Other. Here the Big Other refers to that which structures reality—and so for Lacan and Žižek encompasses both the Christian God and the Symbolic: language, symbols, signifiers, law and the like. For Žižek, Christianity only exists in materialist or atheist practices, such as radical political groups, that negate it. And a true materialism which asserts that only material reality really exists must accept the consequences of the nonexistence of the Big Other. However, it is only Christianity which opens the space for thinking about this nonexistence because it alone is the religion of a God who dies.[6]

This is why Žižek believes the Christian legacy is worth fighting for:

> The only way to redeem the subversive core of Christianity is therefore to return to death-of-God theology … what 'dies' on the Cross is not just the false (positive, ontic) envelope of Divinity, which was obfuscating its evental core; what dies is God himself, the structuring principle of our entire universe, its life- giving force, the guarantee of its meaning … at this point of apocalypse, opposites coincide … his death is the death of Evil, so that crucifixion and resurrection are one event.[7]

Žižek fundamentally argues that the Christian legacy allows the subversion of dominating material political practices because of its focus on the end of matter through the death of God, or the Big Other. It follows from this materialist perspective that 'the reality of the Cross is the only reality there is', since the Cross is the material reality of absence manifesting.[8] So the Resurrection and the Crucifixion are no longer separate events, but one is subsumed into the other. The Resurrection is the 'universalisation of the crucifixion' through Christ turning the act of violence back upon himself, breaking the endless cycle of revenge.[9] The final act is that,

[4] S Žižek, 'The Fear of Four Words: A Modest Plea for a Hegelian Reading of Christianity' in C Davis (ed), *The Monstrosity of Christ: Paradox or Dialectic* (MIT Press, 2009) 92.

[5] Žižek, 'Dialectical Clarity', above n 1, 240.

[6] ibid 287.

[7] ibid 260–61.

[8] ibid 267.

[9] ibid 267–68.

as evil dies through Christ sacrificing himself, so universal love is enacted—or what Žižek might term the law of love. Christ's particular death universalises the refusal of violence by sacrifice, and because sacrifice is sacrificed, the sacrifice is therefore cancelled and love becomes the universal enactment or law.

C. Sites of the Christian Material: Law, Science, Faith

(i) Death and Absence

Let me elucidate these ideas in some more detail. In regard to its particularly legal aspect, according to Lacan and Žižek, the Symbolic Law (or the 'Big Other') regulates the public narrative symbolic space, but what lies 'beneath' the Symbolic Law (the impossible Thing of the Real unable to be contained) is actually that which makes the law—it is unconscious experience, capricious and arbitrary, leaving no guarantee for the subject.[10] In this way, lying actually refers to the Big Other, which lies in the guise of truth, or feigns to feign.[11] As Austin and Derrida observed before Žižek, the authority of law is therefore dependent on its own enunciation, which means that it has no intrinsic authority or reason, but simply relies on its own positing. This traumatic fact is repressed into the unconscious through the imagination that law has its foundation in truth or justice. The law is not to be accepted as true, only as necessary—its authority is without truth, and the solution is not to seek truth by reason but to submit to the regime of the Symbolic so that truth can be seen.[12] For Žižek, then, the supposition of people in law's authority stems from a faith in law, from a belief or confidence in the truth behind law. People only accept that law is authoritative insofar as they already believe in law. However, the belief that truth resides in law is illusory and can be described by the psychoanalytic concept of transference—the reasons we believe law is true are only persuasive to those who already believe law to be true.[13]

Žižek thus articulates the incompleteness of law—that it is never grounded in truth and is necessary without being true—there is always something beyond it (the Real), no fundamental Other that can ground the law or redeem its founding violence. Just as the ancient pagans viewed the state as founded through violence (specifically war), so Žižek, drawing on Freud, sees law as originating through the violence of parricide.[14] This is as an extension of Žižek's definition of materialism; materialism acknowledges the ontological incompleteness of reality, here in a legal

[10] E Casey and J Woody, 'Hegel, Heidegger, Lacan: The Dialectic of Desire' in S Žižek (ed), *Jacques Lacan: Critical Evaluations in Cultural Theory* (Routledge, 2003) 131–32; F Jameson, 'Imaginary and Symbolic in Lacan: Marxism, Psychoanalytic Criticism, and the Problem of the Subject' (1977) 55 *Yale French Studies* 338, 353.

[11] Casey and Woody, ibid, 80–81.

[12] S Žižek, *The Sublime Object of Ideology* (Verso, 1989) 37–39.

[13] J Dean, 'Žižek on Law' (2004) 15 *Law and Critique* 1, 8.

[14] ibid 14.

sense. Žižek finds a solution to this problem in a secular approach to the notions of loving one's neighbour and 'unplugging' found in St Paul, or disengaging oneself from the idleness that constrains the subject to identify with the hegemonic social order or Symbolic. This is not a merely inner contemplative stance, but an active work of love which leads to an alternative community.[15]

It is in this context that, in his typical fashion, Žižek exposes what he claims is the dialectical nature of Christianity. According to Christianity, humans were created by God, but have failed to keep his standard expressed in his moral law. As a consequence, God as a just God must punish this sin, but because of his love for humanity God puts forward his own son Jesus Christ, as God in human form, to take the punishment deserved for sin on the cross. Whoever repents and trusts in Jesus to take their punishment on the cross receives Jesus' righteousness due to his perfect life and, with this, forgiveness, reconciliation with God, eternal life and indwelling of the Holy Spirit until final redemption of the body. Žižek, adopting Hegelian ontology with the terminology of Lacanian psychoanalysis, argues that if the effect of the Crucifixion is God existing as the Holy Spirit in terms of a mere community of believers bound by love (that is, rather than a translation of essence from God the Father and God the Son to God the Holy Spirit, the essence is sublated/disintegrated), it follows that the Big Other is no longer required. As such, if God dies in Christ as his earthly embodiment on the cross, not only does God die, but he disintegrates as the Big Other. This is what Hegel termed the 'monstrosity' of Christ: that the 'insertion of Christ as the Mediator between God and man is strictly equivalent to the fact that there is no Big Other'.[16]

Therefore, the corollary of Christian faith for Žižek is that belief in the God who sacrifices himself on the cross for sin renders one an atheist, for it is in fact belief in a dead God, a non-entity, a thing without substance or essence. The Incarnation teaches us that the Spirit only exists through the finite existence of a community of mortal humans who acknowledge it. Since Christ dies on the cross and Christ is the essence of God, the essence of God is negated and God only exists when subjects contingently and finitely act as if God exists.[17] This implies that the death and resurrection of Christ are contemporaneous—Christ dies on the cross, his tortured, dead body is a material remainder, and he is simultaneously resurrected in us, the collective of believers. 'A materialist does not deny miracles, he just reminds us that they live behind disturbing material leftovers.'[18]

So Christ is resurrected not bodily or literally, but through the spirit of love which binds the believers following his crucifixion.[19] The Holy Spirit is not a distinct person of the Trinity who comes to dwell within believers. Bodily resurrection

[15] ibid 20–21; Žižek, *The Fragile Absolute*, above n 2, 135.

[16] S Žižek, 'Is it Still Possible to be a Hegelian Today?' in L Bryant et al (eds), *The Speculative Turn: Continental Materialism and Realism* (RE Press, 2011) 217–18.

[17] Žižek, 'Fear of Four Words', above n 4, 60–61.

[18] Žižek, 'Dialectical Clarity', above n 1, 287.

[19] ibid 290–91.

and the indwelling of the Holy Spirit are not the true miracle or the essence of the material, according to Žižek. Rather, the true miracle is the love in the collection of believers that constitutes the Holy Spirit and the resurrected Christ, and the material fact of Christ is that this 'resurrection' and 'Holy Spirit' exist against the backdrop of Christ's dead body.

(ii) Life, Presence, Hope

There is much to appreciate about Žižek's reading here. He is insightful in his identification that Christ's death is a sacrifice, in some sense a refusal of violence. Similarly, it is true that at the point of crucifixion opposites coincide—this is the epitome of paradox, manifested in Christ's Incarnation, and ultimately producing a community of love between the believers. However, there are also places where he does not quite hit the mark. These issues can be crudely summarised as a misunderstanding of the Resurrection. For example, Žižek states that

> when Christ dies, what dies with him is the secret hope discernible in 'Father, why hast thou forsaken me?': the hope that there *is* a father who has abandoned me. The 'Holy Spirit' is the community deprived of its support in the big Other.[20]

Žižek is consistent here in the sense that Christ's death appears to be the death of hope, and his conception of the Resurrection means that this hope can never be restored.

But the Resurrection is the very evidence that God our Father has not abandoned us, and hope remains with faith and love. As Jesus says, 'I will not leave you as orphans … I will ask the Father, and he will give you another Helper … the Holy Spirit … to be with you forever'.[21] And after his resurrection, Jesus states that 'I am with you always, to the end of the age'.[22] Žižek should at least admit that believers are not finally abandoned by God but helped by the Holy Spirit, whether or not this is the actual indwelling Spirit of God which comprises and unites the spiritual community through the law of the Spirit as Milbank states or is the mere existence of the spiritual community itself as Žižek says. Milbank, following the Apostle Paul, argues that Christ's resurrection is the basis or foundation for the community of faith. Christ's counter-violence was displayed in utter self-giving, which results in immediate return to us as resurrection. This enables the community of faith to also refuse violence and live in love and peace.[23] But Žižek is saying that Christ is resurrected through the presence of the community of faith which exists in love and peace. It follows that Milbank's and Žižek's structures are practically identical; the only difference is the orientation.

Christ's refusal of violence and giving of himself resulted in immediate return through the Resurrection. Paradoxically, it is through his apparent (but not real)

[20] ibid 171 (original emphasis).
[21] John 14:16, 18, 26.
[22] Matthew 28:20.
[23] J Milbank, *Being Reconciled: Ontology and Pardon* (Routledge, 2003) 100.

abandonment that he is ultimately returned. Conversely, on Žižek's view, Christ's death signals abandonment by God, the final victory of death manifested through the hopeless material remainder of Christ's dead body. We should therefore accept Milbank's ontology over Žižek's, because we only gain hope of the final defeat of death, the final act of violence and final communion with God through the actual resurrection itself.

Against Žižek's claim that Christ's death signals the space for universal love, it is actually his death and distinct resurrection that allows this possibility. As Milbank states, the 'pre-Cartesian Catholic metaphysical vision' of the

> resurrected body ... permits ... the universal possibility of love ... Here one can claim that the Catholic perspective achieves a materialism in a joyful, positive sense ... for matter to 'matter' there must be a recognition of a mediating link between matter and spirit.[24]

Through the quintessential materiality of Christ's resurrection, humanity and divinity (matter and spirit) are mediated and united in one glorified body forever, and by faith we analogically participate in this body. So, rather than a dreary materialism that finishes with the tortured and dead body of Christ, abandoned with no hope, by faith in the Resurrection a Christian materialism joyfully embraces the glorified body of love provided by Christ.

(iii) The Place of Faith (and Reason)

Thus, faith is indispensable to a proper Christian materialism. Hebrews 11:1 states that 'faith is the substance of things hoped for, the evidence of things not seen'.[25] Faith is the material fact, the immanent substance and evidence for the transcendent, and consequently the foundation for a theological Christian materialism which allows immanent and tangible peace from a transcendent and immaterial source—the living, Triune God.

Žižek, too, acknowledges this need for faith, though from a very different perspective. For Žižek, the principle of his analysis which reveals the apparent yet strangely paradoxical affinity between Christian monotheism and atheism demonstrates not that atheism depends upon monotheism, but that 'monotheism itself prefigures atheism in the field of religion'—that 'God is a dead God', a 'sublated nothing'.[26] The very concept of a God who will give himself up for humanity in Christian theism opens the space for atheism to occur as a result. However, it is not simply the case that all paths lead to atheism. Even Žižek, in a series of final comments, makes the radical proposal that atheism is the 'negation of the negation of belief' and so results in a return to faith, but without God—a belief in belief without reference to a particular object, such as God.[27]

[24] J Milbank, 'The Double Glory, Or Paradox versus Dialectics: On Not Quite Agreeing with Slavoj Žižek' in C Davis (ed), *The Monstrosity of Christ: Paradox or Dialectic?* (MIT Press, 2009) 125.

[25] King James Version.

[26] Žižek, 'Hegelian Today', above n 16, 96.

[27] ibid 101.

The implication of a lack of necessity through the death of God which follows from Žižek's critique intersects with Milbank's statements regarding contingency, for Milbank argues that on this view all that exists is contingency, or the contingent remainder—the contingent is absolutised.[28] In other words, the only possibly universal truth that secular reason can entertain is the rule of contingency. Paradoxically, the death of necessity absolutises contingency. In addition, the death of God as the 'necessary being' precludes 'metaphysical mediation', for 'there is no longer any metaphysical to mediate'.[29] This has 'led to a vacuum', and without metaphysical mediation 'various modes of fideistic religion have emerged and rushed to fill this void'.[30] In short, the establishment of necessary contingence inevitably leads to faith without reason. This observation parallels Žižek's earlier critique that since law is not grounded in truth, it is believed by faith without reason. The specific issue is that 'merely fideistic faith mimics rationalistic reason without faith', and there needs to be an alternative structure that unites reason with faith.[31]

This alternative structure is faith in the Resurrection. The true miracle is not the disturbing material leftover of Christ's tortured, dead body, but that this body is itself gloriously resurrected and redeemed, as the prototype for our own resurrection.

> But in fact Christ has been raised from the dead, the first fruits of those who have fallen asleep. For as by a man came death, by a man has come also the resurrection of the dead. For as in Adam all die, so also in Christ shall all be made alive.[32]

Resurrection empowers faith, and by faith we are able to joyfully participate in this bodily resurrection through Christ.

Conversely, Žižek's faith in a non-entity, the dead God, a sublated nothing, fundamentally lacks the requisite materiality sought in Christian theology, and also is at odds with the accounts of the disciples recording the Resurrection. Despite Žižek's claims to the contrary, with faith in Jesus bodily resurrected rather than faith in nothingness, there exists a genuine materiality which can become the basis for a Christian theological materialism. The law, too, is redeemed through the Resurrection. It is no longer a lie, but the truth; it is the revelation of Christ's divinity which can be believed through a faith united with reason, rather than a fideistic or blind faith. This is further confirmed by the disciples themselves testifying about this resurrected body through eyewitness accounts, as well as empirically observing it.

The earliest written account of the Resurrection is probably that of the Apostle Paul in 1 Corinthians 15:3–8, where he describes an early oral tradition of Jesus' appearances to the 12 disciples and others, before alluding to his own experience

[28] Milbank, 'Double Glory', above n 24, 114–15.

[29] J Milbank, *The Future of Love: Essays in Political Theology* (Cascade Books, 2009) 328.

[30] ibid.

[31] ibid 333.

[32] 1 Corinthians 15:20–22.

of seeing the risen Christ.[33] Matthew records the disciples seeing the risen Jesus and worshipping him (Matthew 28:16–17); the accounts of Luke (Luke 24:36–43) and John (John 20:19–21:14) record the risen Jesus appearing before the disciples, inviting them to see and touch his hands and feet, and eating with them. Mark's account records an angel at the tomb informing the women that Jesus had risen (Mark 16:1–8), though verses 9–20 are most likely not original to the gospel of Mark.[34] Nevertheless, Matthew and John were both original disciples and eyewitnesses, Mark was probably recording his account informed by an original disciple and eyewitness (Peter), and Luke interviewed the original disciples and eyewitnesses for his account.[35]

Therefore, the accounts of the Resurrection in the gospels and by the Apostle Paul are given as original evidence through individual eyewitness testimony, not as unreliable secondary hearsay, so from a purely legal perspective are considered to be evidentially trustworthy, where trustworthiness is a belief or faith united with reason. From a 'scientific' perspective, to perhaps anachronistically consider the disciple Thomas, he in particular was not content to simply believe in Christ as a fideist (in the sense of blind faith without any reason), but believed on the basis of the physical evidence provided by touching Christ's pierced feet and hands. Interestingly, he did not even believe the (original evidence of) eyewitness testimony by the other disciples, but needed the physical evidence. Although the actual fact of Thomas touching Christ's hands and feet is not recorded, the invitation by Jesus and the subsequent affirmation of his Lordship and Deity by Thomas indicates that he did accept Jesus' invitation and was satisfied that he had in fact been raised from the dead. Jesus also affirms that those who believe without the physical evidence (unlike Thomas) will be blessed.[36] Perhaps it is those who believe the eyewitness testimony, those who trust in the law of love proclaimed by Christ and Paul, who are blessed in this sense.

In a fundamentally reasonable way, the disciples affirmed that it was the resurrected Christ. They touched him, ate with him and conversed with him, having faith in the legal and physical evidence before them.[37] It is true that these are individual accounts, but they involve eyewitness testimony and physical evidence. Žižek may not admit the Resurrection as a life-giving event distinct from the Crucifixion, but in adopting this approach Žižek's interpretation of what the accounts record about the Resurrection is incomplete.

Bearing in mind the testimony about the Resurrection, faith in the Resurrection is not mere fideism that is against reason, nor is it secular rationality which

[33] J Price, 'The First Letter of Paul to the Corinthians' in C Laymon (ed), *The Interpreter's Concise Commentary on Acts and Paul's Letters* (Abingdon Press, 1983) 229.

[34] See L Pherigo, 'The Gospel According to Mark' in Laymon, ibid, 174–77.

[35] See Luke 1:1–4; John 21:24; R Gundry, *A Survey of the New Testament* (Zondervan, 1970) 78–79, 83–85, 93–94, 101–03.

[36] See John 20:24–29.

[37] John 20:24–21:14.

excludes faith by definition, or belief in nothing. Rather, it is a faith in Christ which is compatible with reason, a faith based fundamentally in truth affirmed by law, and even a faith in law itself. In effect, then, to have faith in the Resurrection is to affirm law. What we therefore see is that, from the perspective of Christian theology, faith in the Resurrection as truth and law produces a genuinely Christian materialism. Through paradox, this can allow faith to be united with reason, as well as producing a peaceful community through implementing the law of love. However, there is one more ingredient required—the sublime.

II. The Sublime Object: Defeating Death

Exploring the idea of the sublime allows further refining of the structure of the Incarnation and Resurrection as paradoxical, and it is a major theme of Žižek's work. He states that

> sublimity excites and agitates … the sentiment of Sublimity is attached to chaotic, terrifying, limitless phenomena … the Sublime must follow Beauty as a form of mediation of its immediacy … the sublime object [is] 'an object raised to the level of the (impossible-real) Thing'.[38]

So for Žižek the sublime is that which is terrifyingly monstrous in the sense that it is beyond any limit or categorisation; it cannot be adequately represented, mediated or apprehended, yet it is the most real of things. Žižek also observes the paradoxical nature of the sublime:

> The paradox of the Sublime is as follows: in principle, the gap separating phenomenal, empirical objects of experience from the Thing-In-Itself is insurmountable—that is, no empirical object, no representation of it can adequately represent the Thing … but the Sublime is an object in which we can experience this very impossibility … by means of the very failure of representation, we can have a presentiment of the true dimension of the Thing.[39]

Although expressed in Kantian terms, the paradox of the sublime indicated by Žižek can also be seen as Incarnational in regard to Christ. Specifically, Christ as the God-man cannot be apprehended; his full glory cannot be countenanced, categorised or expressed in terms of limits. Nevertheless, it is through this utter transcendence of Christ being displayed through the immanent Incarnation that we are actually able to grasp the truth of Christ by faith—that in his sacrifice and love we may have forgiveness of sins and eternal life with him in glory. As Žižek states,

> we can now see why it is precisely nature in its most chaotic, boundless, terrifying dimension which is best qualified to awaken in us the feeling of the Sublime: here, where the

[38] Žižek, *Sublime Object*, above n 12, 202–03.
[39] ibid 203.

> aesthetic imagination is strained to its utmost, where all finite determinations dissolve themselves, the failure appears at its purest.[40]

Purely secular or human reason, in its desire to categorise, to observe and even to imagine, is fundamentally limited and therefore can never experience the sublime. It is only nature enlightened by grace, taken beyond itself by the revelation of truth, that can really see the glory of Christ in his defeat of death.

The defeat of death is the paradigmatic sublime object. Death is the great equaliser, the perennial limit of human existence. Žižek, though, contends that the death of Christ is fundamentally different from the death of a pagan god, a mere 'terrestrial embodiment'. Since the death of Christ is the death of God, the 'positive, transcendent, unattainable entity', the death of Christ means the non-existence or nullity of everything. For Žižek, the death of Christ is a sublime object because it positively embodies the terrifying, limitless void.[41] We saw that Žižek argues that sublimity is attached to terrifying, limitless phenomena, and here he applies death to this definition in the sense that death means the terrifying, endless void of nonexistence. However, sublimity is more intrinsically found not in death and the consequent emptiness or nothing, the lack, but in the eternal presence; through Christ's resurrection, even death is no limit: there is only endless life. This, perhaps, is the real terror, the magnificent monstrosity, the truly sublime—the death of death, that even death has no limit on us. It is not death and its final, finite nothingness that is sublime, but eternal, unlimited, unparalleled life by death.

So, for a genuinely sublime Christian materialism, the Resurrection and the glory (light) of Christ is again rendered central, for it is through the resurrection of Christ that death is truly defeated:

> When the perishable puts on the imperishable, and the mortal puts on immortality, then shall come to pass the saying that is written: 'Death is swallowed up in victory.' 'O death, where is your victory? O death, where is your sting?'[42]

The sublime is not merely the obscure background of divine nothingness, but also the revelation of a glorious, limitless, terrifying light.[43] This sublime event is precisely the resurrection of Christ, who displays his infinite glory through defeating death in the resurrected body. The event can be truly sublime only if it is in itself beautiful, and embraced by the community. In fact, the sundering of the sublime from the beautiful (which is assumed by Žižek when he says that the sublime follows beauty) was actually an arbitrary gesture motivated by distorted theology and political economy.[44] The sublime does not follow the beautiful but is the beautiful, and through the universality of Christ's resurrection by faith we too

[40] ibid.
[41] ibid 206.
[42] 1 Corinthians 15:54–55.
[43] J Milbank, 'Sublimity: The Modern Transcendent' in R Schwartz (ed), *Transcendence: Philosophy, Literature and Theology Approach the Beyond* (Routledge, 2004) 215.
[44] See ibid 211–34.

can participate in this sublimity. The Apostle Paul underscores this point that the resurrected body has a unique glory:

> What is sown is perishable; what is raised is imperishable. It is sown in dishonor; it is raised in glory. It is sown in weakness; it is raised in power. It is sown a natural body; it is raised a spiritual body. If there is a natural body, there is also a spiritual body. Thus it is written, 'The first man Adam became a living being'; the last Adam became a life-giving spirit. But it is not the spiritual that is first but the natural, and then the spiritual. The first man was from the earth, a man of dust; the second man is from heaven. As was the man of dust, so also are those who are of the dust, and as is the man of heaven, so also are those who are of heaven. Just as we have borne the image of the man of dust, we shall also bear the image of the man of heaven.[45]

In the final analysis, then, the defeat of death through Incarnational Paradox is the sublime object, as it produces infinity, an eternal, glorious life without limits. In conflating the Crucifixion with the Resurrection, Žižek denies the sublime element—the infinite miracle. Žižek fails to see that the Incarnation, incorporating both the Crucifixion and the Resurrection as distinct events, combines the ordinary with the extraordinary through miracle to display the sublime.[46] It was necessary that Christ died and then was resurrected by miracle in order to provide life. Apart from the paradox of Christ as the infinite God and finite man, this too is the defining paradox of a sublime Christian materialism—that just as Christ died a finite death to defeat death and infinitely rose to live forever, so must we die to defeat death in order to truly live.

III. The Sublime Truth of Faith: Paradoxical Law, Love and Life through Resurrection

A. Reconciling Reason and Faith through Incarnational Paradox

The framework of paradox also reveals a way in which faith and reason can be reconciled. Milbank prefigures a solution by stating that the only alternative to nihilism and fideism is the return of a metaphysic which is able to mediate between faith and reason, a 'reasonable faith' or theology.[47] The key to this metaphysic is the Incarnational Paradox. The paradox of the Incarnation is, in essence, the paradox of the absolutisation of contingency—for Christ is the interface of absolute and contingent as the God-man. Furthermore, the meeting of the temporal and the eternal in Christ leads to the recovery of reason, for reason is recovered in the 'betweenness' or paradox of (incarnational) being, where 'finite belonging to

[45] 1 Corinthians 15:42–49.
[46] Milbank, 'Double Glory', above n 24, 211.
[47] Milbank, *Future of Love*, above n 29, 328, 333.

the infinite is the order of things', where time meets eternity, absence meets presence and immanence meets transcendence.[48]

Reason is united to faith at the paradoxical interface of the universal (reason) and the particular (faith), which is the event of Christ. This is why Milbank states that the 'absolutisation of contingency' has a 'uniquely disclosive relationship to eternal truth' and is 'absolute truth'—it is the paradoxical event of Christ which is truth.[49] The event of Christ moderates and instantiates the paradox of a contingent law, or necessary contingence, for the event of Christ dying on the cross and rising again was an event both contingent and necessary. It was contingent in the sense that it was unexpected, as evidenced by the Apostle Peter's reaction when first informed by Christ that this is what would occur, and it was necessary in the sense that it was predicted by prophecy, foreordained by God and required in order for the sins of humanity to be forgiven and reconciliation with God to occur. Thus, the Event of Christ (truth), which is simultaneously necessary and contingent, can restore reason to faith and unite the two.

More precisely, Milbank argues that truth is the 'stability of the eternal' and identifies this truth with paradox 'through the recollection backward and repetition forward of temporality'. He also identifies reason with 'negotiation of the paradoxical'.[50] It was not simply faith that 'believed the absurd', but reason, whose 'ungrounded presupposition was the paradoxical coincidence of eternity and time as the truth'.[51] Therefore, the only serious location of truth where reason and faith are united must lie in the 'coincidence of the eternal and the temporal' in the event of Christ.[52] For paradox is 'infinitely accentuated in the Incarnation', since the 'eternal God is identified with temporal man', and in this way we can have truth, the infinite (God) giving back to the finite (man).[53]

Incarnation also means that participation in the divine relational life is restored. In this sense, truth is recovered by a repairing of the asymmetrical relation to God of the creation by the action of God himself. Since God is identity and the infinite/finite, he is also the 'paradox of relational reconciliation'.[54] Therefore, truth, which is 'itself relational', is 'relationally restored'.[55] Truth is inextricably tied to participation in the life, death and resurrection of Christ. The 'truth of truth', ontological truth, can finally be found in 'transcendent metaphysics or theology': the 'Trinitarian play' between the one and the many, the infinite and the simple.[56]

[48] C Davis, 'Introduction: Holy Saturday or Resurrection Sunday? Staging an Unlikely Debate' in C Davis (ed), *The Monstrosity of Christ: Paradox or Dialectic?* (MIT Press, 2009) 11, 19, 21.

[49] Milbank, 'Double Glory', above n 24, 114–15.

[50] ibid 169–70.

[51] ibid.

[52] ibid.

[53] ibid.

[54] J Milbank, 'The Thomistic Telescope: Truth and Identity' (2006) 80 *American Catholic Philosophical Quarterly* 193.

[55] J Milbank, 'The Return of Mediation' in J Milbank et al (eds), *Paul's New Moment: Continental Philosophy and the Future of Christian Theology* (Brazos Press, 2010) 225–26.

[56] Milbank, 'Thomistic Telescope', above n 54.

This 'truth-as-disclosure is also the bond of being'—'exchange between the infinite and the finite'.[57]

B. Revealing the Law of Love through Incarnation

This paradoxical exchange of infinite and finite, particularly in the context of Christ dying so that he may live, reveals the law of love. God has not abandoned us. Rather, through the truth of the Resurrection, that in Christ we die so that we may live, the law of intimacy, love, forgiveness and mercy is demonstrated so that it can be reflected and performed by us. In this sense that truth is the manifestation of divine being beyond the mere mirroring, it also communicates peace and the good. Indeed, 'love and truth are co-equal in God'.[58] So in Christ, the specifically exceptional in time where the divine being incorporating love and peace is disclosed, there is the establishment of the law of true human life (the law of love) against the old law, which is the law of sin. This is paradoxically based upon Christ as the exception to human law, and upon faith in the criminal death of the one who first identified himself as this exception. Up to this point, Žižek agrees with Milbank. Žižek also rightly sees that for justice and truth to be possible, it was necessary that one man be recognised as God. However, he should go further and accept that 'this necessity in its actuality really is conjoined to the paradox of the infinite', which is of the order of resurrection.[59]

In other words, against Žižek, only in the necessity of the paradoxical Incarnation and Resurrection can truth and justice which undergird law be possible—that is, the law of love, which removes the violence of antagonism and alienation, and loves the individual as different while also uniting them to the community. Ultimately, it is because of the Cross, the 'event of the judgment of God', that 'no return to the law of death', to the 'antique compromise of inhibition of violence', remains possible—and that the Christian outlook of ontological peace now provides an alternative to nihilism, or secular reason.[60] 'Humanity can only be united through the arrival of Christ, the concrete event, beyond all laws'—the 'arrival of fully restored human truth'.[61] Furthermore, with faith in this event necessarily comes charity, so receiving the love of God manifested in the Incarnation, Crucifixion and Resurrection means to pass it on as love for your neighbour. Hence, it is the Pauline law of love, to love your neighbour as yourself, which provides the foundation for a peaceful legal community based in the truth of Christ, and unites reason and faith.

The only alternative to a secular approach which sunders faith and reason is the return of a theology which is able to mediate between faith and reason,

[57] ibid.
[58] Milbank, 'Thomistic Telescope', above n 54.
[59] Milbank, 'Double Glory', above n 24, 215.
[60] J Milbank, *Theology and Social Theory: Beyond Secular Reason* (Blackwell, 1990) 442.
[61] ibid 318.

and unite them. This theology arrives in the form of the Incarnational Paradox, where reason is recovered through faith in the truth of divine being, and this is revealed in Christ as the interface between the finite and the infinite, eternal God and temporal man. In the disclosure of divine being as love and ontological peace through the incarnation, crucifixion and resurrection of Christ, the law of sin and death is replaced by a new law, the law of love, which can then become the theological truth which grounds the community and restores reason to faith, allowing peace.

For 'in Christ peace is proleptically given', because 'only the perfect saving of one man from the absolute destruction of death' through the resurrection of Christ, the 'refusal of the loss of any difference', can 'initially spell perfect and infinite peace', leading to the institution of love.[62] This is the normative dimension to the law of love: love is paradoxically both a commandment of the law and obedience to that commandment—love of God and of neighbour is commanded as the greatest commandment of the law by Christ, and Christ also says that if you love him you will obey his commandments. So divine love both presupposes and is the necessary condition for obedience and the law, and is located in the Incarnational Paradox. This paradox of law and love also points the way to how the law of love may prove to be a foundation for the peaceful legal community: it simultaneously fulfils the law by obeying the commandments, since love does no wrong to a neighbour, and reflexively transcends the law by producing its own obedience. This descriptive dimension to the law of love is explored in the final chapter.

C. Empowering the Law of Love: Participation through Faith in the Resurrection

There is a type of paradoxical and symbiotic relationship between law and truth. It is the law of love that presupposes the truth yielded through the Incarnational Paradox and the Resurrection. This, in turn, provides the foundation in truth for the loving and peaceful legal community to be instantiated. In this way, law and truth establish and maintain the other. The Resurrection in particular gains significance when considered in relation to how Milbank explains it in the Pauline context.

The first relevant theme in this regard is that 'Paul pursued law beyond law': the law of love, which is the 'basis for natural justice in symbolic law'.[63] Though justice, according to Derrida, transcends law and cannot be deconstructed, it still 'must be given expression in the legal'.[64] Paul therefore linked natural justice with the 'invocation of a supreme divine king' (Christ, the fulfilment of the law)

[62] J Milbank, 'A Response' in R Gill (ed), *Theology and Sociology: A Reader* (Cassell, 1996) 468.

[63] Milbank, *Future of Love*, above n 29, 170.

[64] J Milbank, 'Paul against Biopolitics' in J Milbank et al (eds), *Paul's New Moment: Continental Philosophy and the Future of Christian Theology* (Brazos Press, 2010) 35; *cf* J Derrida, 'Force of Law: "The Mystical Foundation of Authority"', paper presented on Deconstruction and the Possibility of Justice, Cardozo Law School (1989) 14–15.

who 'exceeded the law as embodying a living law', and he did so with particular regard to the Resurrection as the display of a living law of love.[65] This leads into the second theme, and returns us to the question of the law of love and its relationship to the Resurrection. Justice lies 'before the law' and is 'attainable through the truth of the resurrected man', for 'with death to the old law comes resurrection to a living law', the law of the spirit or the law of love, which 'renews and redistributes the good'.[66] So the determining factor in the symbiosis and paradox of law and truth, the reconciliation of reason and faith, and the removal of violence is the event of the Resurrection itself. Paul's own writings support this:

> Now if Christ is proclaimed as raised from the dead, how can some of you say that there is no resurrection of the dead? But if there is no resurrection of the dead, then not even Christ has been raised. And if Christ has not been raised, then our preaching is in vain and your faith is in vain. We are even found to be misrepresenting God, because we testified about God that he raised Christ, whom he did not raise if it is true that the dead are not raised. For if the dead are not raised, not even Christ has been raised. And if Christ has not been raised, your faith is futile and you are still in your sins.[67]

Paul argues that the basis of the law of sin and death being defeated is Christ himself actually being raised from the dead (it alone defeats death and brings life), for if Christ was not actually raised, Paul's preaching is in vain and he is a false witness, faith is futile and sin is not dealt with. Most importantly, since Christ has in fact been raised, he is the prototype and guarantee for the defeat of death and the general resurrection.[68] As such, truth as participation in the divine is only revealed through the Resurrection, giving the spirit of life rather than death. Hope is only given through Christ in the Resurrection, and this itself is the basis for true peace. Most importantly, since loving others requires loving God, loving God involves trust or faith in God and faith is futile without the Resurrection, it follows that the law of love presupposes the truth revealed through faith in the entirety of the paradoxical Christ Event—life, death and resurrection, God and man.[69]

IV. Manifesting the Peaceful Community: Faith and Practice

It is perhaps this which allows Christianity to be embraced so readily by the counter-intuitive postmodern and Lacanian registers.[70] Truth is finally revealed

[65] Milbank, 'Paul against Biopolitics', ibid, 42–43.
[66] ibid 56.
[67] 1 Corinthians 15:12–17.
[68] 1 Corinthians 15:20–22.
[69] 1 Corinthians 15:17.
[70] See Chapter 3's discussion of Derrida; see also J Lacan, *The Triumph of Religion Preceded by Discourse to Catholics* (Polity, 2013).

through the anti-foundationalist paradox of the Incarnation, which is the meeting of the eternal and the temporal in Christ, his crucifixion and his resurrection—an identity in difference, a hole made whole—cosmic paternal reconciliation. Since true reason is recovered in this paradoxical revelation of the divine being as the law of love, in Christ reason and faith unite to yield truth, and provide the foundation for a peaceful legal community. In this disclosure of the divine being in Christ is revealed the love and peace inherent in Trinitarian relations, particularly the law of love, which is the basis of the divine relationship. Thus, the law of love in the divine being ultimately yields truth in the Incarnational Paradox.

The proposition that the peaceful legal community is based on the emergence of truth through the Incarnational Paradox, the moment of intersection between faith and reason, raises the question of what this may point towards. It could be that truth is the interstitial space simultaneously separating and connecting the fundamental parallel and so-called 'binaries' of reason and faith, presence and absence, immanence and transcendence, self and other—the space where faith and reason become one through the operation of the law of the Trinity, or the law of love: the reconciliation of the one and the many, diversity in unity. This is the crucial jurisprudential insight which the crude and popularised formulations of fideism and secularism omit, that God is both personal and wholly Other, the moment of simultaneous sameness and difference: the moment of truth. Indeed, it is the paradoxical resurrection of the personification of truth, Jesus Christ, which allows this insight. For it is Christ, the transcendent and the immanent, the one in whom divinity and humanity is united forever, who is the only mediator between God and man, and who dies in order to live. So Christ, as the truth that mediates between faith and reason, also provides a new law. Instead of the law of the letter, which kills, it is a law of the Spirit, a law of love, which gives life.

In this sense, it is indeed the Trinitarian relationship, and Christ as the revelation of that relationship, which resolves the problem of the one and the many, or the problem of how to love the individual in a community stricken by antagonism and alienation. When such problems are approached from a purely secular perspective, there is no recourse to divine love, and the exclusion of God means the exclusion of divine love in the community. But Paul's outlook is more optimistic—we relate to the law through God by divine love, so by the spirit the law is uplifting and can instruct us in righteousness. Thus, the law is rejected in the flesh to be redeemed in the spirit. True community is to be oneself but more than oneself, to be needed by the community, assimilated in the spirit. This happens through love, not submission to a higher sovereign authority—according to Christ, we love one another and believe God loves each member of the community.

At this point, those who disagree with the position adopted in this book may be wondering how they may be equally loved in this 'Christian' community. This may occur through one final paradox—faith and practice. Normally, practice follows faith, but there is also the possibility of faith following practice. For example, Blaise Pascal argues that 'if you perform religious rites with enthusiasm … you will come to be devoutly religious. "Go then and take holy water, and have masses said; belief will come and stupefy your scruples.'"[71] Žižek, too, appears to allude to this paradoxical notion of belief following practice.[72] Therefore, I encourage even those who disagree with Christianity to continue discussing it. It may well be the way that the secular is not alienated and antagonised. By engaging in the Christian practice of loving your neighbour (which includes those of differing belief) as yourself, the peaceful legal community of harmony and reconciliation will be instantiated, and belief may come.

[71] Blaise Pascal, cited in J Cargile, 'Pascal's Wager' (1966) 41 *Philosophy* 250, 250.
[72] Žižek, 'Dialectical Clarity', above n 1, 287.

7

'Love Your (Legal) Neighbour as Yourself': Producing Peace through a Theological Jurisprudence of Truth

This book has engaged in a theological critique of the secular foundation undergirding the modern system of law, arguing that the secular division of reason and faith leads to antagonism and alienation. The Christian revelation of theological truth (the law of love) through the uniting of reason and faith in the Incarnation produces a vision of ontological peace which redeems law and removes this violence—in other words, the Christian law of loving one's neighbour provides the foundation for an ontologically peaceful legal community in which difference operates harmoniously.

In section I of this chapter the notions of secular reason as blind faith and true reason being recovered and united with faith through the Incarnational Paradox will be explained and explicitly connected to notions of the peaceful community. Section II contains a more unified explanation of truth incorporating revelation, correspondence and rhetoric, in conjunction with further exploring the conclusion that truth and law are symbiotic and produce peace in the context of Christ's incarnation, crucifixion and resurrection. Finally, in section III the nature of this ontological peace resulting from theology is more exactly articulated in contrast to the specific nature of pagan (secular) violence.

This chapter (and the book) concludes by critiquing the application of the law of love to the modern (secular) legal system. In particular, section IV considers the relationship between the Christian polity of love and the secular legal system, arguing that forgiveness is the key to establishing a peaceful legal community. Section V specifically applies these notions to a particular system of private law which governs relationships between individuals through contrasting theological and (secular) legal interpretations of the Parable of the Good Samaritan, arguing that the neighbour principle in negligence as derived from the parable lacks and ultimately distorts the theological principle. Finally, section VI proposes that it is only through recovering this principle of love that we may redeem and regenerate the legal system and attain a peaceful legal community.

I. 'The End of Reason': The Blind Faith of Secular Reason and Recovering Reason through the Incarnational Paradox

Christian faith is not merely intellectual assent, but a trust in or reliance on God. This faith is not so-called 'blind faith', or belief despite lack of evidence or in defiance of contrary evidence, but rather is a personal trust in the character of God which has been revealed in Christ. Such trust is in accordance with reason and the faculties of the mind, and indeed without the foundation of Christian faith with the divine mind and reason, the faculties of the human mind and the power of human reason cannot operate. It is this premise of reason based in faith which secular reason rejects, and consequently it sunders faith from reason. So secular reason, by separating faith from reason, actually renders itself blind faith. Secularised reason provides no reason to think that it is reasonable—it is mere belief in its own reason without evidence. Conversely, Christian faith unites itself with reason and recovers both through the Incarnational Paradox.

A. The Blindness and Violence of Secular Reason

When reason was isolated from faith (thus producing 'secular reason') and became the foundation of modern science, its nature as de facto blind faith was revealed. Milbank notes this as emblematic of the fact that 'once secular reason has exposed its own efforts to ground itself in the universal, then its advocacy of a polity and an ontology which is confined to the (non)regulation of conflict through conflict emerges clearly to view'.[1] In any discipline governed by a universalising secular reason which excludes faith, the 'regulation' of the discipline through violence surfaces.

Furthermore, since reason has turned against itself and discovered no universal foundation for reason (ie that it is blind faith), the question may be asked whether there is anything at all. This kind of postmodern deconstruction produces the perfect or mature form of secular reason: a nihilistic mythos antithetical to reason.[2] Furthermore, it sustains its ontology as a mythos through violence, for it has no other means—it cannot use persuasion due to its own unreason, so it must use coercion.[3] Therefore, secular reason is ultimately unreason, nihilistic mythos and blind faith, and tends to sustain itself through violence.

The orientation of the secular to the nihilistic cannot be opposed by simply redeeming enlightenment reason. Rather, this secular reason can be confronted with the faith of Christian theology manifesting in virtue reconciled with

[1] J Milbank, *Theology and Social Theory: Beyond Secular Reason* (Blackwell, 1990) 327.
[2] J Milbank, *The Future of Love: Essays in Political Theology* (Cascade Books, 2009) 156.
[3] See Milbank, *Theology and Social Theory*, above n 1, 260–63.

difference.[4] This is because a Christian perspective saves the human bias towards reason, for reason in the framework of virtue and difference is consistent with the infinite through participation in the divine virtue, and leaves no residue of chaos by allowing antagonistic difference. Rationalism is linked to the biblical mythos in particular, and to save reason in this fashion requires the supplementation of reason by faith, including faith in infinite reason.[5]

There are two ways in which this occurs. The first is that, according to Aquinas, all human rationality is participation in the divine reason, and therefore all knowledge requires faith. The light of revelation strengthens our grasp of natural principles, and consequently theology mediates knowledge in all other disciplines.[6] Therefore, to reason truly, one must be already illumined by God, while revelation itself is just a higher measure of illumination, conjoined intrinsically and inextricably with a created event which symbolically discloses that transcendent reality, to which all created events to a lesser degree point. This event is the incarnation, crucifixion and resurrection of Jesus Christ, the God-man. Instead of grafting faith onto a base of reason, faith is fundamental in seeking to elaborate a Christian *logos*, or a reason which bears the marks of the Incarnation.[7]

The nature of the Incarnation and the Trinity itself is the second, and probably more fundamental, method of confronting secular reason with faith and reason united in Christian theology. In terms of the nature of the Trinity, thinking an infinite differentiation which is also harmony is what grounds the reconciliation of difference with virtue. For the paganism of antiquity, the absolute was chaotic, and Being is infected with this chaos since the only discourse which can include both the same and the different is itself a discourse of difference, not a discourse of reason.[8] The extreme response of Voluntarist theology and the emphasis of the absolute unity and simplicity of God (ie equating him with Being) are also sources of secular reason since they do not take account of difference. Hence, the only transcendental, self-identical reality is an empty will or force which returns as the arbitrary and chaotic different. To save reason, one must derive it from an entity which lies beyond Being and beyond mere difference.[9] The Trinitarian God of Christian theology fulfils this by simultaneously being the divine and the difference in the divine persons, peace in unity and diversity, and the reconciliation of virtue and difference. A Christian ontology can therefore provide the foundation for taking account of difference and producing a reason compatible with faith which is ontologically peaceful as a function of the Trinitarian relations. Such cannot be arrived at by the operation of secular reason, but is rather revealed through faith and is a result of faith.[10]

[4] ibid 320–21.
[5] ibid xvi–xvii.
[6] ibid 252.
[7] ibid 383.
[8] ibid 434–35.
[9] ibid.
[10] ibid 437.

B. Kant on Pure Reason, or the Need for Faith

Secular reason attempts to discern the truth of reality independent of faith or revelation. Milbank proposes that pure (or secular) reason is supposedly able to resolve the four fundamental Kantian antinomies and uncover the truth of reality: beginning/no beginning, freedom/causality, ultimate constituent parts/no such parts and necessary being/contingent being. In addition, Christian theology needed to show that the way things are is a mode of perfection. Here, 'faith achieved what reason could not' by transcending the antinomies, and it did so by claiming such perfection in terms of the 'derivation of things from a perfect being, however inscrutable'.[11] Since God is perfect being, the way things are (truth as revelation of being) is also a mode of perfection. Consequently, the Kantian antinomies can never be resolved through pure or secular reason, but may be transcended through faith in the divine.

Immanuel Kant specifically indicates ways in which reason is unable to fully comprehend reality, opening the space for a reason combined with faith. In *Critique of Pure Reason*, Kant constructs each of the antinomies by firstly outlining arguments for a thesis and then arguments for an antithesis.[12] The first thesis is that 'the world has a beginning in time, and in space it is also enclosed in boundaries'; the first antithesis is that 'the world has no beginning and no bounds in space, but is infinite with regard to both time and space'.[13] The second thesis is that 'every composite substance in the world consists of simple parts, and nothing exists anywhere except the simple or what is composed of simples', while the second antithesis is 'No composite thing in the world consists of simple parts, and nowhere in it does there exist anything simple'.[14] The third thesis is 'Causality in accordance with laws of nature is not the only one from which all the appearances of the world can be derived. It is also necessary to assume another causality through freedom in order to explain them'; the third antithesis is 'there is no freedom, but everything in the world happens solely in accordance with the laws of nature'.[15] The final thesis is that 'to the world there belongs something that, either as a part of it or as its cause, is an absolutely necessary being', while the final antithesis is 'there is no absolutely necessary being existing anywhere, either in the world or outside the world as its cause'.[16]

Kant observes that the arguments for these positions represent the 'glittering pretensions' of reason, yet they 'do not even permit reason to think them'.[17] 'Unfortunately,' he argues,

> reason sees itself, in the midst of its greatest expectations, so entangled in a crowd of arguments and counterarguments that it is not feasible, on account either of its honor

[11] ibid 135.
[12] I Kant, *Critique of Pure Reason* (Cambridge University Press, 1998) 470–95.
[13] ibid 470, 471.
[14] ibid 476, 477.
[15] ibid 484, 485.
[16] ibid 490, 491.
[17] ibid 496.

> or even of its security, for reason to withdraw and look upon the quarrel with indifference, as mere shadow boxing, still less for it simply to command peace, interested as it is in object of the dispute; so nothing is left except to reflect on the origin of disunity of reason itself.[18]

Even Kant acknowledges that pure reason produces violence and endless strife, lacking the ability to command peace. It has a fundamental antagonism within itself. Since reason fails in this way and the antinomies cannot be conceptualised by the understanding, it follows that any transcending of the antinomies becomes a pure act of faith, not a necessity of reason. However, through the Trinity and Incarnational Paradox of Christ (or specifically Christian faith), these antinomies can be transcended.

For example, as we have already seen in the Trinity, the second antinomy, of difference and sameness, or ultimate constituent parts/no such parts, is transcended. The Trinity is one in the sense of the Godhead and so does not consist of simple parts, but simultaneously the Godhead is composed of the three divine members, Father, Son and Holy Spirit; so the Trinity does consist of simple parts. The Incarnational Paradox transcends the other antinomies. For the first antinomy, of time and space, Christ as God is the eternal *logos*, unbounded by time and space. However, as a man he is temporal and spatial. For the third antinomy, of freedom and causality, Christ's Incarnation was causally necessary (though not in the sense of being in accordance with immutable natural laws) as a matter of fulfilling Scripture and the will of God, but was also simultaneously an act of freedom as a voluntary sacrifice in love. Finally, for the fourth antinomy, of necessary or contingent being, Christ is a necessary (eternal) being as God, but as a man is simultaneously a contingent human. The fact that in the Trinity and Incarnation the thesis and antithesis of each of the antinomies are fulfilled implies that with Christian faith comes the transcending of the antinomies and the sublating of the binaries. And with that destruction of secular structure comes the recovery of reason—for the eternal/becoming distinction in Christ is universal and is what makes reason possible.[19]

Reason is united to faith at the paradoxical interface of the universal (reason) and the particular (faith), which is the event of Christ, for this allows the reconciliation of virtue and difference. The discourse of poetry in Christian theology promotes the recognition of difference through subjectivity and particularity, and the creative difference of the Trinity, in contrast to the pure, universalising nature of secular reason. Thus, secular reason is ultimately blind faith and leads to violence, while reason united to faith in Christian theology is unique in allowing true reason to flourish through the reconciliation of virtue and difference, producing an ontology of peace.

[18] ibid 497.
[19] Milbank, *Theology and Social Theory*, above n 1, 375.

C. Faith, Reason, Peace: A Sacred Polity

The positive combination of faith and reason has a particular distinctive quality when applied to the social or political space. In Enlightenment thinking, political constitution must balance the tension between an absolute sovereign centre and the mass of atomistic individuals. Either the political reality is natural, where the individuals compete in an agonistic market economy, or it is artificial, where the individuals are subsumed under the singular judgment of a sovereign head.[20] At this point, 'the whole is mystically elevated as greater than the parts, in such a fashion that the totality is held to transcend the grasp of reason, and must be regarded as the work of an unfathomable nature or providence'.[21] The secular approach fails to take proper account of this tension between the particular and the universal, atomic individualism and absolute sovereignty. The secular response is simply to extend and expand sovereign power, producing violence; it is an 'abstracting, idealising project'.[22] The existence of irreconcilable difference means that these must be mediated, and this occurs through increased regulation; people are treated as abstract commodities ruled by violence.[23] Therefore, rather than acknowledging the theological foundations of the society in faith, noting the mystical elevation of the sovereign through unfathomable providence, the secular space tends to alienate.

The key, then, is to seek a sacred space in which the individual and the community can be harmoniously connected; rather than faith or reason, it is faith and reason. It is not a matter of purely secular categories which divide, but the embrace of transcendent truths of faith which unite and allow peace.[24] As Milbank says, 'without "community", without its self-sustaining affirmation of objective justice, "excellence", and transcendental truth, goodness and beauty, one must remain resigned to capitalism and bureaucracy'.[25] The society here envisioned is not an endless series of legal rules which can never hope to properly regulate human behaviour (and so only produce violence), but a sacred community. Importantly, this is not a theocratic society based in some kind of legalistic church canon; it is both the model for an ideal society and a way of living within a given society, characterised by love. The aim, ultimately, is to exist harmoniously within a community of difference.

[20] J Milbank, *The Word Made Strange: Theology, Language, Culture* (Blackwell, 1997) 275.
[21] ibid.
[22] ibid 281.
[23] ibid 281–82.
[24] ibid 279–80.
[25] ibid 281–82.

II. 'Faith in the Truth of Christianity': Correspondence through Revelation and Rhetoric

A. Correspondence as Analogical Participation in Revelation

This raises the question of how we may arrive at and implement the transcendent truths which unite a peaceful community. Christian truth is not merely correspondence in the abstruse and atheological sense of propositions corresponding to states of affairs in reality, but is correspondence in the far richer sense that it is *aletheia*, revealed by God. In particular, the Trinitarian relationship is that of self-giving love, or loving the other as oneself, and it is perfect peace because it is the epitomic display of the reconciliation between the One and the Many, or the universal and the particular. The members of the Trinity coexist in perfect harmony as one God, but three Persons. This is superlative unity in diversity and community: unity in common with others. The Tri-Unity, then, is the consummate example for love and ontological peace.

This truth is primarily revealed through the Incarnation of Christ, the second member of the Trinity. The Incarnation, God in flesh or becoming human, perfectly displays the grace of God through demonstrating the unmerited favour of Christ loving the created order by sacrificing and giving himself for the forgiveness of sins. Christ taking on human form and volunteering to die on the cross for people is the ultimate display of the self-giving love characteristic of the Trinity. Its concern is for other and not self, and so it reveals a law beyond formal law, a law of grace which becomes the law of love—to love your neighbour. It is this revelation of God's love in Christ which is truth, or *aletheia*.

In addition, the Incarnation of Christ reveals the peace inherent in the Trinitarian relations by reconciling the temporal and the eternal. For Christ as fully God is eternal, but simultaneously as fully man is temporal, and this also recovers the reality of reason united with faith. Consequently, though reason is directed towards truth, it is not in the crude sense of secular reason discovering the nature of physical reality and systemising it to a set of propositions. Instead, the process is inverted and theologised, with truth revealing itself through the Incarnation of Christ, reconciling reason with faith and recovering it. This revelation is subsequently apprehended and participated in by faith.

B. Participation through Faith

So, although truth-as-correspondence is an appropriate theological definition of truth, it is fundamentally different from the typical meaning of the phrase. One of the more important aspects of this difference is the relationship between revelation and rhetoric. Historically, Christians have always understood that the beliefs grounding their ethics are matters of faith, or persuasion (rhetoric).[26] In particular, as the glory of Christ is revealed to the mind, the mind is persuaded, which is the same as saying the mind appropriates this revelation by peaceful persuasion or rhetoric, rather than the violent coercion of secular reason. As the mind is transformed by faith, it participates in the glory of Christ by imitating Christ and then loves one's neighbour as a reflection of the Trinitarian relations. So the truth of Christianity is that the divine mind of the Trinity in its perfect love and peace as revealed in Christ recovers reason and corresponds to the created order through participation in the Trinitarian relations resulting from faith, the persuasion of the mind by the glorious truth of what has been graciously revealed.

In this sense, the concrete virtue of loving one's neighbour seeks its notion of what it means to have truly human character in a place beyond or above what is human, rather than in or beneath.[27] Ultimately, then, it is this necessary transcendence in human relations which challenges the secular and opens the space for faith, for scholars have historically found it difficult to simultaneously point to the

> universally valid and objective and to the customary particulars which instantiate it … a solution is only really possible in terms of a tradition like Christianity, which starkly links particular to universal by conceiving its relationship to transcendence (truth) in a rhetorical fashion (faith).[28]

C. A Legally Incarnated Truth

The relation of transcendent truth to immanent faith or persuasion is proclaimed most forcefully in the Incarnation of Christ, and more specifically in the Crucifixion and Resurrection. As Milbank observes,

> Most forms of persuasion (and if we eschew violence, but still want to encourage virtue, only persuasion is left) are thoroughly coercive. We need in consequence to find a language of peace, and this is presumably why we point to *one* drama of sacrifice in particular. Truth and persuasion are circularly related. We should only be convinced by rhetoric where it persuades us of the truth, but on the other hand truth *is* what is persuasive, namely what attracts and does not compel. And Christians only see this *entire* attraction in the figure on the cross, a specific and compelling refusal to return evil for evil.[29]

So truth is most effectively revealed and people most ably persuaded by what attracts, namely that Christ's refusal of violence draws people to Christian peace. According to the Gospel According to John, Jesus himself said 'when I am lifted up

[26] Milbank, *Theology and Social Theory*, above n 1, 329.
[27] ibid 328.
[28] ibid 330.
[29] Milbank, *Word Made Strange*, above n 20, 250 (original emphasis).

from the earth, [I] will draw all people to myself', and he 'said this to show by what kind of death he was going to die'.[30] Moreover, the Christian message is affirmed as a way of revealing truth, of indicating the way things really are, through Christ's resurrection. Only in resurrection does the gap between history and nature that we call mythology close, and at this moment the myth ceases to be myth and Christianity becomes more than mere perspective. If the entire narrative of Christianity cannot explain the way things are, there exist no other viable means of determining the question.[31]

These notions are central to understanding the symbiosis of truth and law. In particular, at the end, Christian theology provides a unique post-secular legal community. Truth is the revelation of the law of love and peace in the Trinity through the Incarnation (Crucifixion and Resurrection), and by persuasion and participation this provides the basis and model for peaceful and loving human relations governed by the law of love. Similarly, the truth of correspondence, the way things are between the Trinitarian relations and human participation in terms of a loving but diverse community, is based on the law of love, to love one's neighbour as oneself. Thus, truth is achieved by imitating the divine being in love and peace as enabled and modelled by Christ, and this institutes the legal community in such a way as to remove the prevailing violence characteristic of the secular and to allow in its place the possibility for peace.

III. Revealing an Ontology of Peace: The Nature of Peace and Violence in Christianity

A. Back to the Future: Augustinian Peace and Pagan Violence

Augustine describes the incomparable good of this kind of peace:

> For peace is so great a good that even in relation to the affairs of earth and of our mortal state no word ever falls more gratefully upon the ear, nothing is desired with greater longing, in fact, nothing better can be found … (it) is dear to the heart of all mankind.[32]

For Augustine, this true, heavenly peace may be defined as suffering no attack from within or from any foe outside. It surpasses all understanding (except that of the divine mind) and is only appropriated by faith.[33] Hence, as the truth of Christ is revealed, our mind is persuaded and we are made partakers of this peace, so we

[30] John 12:32–33.
[31] Milbank, *Word Made Strange*, above n 20, 250.
[32] Augustine, *Concerning the City of God Against the Pagans* (Penguin, 2008) 865–66.
[33] ibid 1081, 1088.

know the perfection of 'peace in ourselves, peace among ourselves, and peace with God'.[34] Reconciling virtue with difference also involves the justice of a city where differences exist harmoniously as a community, based on Augustine's model of the City of God, where the individual is loved and not alienated, and the universal is reconciled with the particular. As Milbank notes, 'the justice secured in this city constitutes a more reliable sort of peace: not a mere suspension of hostilities, but a peace founded upon agreement and organic harmony, when each person sticks to his[*sic*] allotted task'.[35] In this sense, one is reminded of the Apostle Paul's description of the Christian community in 1 Corinthians 12 as members of a body, each with particular functions working in an organic harmony. The absoluteness of the community (it has justice, peace, truth and so forth) presupposes that it reflects an eternal order, and its organic harmony allows the particular different members of the community to be individually virtuous.[36] Thus, virtue is reconciled with difference, which gives peace. Such peace originated with the God who created all in peaceful donation, and is reflected in the heavenly city where the inhabitants remain in a state of selfless generosity. This peace was disrupted by the sinful assertion of prideful self, leading to domination, conflict and a spurious 'peace' of suspended hostilities in a context of chaos. In the Christ Event, however, peace is realised through the unconditional offer of forgiveness, reconciliation and love.[37]

In contrast with Christian theology, the secular is described as neo-paganism by Milbank, 'because it is an embracing of those elements of sacred violence in paganism which Christianity both exposed and refused, and of which paganism, in its innocence, was only half-aware'.[38] In this sense, the secular is a post-Christian paganism, which must be negatively defined as a refusal of Christianity and the invention of an anti-Christianity. The so-called violence of paganism is 'a certain universal primitive religion of an immanentist character, which involves sacrifices, games, and wars, a religion resigned to the "circulation of blood"', such as that described by Benjamin.[39]

Augustine compares pagan religion and practice, incorporating a demonstration of how the nihilistic competition of power with power is itself trapped in a mythos with Christian religion and practice, which is based in faith and the ontological priority of non-antagonistic peace over violence. He concludes that the former is but a dim and distorted echo of the latter.[40] This violent ontology of difference 'teaches the needlessness of regret, and the necessity of resignation to the whole process, where all is equally necessary and equally arbitrary; where

[34] ibid 1082.
[35] Milbank, *Theology and Social Theory*, above n 1, 335.
[36] ibid.
[37] ibid 394.
[38] ibid 280.
[39] ibid 285.
[40] ibid 392.

everything depends on everything else, and this dependence is enacted through constant struggle and counter-resistance'.[41] Against the God of Christian theology, in paganism the gods emerge as a response to an alien voice, reinstating a mythical consciousness of many gods and heroes. To exercise freedom, then, one must submit oneself to the arbitrariness of myth, and find oneself within its uncontrollable power and its violent combat.[42]

For example,

> [the Roman god Jove's] first words are a fateful 'restriction' and binding of his own anger, and at the same time a command to feral human begins to 'contain' their passions ... this is a gloss upon Augustine's view that 'pagan virtue' was always limited to the mere 'restriction of anger' through self-control

so that, for the pagans, the 'primal signifiers were weapons, and the basic language was war'.[43] By contrast, 'the virtue of the City of God, being able to root out anger and bad passion altogether, is most profoundly the power of charitable donation'.[44] The Trinity as a kind of natural law embodies the rules for peaceful society by suggesting that true personhood is only enabled by mutual sharing through universal association. This social principle surpasses the pagan where self-preservation is prior to relation and communication.[45] Indeed, the Trinitarian perspective actually reveals the true nature of the pagan as a theological distortion 'where the supposed "primary self" conceals the constitution of this self through delayed and postponed violence'.[46]

In Christianity, the transcendent is peacefully revealed through faith and forgiveness in Christ. Indeed, for Augustine, the pagans were unjust, violent and lacked virtue precisely because they did not give priority to peace and forgiveness.[47] Justice that is content with less than complete social consensus and harmony is therefore not true justice, because one has faith in an infinite justice, that there is a temporally proper (if changing) position for everything, without any chaotic reminder.[48] Furthermore, against the pagan religion, just as God loses nothing in creating the world, so Christians lose nothing by offering love for God. Instead, the self-giving is a new reception of being fundamentally in orientation with the other.[49] Thus, Christian theology in the peaceful gift of self-giving provides a unique way of reconciling difference with virtue and producing peace, in contrast to the violent antagonism of the pagan and the secular.

[41] ibid 317.
[42] ibid 320–21.
[43] Milbank, *Word Made Strange*, above n 20, 108.
[44] ibid 109.
[45] ibid.
[46] ibid.
[47] Milbank, *Theology and Social Theory*, above n 1, 415.
[48] ibid.
[49] ibid 395.

B. Confronting History and the Present: Peace and Violence in Christianity

However, the teachings of history starkly belie the conclusion that Christianity inherently and necessarily possesses an ontology of peace. The religious wars of the Reformation and Counter-Reformation are notable examples of the myriad and extensive catalogue of violence perpetrated in the name of Christianity. Others include the celebration of violent resistance against idolatry and persecution of unbelievers characteristic of early imperial Christianity, where a Christian ruler's faith was expressed through their willingness to pursue and violently punish those who were viewed as enemies.[50] This was eventually extended to include holistic persecution and forced conversion of non-Christians, manifested through later events such as the Crusades and the Inquisition. The Crusades in particular, despite being 'holy wars' allegedly waged on behalf of God for the sake of winning converts and defeating ungodly enemies, were marked with atrocities, which Riley-Smith claims were not aberrations, but rather constitute the norm of violence in Christian history.[51]

It is worth noting that there is a distinction between the violence of the secular, liberal enlightenment (which has violence as a presupposition and universal coercion as an end goal) and the violence allowed by faithful Christianity with an ultimately redemptive purpose: to establish genuine peace. The liberal 'peace' assumes the priority of the individual will through law in the sense of formal generality, and so exists in a universalised vision of coercion. The Christian peace in a sense subverts this law in favour of unregulated, self-giving charity; but by doing so, it opens itself up to violence. Therefore, though violence is not unavoidable, it is allowed in order to facilitate educational redemption and ultimate peace.[52]

So 'in some circumstances, passively refusing to intervene with physical violence to address violence may be more violent'.[53] Just as Christ volunteered to suffer (and thus in a sense allow or coordinate) violence for a redemptive purpose, to re-establish and redistribute the good, it may be necessary to allow or endure violence for the sake of opening the possibility for true peace. Our imperfection intimates that violence may sometimes be necessary to appropriate and instantiate the good.[54] Though any good that needs you to fight for it is not an absolute good, and the absolute Good is never threatened, our comparatively limited apprehension of the absolute good implies that participation in the eternal is not 'cheap and easy'.[55] Given the reality of evil in the world, we must actively seek to oppose it (even to the point of violence), and in the very act of opposing evil and violence

[50] T Sizgorich, *Violence and Belief in Late Antiquity* (University of Pennsylvania Press, 2009) 21–24.
[51] J Riley-Smith, *The Crusades, Christianity and Islam* (Columbia University Press, 2008) 2, 4, 9.
[52] J Milbank, *Being Reconciled: Ontology and Pardon* (Routledge, 2003) 38.
[53] ibid 29–30.
[54] ibid 39–40.
[55] ibid 40.

to pursue and implement some semblance of the good, we remove ourselves from being mere spectators, from a disinterested pacifism which is in fact even more violent. Sometimes violence ought to be refused (opposed) by a type of counter-violence so that final, perfect redemption may occur.

This point can be clarified with reference to the important critique of Milbank by the late Gillian Rose. Milbank acknowledges both that Rose is fundamental to his work and that she has also disagreed with it.[56] Rose's desire to 'retrieve and rediscover' a tradition of law that the 'post-structuralist wave' has 'overcome', particularly through her review of Nietzsche, Foucault and Derrida, provides an important foundation for Milbank's theologically parallel work in theology and social theory.[57] Both Milbank and Rose contend that modernism has gone awry and that post-structuralist nihilism is no solution.[58] Although Rose is initially concerned with law in the context of nihilism and deconstruction, she also importantly identifies that there is a tension that exists in law involving the universal and the particular, namely that 'the other, unknowable, law ... is precisely ... the law of the person'.[59] The formal law is necessary to our self-consciousness and utterly intimate, yet we have no acquaintance with it and it is entirely remote. We obey it only because of its 'universal practical validity'.[60] This is manifested in particular through what Rose calls the 'antinomy of law', or the 'inscrutable encounter with form in general'.[61] Rose expands this idea to mean the 'dual implication of law and ethics' in *The Broken Middle*, and states that where *Dialectic of Nihilism* argues that 'post-structuralist nihilism completes itself as law—unreflected but always historically identifiable'—here 'post-modern antinomianism completes itself as political theology, as new ecclesiology, mending the diremption of law and ethics'.[62]

Where Rose and Milbank part ways is in their conception of the necessity of violence in law. Rose argues that the notion of love without violence is a 'sect mentality' which becomes 'the only refuge for humankind's invincible enslavement to violence'—it displays a 'lack of faith in the violence to be found in love, the love to be found in violence—the law to be found in both'.[63] Fundamentally, contrary to Milbank, violence is 'not being posited as prior to law: it is presupposed as the call of law'.[64] Rose specifically engages Milbank on this point.[65] She argues that Milbank's conception of a heavenly city of peace 'effectively destroys the idea of a city: its task of salvation deprives it of site; while its inclusive appeal deprives it of limit or boundary that would mark it off from any other city and their different laws'.[66]

56 J Milbank, *Theology and Social Theory: Beyond Secular Reason*, 2nd edn (Blackwell, 2006) viii, xii.
57 G Rose, *Dialectic of Nihilism: Post-Structuralism and Law* (Blackwell, 1984) 1.
58 ibid; Milbank, *Theology and Social Theory*, above n 1.
59 Rose, *Dialectic of Nihilism*, above n 57, 23–24.
60 ibid 24.
61 ibid 2.
62 G Rose, *The Broken Middle: Out of Our Ancient Society* (Blackwell, 1992) xv.
63 ibid 147.
64 ibid 151.
65 See ibid 277–96.
66 ibid 281.

It is, as Milbank admits, 'a paradox, a nomad city'.[67] Milbank would even see these attributes as virtues; the heavenly city has no alienating and dividing (violent) boundaries, and, as an eternal community, has no specific site—though it can be arguably instantiated on earth, so it is situated to some extent. The disputed issue therefore seems to be the ethereality of Milbank's city, its lack of basis in the reality of socio-legal relations due to its salvific escapism and lack of concrete definition.

Rose claims that we should not embrace either the Athenian tradition of the Greeks, which takes the existing law as transcendent and beyond critique, or the Jewish tradition, which opposes the law of the city to revelation, which then becomes a law that is transcendent and beyond critical evaluation. According to Rose, we should instead take a middle path which engages critically with both extremes. This path is the true realm of law, for the middle is always broken: legal institutions always do some harm, and we should not attempt to either accept it or escape it.[68] True faith is to grapple with this difficulty of the broken or violent middle.[69] Rose understands faith in this context as being (that is, existing) in the midst of uncertainties and mysteries without grasping for facts and reason, in conjunction with the enlarging of inhibited practical reason.[70] Faith is not about any object in particular (it is not a faith 'in' God as Milbank might have it), but rather an inflection or attitude of being and action in the world.[71] So the middle is the realm of the necessarily violent law, and to simply accept it and mask it without critique (as liberalism does) or escape it without a struggling engagement (with Milbank's heavenly city) is to lack faith and actually reinscribe this violence.[72]

Rose ultimately contends that 'mended middles betray their broken middle', presenting a 'holy middle' which ultimately 'corrupts' because it claims to repair the relation between the universal and particular, 'drawing attention away from the reconfiguration of singular, individual and state'.[73] The middle is always 'broken—because these institutions are systemically flawed'—and this implies that 'this holiness will itself be reconfigured by the resource and articulation of modern domination'.[74] In other words, Milbank's (false) claim of a perfectly peaceful city with a holy relation between individual and state will be utilised to perpetrate even greater violence.[75] 'If the broken middle is abandoned instead of thought systematically, then the resulting evasive theology, insinuated epistemology, sacralised polity, will import the features of the City of Death remorselessly.'[76] In short, the

[67] ibid.

[68] V Lloyd, 'On the Use of Gillian Rose' (2007) 48 *The Heythrop Journal* 697, 699; *cf* V Lloyd, 'Complex Space or Broken Middle? Milbank, Rose, and the Sharia Controversy' (2009) 10(2) *Political Theology* 1, where this is applied to the tensions which exist between the individual and the state.

[69] Lloyd, 'On the Use of Gillian Rose', ibid, 700.

[70] V Lloyd 'The Secular Faith of Gillian Rose' (2008) 36 *Journal of Religious Ethics* 683, 692.

[71] ibid 697.

[72] Lloyd, 'On the Use of Gillian Rose', above n 68, 701.

[73] Rose, *The Broken Middle*, above n 62, 285.

[74] ibid 284–85.

[75] ibid 307.

[76] ibid 293.

telos of their critical projects differ; Milbank concludes with a vision of ontological peace, while Rose calls us to be content with the struggle within the world we have.[77]

Importantly, Vincent Lloyd argues that, for Rose, law can be identified with social norms, and since violence is always implicated in law, this implies that social norms never completely match with social practice. This is why Rose is so opposed to any theory which may suggest that a (legal) authority is beyond question—it will result in the violence of unwarranted and unjustified penalties.[78] That is a formidable objection, given Milbank's emphasis on the ultimate or heavenly social peace, which presumably is beyond question because for Milbank it represents the culmination of social ontology. However, it is not an insurmountable one in the sense of considering the possibility that social norms could match with social practice. If this occurred, the broken middle would be repaired, and there would no longer be an inevitable violence of law. This may exist in the idea of the law of love itself. 'Love your neighbour as yourself' is a unique norm because it is a command which may govern human society, but one which can also be seen as a practice of loving your neighbour as yourself. Therefore, in this framework there is scope for social norm(s) and social practice to match, repairing the middle and removing the invincibility of violence. With Rose, we can continue evaluating and interrogating the extent to which these do in fact coalesce, but this does not exclude the possibility of their doing so.

Even Rose seems to acknowledge this to some extent according to Lloyd, since to love is an act of faith, the suspension of usual relational norms; love relationships do not have the usual normative quality, nor do they have any mechanisms of protection.[79] Rose relays the story of Abraham's (near) sacrifice of Isaac as acknowledging the love in violence and the violence in love, with the law being in both. She goes on to say that it is this 'free offering', this 'already knowing yet being willing to stake oneself again' that 'prevents one … from acting with arbitrary violence'.[80] Such an idea culminates in the willing sacrifice of Christ, the ultimate act of faith through suffering of violence and the violent refusal of violence, which implies that we too can choose in faith not to engage in violence. Like Christ, we may be called upon to suffer violence or violently refuse violence when norms do not match practice, but because of his resurrection we are able to do this—and we can also consequently continue a community of love and peace.[81] So, in one sense, Rose's insight is absolutely right: violence is inevitable because Christ always has to suffer. But it is in this very act of violent love, or the paradoxically violent resistance of violence, that the law of love is instituted, and norms can match practice: the possibility for peace remains.

77 Lloyd, 'On the Use of Gillian Rose', above n 68, 697.
78 Lloyd, 'The Secular Faith of Gillian Rose', above n 70, 686.
79 ibid 701–02.
80 Rose, *The Broken Middle*, above n 62, 148.
81 See Milbank, *Being Reconciled*, above n 52, 100, 102–03.

C. Future Glory: The Hope of Communal Peace

All this is not to say that violence is ontologically fundamental, nor does it justify the inordinate arbitrary violence perpetrated during religious wars in which Christianity was involved or even the perpetrator. Such acts must be categorically condemned. The fact that the argument centres upon the proposition that Christianity is ontologically peaceful, in conjunction with the historical observation that it has not produced peace, raises what is both an extremely obvious and an extremely fundamental issue. If it is established that Christianity has an inherent ontology of peace rather than violence, this implies that those who perpetrate capricious or excessive violence in the name of Christianity or as Christians have neglected some aspect of Christian theology.

It was proposed earlier that the wars and violence resulting from the Reformation and Counter-Reformation stemmed from the violent divorce of reason and faith. That claim is qualified here in the sense that it is partly correct, though not completely. Rather, those who perpetrate that sort of violence in the name of Christianity ultimately fail to comprehend the implications of Christianity's Trinitarian theology. One of these is the reconciliation of reason and faith, but even more fundamentally, the nature of the Trinity reveals the reconciliation of difference and sameness through the law of love. In the Trinity, difference exists as one, harmoniously and peacefully, and this is concretely enabled and modelled in the selfless Incarnation and sacrifice of Christ, who died for people rather than committing violence against them. In this way, those whose minds are transformed with the revelation of the Trinity will participate in the divine love, reconciling difference and living in harmony. Hence, it follows that the truth (revelation) of the law of love in the Trinity results in participation by faith, and this entails peace rather than violence.

Given our human weakness and fallen nature, however, some type of violence seems necessary on the path to ultimate peace, redemption and reconciliation. There must therefore be a distinction between the unrestrained and evil (pagan) violence, which detracts from the good, and violence which communicates some substantive good. As Milbank observes, violence may be a 'stay' or 'a rebuke or a caress'—not all apparent violence is actually violence, for violence must be judged as to whether 'a substantive good has been impaired'.[82] How, then, do we determine whether a particular type of 'violence' is of the former kind or the latter? Milbank gives us some clues:

> Every occasion for every good act is always like this—there is always some initial evil, some deficiency, some threat, some terror, something to be warded off … hence virtue is paradigmatically heroism … to be brave … virtue is always reactive: it always secretly celebrates as its occasion a *prior* evil, lives out of what it opposes … Here, at the beginning of every virtue, lies a failure to turn the other cheek … worse still, no … encroachment,

[82] ibid 26–27.

> no seeming violence, is obviously violent in an objective and unquestionable sense. No, violence has always to be judged, since every encroachment, every invasion, including an imperial one, may be a gift, an alien strengthening; we have to decide whether it strengthens us or weakens us ... is there a violent tearing apart of our true self here? Or to the contrary, does our true self only emerge on this journey out of itself?[83]

So the delineation is between violence that presupposes a prior evil and/or aims towards some ontologically necessary evil, and so leads to an individual heroic virtue, and violence in a sense that is gift or strengthening, allowing our true self to emerge, which results in humility and a fundamental peace with the community. This is why communal peace and the good is an attainable ontological reality, and atomistic, individual peaceableness or pacifism must be counter-intuitively rejected—pacifism tends to gaze upon violence without refusing it.[84]

Though this scenario is 'apocalyptic' rather than 'utopian' in the sense that we may require violence to bring the ultimate good of repentance, redemption and reconciliation, the fact that this remains an attainable ontological goal retains some utopian elements. It implies that consistent Trinitarian Christian theology opens the possibility for the final reconciliation of the universal and the particular, through revelation and the Incarnation, and provides true peace and the good. Any other differential ontology is non-Christian, presupposing transcendental violence and contending for the necessity of reading reality as ontologically conflictual—the failure to take account of difference is violence, for in the jostling of difference(s) there is agonistic conflict.[85] However, what is sought is not conflict but peace. Peace is the ultimate good; it is delightful, and what will be found in heaven—a peace and life everlasting. Real peace is a state of harmonious agreement, based on a common love and a realisation of justice for all, and it is Christian theology which allows the possibility for this peace through the truth of the law of love. So reconsidering and implementing the law of love in the modern legal system offers a way of rethinking and redeeming the system, reducing its violence and rendering it ontologically peaceful.[86]

IV. Christian Theology and the Modern Legal Community: Proposing the Law of Love

A. Christ against Leviathan

Augustine argues that the eternal city, or the Christian community, possesses heavenly peace by faith. This ideal heavenly peace is attainable, at least in part, on earth

[83] ibid 220–21.
[84] ibid 42–43.
[85] Milbank, *Theology and Social Theory*, above n 1, 297, 313, 315.
[86] ibid 393.

and refers to an ordered harmony in the community of the city, where all citizens contribute and fulfil their role.[87] In such a community, the individual is not alienated and antagonised, but is loved by the community comprising individuals as a function of the law of love, and performs their designated role as an act of love towards all other individuals of whom the community is comprised.

Augustine concludes that without love based in faith (and consequently based on the revelation of God in Christ, the mutual bond of spirit) there is no commonwealth, or legal community. As such, not only is the theological law of love the most desirable ontological basis for a legal community of peace, it is the only basis for such a community. Augustine's point also holds true for our modern system of law. That is, without a peaceful ontology—which involves loving your neighbour as yourself—it is not possible for the legal system to create peace, and it is rendered inherently violent in its attempt to keep violence at bay.

This is because 'the distinctiveness of Christianity, and its point of difference with antiquity and modernity, is its reconciliation of virtue with difference'.[88] The antique (pagan) closure against difference (ie antagonism and alienation of individuals) meant it really promoted a heroic, exclusive, aristocratic freedom.[89] Pagan ethics are therefore not really ethical, because they were not oriented towards a harmonious, relational community as an end goal. Instead, the pagan ethic celebrated control, force and violence over members.[90] The division between the whole and the part, as the division between the soul and the body, perpetuates a fundamental discontinuity, where subordination of one by the other can only be by force. In contrast, Christian ontology abolishes this division and duality, which supports the notion of an ineradicable ontological violence.[91] Christianity is therefore something like the peaceful transmission of difference, or differences in a continuous harmony.[92]

The contrast here is between Hobbesian assumptions of primitive atomistic violence controlled by excessive sovereignty and the loving and peaceful Christian community. The modern state attempts to sovereignly coerce peace as the mere absence of conflict between individuals, but the framework of the church as the city or legal community has authentic relations of love between God and neighbour by the Holy Spirit through the redemption effected by Christ.[93] This is really a contemporary articulation of Augustine's argument. Rather than the state establishing a spurious peace based on the suppression of an allegedly prior

[87] Augustine, above n 32, 876.
[88] Milbank, *Theology and Social Theory*, above n 1, 423.
[89] ibid.
[90] ibid 416.
[91] ibid.
[92] ibid 422.
[93] JKA Smith, *Introducing Radical Orthodoxy: Mapping a Post-Secular Theology* (Baker, 2004) 236–37.

violence, the church as the state or community establishes authentic relations of love through the revelation of truth in Christ and the transformation or persuasion of people through faith. The Church as persuading rather than coercing is important, for this allows the proclamation of a new political event: that of the cross, which replaces the sovereign power of the secular state with a different type of power or strategy of governance.[94]

Paradoxically, the power of the cross is in its complete lack of sovereign power—Christ refuses to exert the power he possesses, instead resisting violent rule and establishing peace through service and the sacrifice of self; this in itself is far more powerful, and through Christ we can envisage the possibility of a similarly loving community. In this community to rule is to serve, and people are not merely individual contracting entities regulated by legal violence, but redeemed people who are part of a community operating under grace beyond legalism and characterised by mutual love, empowered and demonstrated through Christ the King, who gave himself for us.[95]

B. The Law of Love as the Person and Work of Christ

(i) Gift versus Legality

So we specifically find the law of love as applied in the legal community through considering Christ himself as the embodiment and fulfilment of that law. Here, gift can be contrasted with law—or at least can allude to the need to go beyond the law to truly establish the gift of love as the common good. The problem is that this (secularised, enlightenment) law assumes a prior violence, which it is trying to prevent through the stringent regulation of life, liberty and truth.[96] The danger of such an approach is that it really detracts from or prevents the overflowing of divine Good, so is actually evil in the Augustinian sense of privation. Rather than the fullness of life, freedom and truth revealed through the Spirit, the law constrains, alienates and antagonises; as Paul realised, it holds out a formal, abstract standard which can never be fulfilled, thereby spelling out judicial violence.[97]

Conversely, through Christ and his manifold gifts, we can understand our role in society. Where law is said to apply to everyone equally, denying difference and constraining intersubjective relationships, the particular nature of divine gift(s) allows difference to be harmonised and promoted, producing peace in the body, as Paul described in 1 Corinthians 13.[98] It follows that this giving of ourselves

[94] Milbank, *Word Made Strange*, above n 20, 251.

[95] J Milbank, 'The Gift of Ruling' in J Milbank and S Oliver (eds), *The Radical Orthodoxy Reader* (Routledge, 2009) 358.

[96] Milbank, *Word Made Strange*, above n 20, 220.

[97] ibid 227.

[98] ibid.

through the receiving of gifts actually increases our subjectivity, so that the sacrifice of the gift is really no sacrifice at all.

> A genuine gift is excessive since it is not required, and it occasions not a loss but a gain in subjectivity for the giver which is reinforced by the counter-gift of gratitude from the recipient. In *this* virtue is to be found no sacrifice.[99]

Hence the society can continue perpetually in peace, forever giving and receiving the gift of love through the law of love, specifically empowered and modelled through Christ's resurrection. With the vision of the resurrected Christ, the presupposition of death is cancelled, along with pagan virtue and death-limiting law. All that remains is charity.[100]

(ii) *Gift as Forgiveness*

The second element of the law of love in the legal community as embodied in Christ is the way in which Christ inaugurates and endows the gift of forgiveness. The person and work of Christ is 'necessary for the redemption' because he 'enacts and enshrines the *viability* of the new, forgiving practice, by virtue of its unique and universal "attractiveness"'—that in being put on the cross Christ draws all people to himself.[101] Only Christ can end all violence, because his death is not only an example but an enabling metaphor for refusing violence and pursuing forgiveness.[102] Furthermore, if Jesus' death is fully effective, it is not limited to ethereal spirituality. It is also the '*inauguration* of the "political" practice of forgiveness; forgiveness as a mode of "government" and social being'.[103] This produces a state of perpetually giving forgiveness or infinite gift-exchange, what Milbank calls an 'atoning practice', which can only arise in a community which prioritises human relationships in a way which images Christ as God.[104]

Christ as the embodiment of the gift of forgiveness creates the space for a community practice of atonement in the law of love through projecting the image of God from heaven to earth—the practice of the gospel which is peace rather than violence. The event of the Incarnation, Crucifixion and Resurrection exceptionally allows this because Jesus as the God-man, the omniscient and innocent divine *logos*, represents the singular suffering of all humanity, a maximally sovereign suffering which is capable of instituting forgiveness on behalf of all.[105] So, through representing universal suffering, Christ also provided the possibility for universal forgiveness by participation through faith and the spirit in the law of love, leading to reconciliation of human relationships. Since we participate in the Trinity and

99 ibid 226 (original emphasis).
100 ibid 229.
101 ibid 160 (original emphasis).
102 ibid.
103 ibid 161 (original emphasis).
104 ibid 162.
105 Milbank, *Being Reconciled*, above n 52, 61.

Incarnation by faith, we also participate in the giving of forgiveness initiated by the divine love. We receive the divine authority to give and accept forgiveness as part of intrahuman reconciliation.[106]

C. Coercion and Love

At this point, a question may be asked regarding the place of punishment and deterrence in this kind of community. The answer is that Christianity can still allow coercion, for the goal of coercion is final peace, and the coercive action to prevent a person damaging themselves or others can be redeemed through their retrospective acceptance of the means taken to reach this final goal of peace. However, the coercion used by the pagan, earthly city does not have the final peace in view, but only the peace of compromise between wills, which consequently contains an arbitrary element open to the exercise of power.[107] Indeed, secular reason appropriated this arbitrary element and pervaded law by engendering a newly rationalistic and formalised approach, one which resulted in pure possession and control, and in the regulation and balancing of power. This, in turn, led to liberal conceptions of property rights, a doctrine of unlimited sovereignty and relationships between legal bodies (both persons and corporations) being conceived on a contractualist basis.[108] In particular, Milbank argues that Hobbes

> traces the origins of human society to individual self-seeking, which eventually gives rise to laws which merely protect established power. Against this background, crime is partly 'rational', because it protests against an undeveloped notion of right and subjectivity. And punishment at this level is virtually indistinguishable from 'revenge': the reassertion of the right of force. Crime and punishment, like revenge, belong to an endless 'fatal' process, because in the realm of force, which is a realm of sheer quantitative 'indifference', one action is only 'equivalent' to another, or 'compensation' for another, in a purely arbitrary sense. No-one is ever satisfied that justice has been done; there is always a balance to be rectified; the punishment can never fit the crime.[109]

Such is at fundamental odds with the Christian vision of loving one's neighbour personally, seeking communal peace and reconciliation, rather than as an abstract legal entity doomed to an endless repetition of violence. In a specifically judicial context, it is more important to investigate than to punish, for once the offence is discovered, the aim is always to restore the offender and promote reconciliation and redemption.[110] Here, the practice of forgiveness nevertheless involves a practice of restitution, because forgiveness is a gratuitous self-offering beyond the demands of the secular law. Christ is the ultimate model for this, since he offered

[106] ibid 62.
[107] Milbank, *Theology and Social Theory*, above n 1, 424.
[108] ibid 441.
[109] ibid 170.
[110] ibid 424.

himself for forgiveness of sins when he was under no legal obligation to do so. Hence, wrongs must be put right by rectification and restoration, or if this is not possible, some other means which demonstrates a will to harmony among human beings.[111] 'The practice of forgiveness, as surplus to any system of desert or obligation, is able creatively to break out of the blindness induced both by the wrong act of the offender, and by the corresponding anger of the victim.'[112]

This emphasis on harmony and mutual trust through the Christian practice of forgiveness recalls statements made by Benjamin and Cover, who saw the need to redeem law through non-violent enforcement with the preconditions of (communal) peaceableness and trust by virtue of unity within Christian practice. These preconditions are met both at the transcendent level and the immanent level. At the transcendent level, the perfect peace that consists between the Trinitarian relations is revealed in Christ and is imparted to the mind by faith, which is a synonym for trust. The preconditions are subsequently met at the immanent level since the persuasion of the mind and participation in the law of love by the subject open the possibility for a community of peace between individuals, a constantly atoning practice, based on a mutual trust. Such a redeemed legal community which exists in love beyond law is exemplified through the Good Samaritan, the paradigm of loving your neighbour as yourself.

V. The Law of Love, or Love beyond Law: Releasing the Spirit of the Good Samaritan

A. Kelsen and the *Grundnorm*

It is possible to conceive the law of love (loving obedience to the law through transcending the rules of law) as providing the foundation for civil law and the community found in the Apostle Paul through comparison with Hans Kelsen's *Grundnorm*, or basic norm. For Kelsen, the idea of the basic norm is a presupposed, fundamental norm that authorises and founds any coherent and valid legal system. It gives meaning to a legal system and bestows the legal power to create such a system.[113] At one level, some may note the apparent absurdity of using Kelsen, the high positivist and anti-moralist, as a model for how a theological truth such as the law of love may found the civil law. However, Kelsen himself notes that the law of love is an example of the basic norm, illustrating that the neighbour principle contains content from which other norms can be logically deduced, resulting

[111] ibid 422, 428.
[112] Milbank, *Word Made Strange*, above n 20, 164.
[113] M Green, 'Hans Kelsen and the Logic of Legal Systems' (2003) 54 *Alabama Law Review* 388, 388.

in the establishment of an entire system of valid norms.[114] Given that Kelsen can observe the fact that the law of love is an example of the basic norm, it might seem that theology should also be able to begin implementing such a process.

The most powerful example of how this may work is found in Romans 13:8–10. In this passage, immediately following Paul's injunction to render obedience to the civil authorities, he clarifies it by stating that this should be achieved by loving one another, for love fulfils the law. He proceeds to show that the commandments are all summed up by the law of love: to love your neighbour as yourself. Thus, Paul is arguing that, in addition to the reasons given in Romans 13:1–7, the civil authorities should be obeyed as a function of the law of love. Furthermore, the law of love legitimises and validates the commandment system in conjunction with the civil authorities, for Paul uses it to justify his instruction to obey them by stating that this law of love fulfils obedience. It is the law of love that vindicates and gives meaning to the civil authorities and the series of commandments by ultimately transcending and fulfilling them. Paul also demonstrates that the law of love provides the content from which an entire system of valid norms can be logically deduced. In Romans 13:10, he states that love does no wrong to a neighbour. In this way, all the commandments, such as not to murder or steal, are contained by this principle, since if you love your neighbour according to Paul you will not murder them or steal from them. Therefore, the axiom to love your neighbour as yourself can plausibly provide the content of 'doing no wrong to a neighbour', from which a series of norms can be promulgated and a harmonious legal community which loves the individual can be created.

However, there is great danger in this approach. I have already noted the counter-intuitive nature of considering Kelsen in this context, given his positivistic framework. The effect of having the foundation of law as a norm (even a 'good' norm, such as loving your neighbour as yourself) through which a series of norms can be logically deduced reintroduces the problem of juridification. The risk of legalising and systematising the law of love in a legal context renders the principle into a rigid code which becomes inflexible, secular and formal—the precise issue with the secular modern law that we have already identified. Like the legalism of the Pharisees that Christ confronted, or even like the rigid equitable principles of our own time, such a law invites transgression by articulating itself in terms of formal boundaries; in other words, such a law is intrinsically violent.[115]

To pursue the law of love as the foundation for a legal community is the right idea, but to approach it through Kelsen's *Grundnorm* maintains a secular form or secular *logos*, which will reproduce violence. What is needed is to go beyond law, to love: the theological *logos*. For in the spiritual bond of love, we are freed from the violent constraints of the law of the letter, yet we are able to fulfil the law of the

[114] H Kelsen, *Pure Theory of Law* (University of California Press, 1967) 195–96.

[115] See A Deagon, 'Rendering to Caesar and God: St Paul, the Natural Law Tradition, and the Authority of Law', *Law, Culture, and the Humanities*, first published on 10 March 2014 as DOI: 10.1177/1743872114524324, 3–4, 24, where this problem has been identified.

spirit. This problem of attempting to implement the law of love as a legal norm within a secular, formal legal system can be explicitly seen through the (secular) legal understanding of the Parable of the Good Samaritan in modern negligence.

B. Understanding the Parable

(i) The Legal Interpretation

Although there are examples and illustrations of common law having a foundation in Christian theology and the law of love (the importance of truth in evidence, trust in contract, principles of equity, establishing peace through criminal law, rehabilitation as a sentencing purpose), these tend to be traces and distortions, a residue of an earlier, pre-secular period that is now long gone. Rather than demonstrating the potential to have a secularised civil law based in the theological truth of the law of love, these examples tend to be the exceptions which prove the rule that secular law seeks to eliminate faith, theology and, ultimately, love. They are part of a mere Christian residue, a malformed vestige which limits the radical selfless love modelled by Christ and puts in its place what amounts to little more than altruistic self-interest. Such can be observed in the seminal case for modern negligence, *Donoghue v Stevenson*.[116] Here, Lord Atkin articulated the rule which has provided the foundation for much of negligence law over the past 80 years. He stated that:

> The liability for negligence … is no doubt based upon a general public sentiment of moral wrongdoing … the rule that you are to love your neighbour becomes in law that you must not injure your neighbour; and the lawyer's question, Who is my neighbour? receives a restricted reply … the answer seems to be—persons who are so closely and directly affected by my act that I ought reasonably to have them in contemplation as being so affected when I am directing my mind to the acts or omissions which are called into question.[117]

Lord Atkin bases his articulation of the (civil) law of negligence on the (theological) rule, or truth revealed, that you are to love your neighbour—the law of love, to love your neighbour as yourself. In the context of understanding what Lord Atkin precisely intends to convey by invoking this principle, it is worth noting the later observation by Lord Diplock that it was 'the Parable of the Good Samaritan evoked by Lord Atkin in *Donoghue v Stevenson*'.[118] The situation of the parable is reproduced in full below:

> And behold, a lawyer stood up to put [Jesus] to the test, saying, 'Teacher, what shall I do to inherit eternal life?' He said to him, 'What is written in the Law? How do you read it?' And he answered, 'You shall love the Lord your God with all your heart and with

[116] *Donoghue v Stevenson* [1932] AC 562.
[117] *Donoghue v Stevenson* [1932] AC 562, 580 (Lord Atkin).
[118] *Home Office v Dorset Yacht Co Ltd* [1970] 2 All ER 294, 326 (Lord Diplock).

> all your soul and with all your strength and with all your mind, and your neighbour as yourself.' And he said to him, 'You have answered correctly; do this, and you will live.' But he, desiring to justify himself, said to Jesus, 'And who is my neighbour?' Jesus replied, 'A man was going down from Jerusalem to Jericho, and he fell among robbers, who stripped him and beat him and departed, leaving him half dead. Now by chance a priest was going down that road, and when he saw him he passed by on the other side. So likewise a Levite, when he came to the place and saw him, passed by on the other side. But a Samaritan, as he journeyed, came to where he was, and when he saw him, he had compassion. He went to him and bound up his wounds, pouring on oil and wine. Then he set him on his own animal and brought him to an inn and took care of him. And the next day he took out two denarii and gave them to the innkeeper, saying, 'Take care of him, and whatever more you spend, I will repay you when I come back.' Which of these three, do you think, proved to be a neighbour to the man who fell among the robbers?' He said, 'The one who showed him mercy.' And Jesus said to him, 'You go, and do likewise.'[119]

So the law of love as the revelation of Christian theology was appropriated by Lord Atkin as the foundation for a duty of care in modern negligence. However, despite its promise, it is a mere trace, a distorted, pagan version of the 'law of love'. Atkin's appropriation of the theological principle to love one's neighbour applied to the legal principle that one should not injure one's neighbour implies a far more restricted sense of conduct than Christ advocates in the parable (which Atkin explicitly acknowledges in the above quote). For example, in the case of *Hargrave v Goldman*, it was found, after a brief discussion of Lord Atkin's neighbour principle and its origin in the Parable of the Good Samaritan, that:

> The dictates of charity and of compassion do not constitute a duty of care. The law cast no duty upon a man to go to the aid of another who is in peril or distress not caused by him. The call of common humanity may lead him to the rescue. This the law recognises, for it gives the rescuer its protection when he answers that call. But it does not require that he do so …[120]

Christ's commandment to love your neighbour as yourself extends to showing mercy to people in peril not caused by you (such as the example given in the parable, which we are called to imitate), but this is not the case in the legal adaption of the theological principle. Thus, far from the love of neighbour being the ostensible foundation for modern negligence, in fact 'the dictates of charity and compassion' (love) are explicitly distinguished from law, and separated from law. Though the law acknowledges that 'the call of common humanity' may compel a rescue and provides protection to this end, it nevertheless excludes charity and compassion from the operation of law. This promotes a law or legal system not modelled after Christ in the fashion of selfless love, but rather a cold, calculating law, one based on an ultimately selfish desire to avoid helping one who is in need. The law of love has been twisted and secularised, reified, by modern law. The trace remains, but contains none of its power.

[119] Luke 10:25–37.
[120] (1963) 110 CLR 40, 66 (Windeyer J).

(ii) The Theological Interpretation

In contrast to Lord Atkin's restrictive and self-interested duty of care, which tends to promote an attitude of eschewing the boundary of least convenience, or even the pursuit of minimum effort just to satisfy some formal goal, we should seek to articulate the neighbour principle in a way which is consistent with Christian theology. Specifically, we need to go beyond mere legal duty and selfish interest, and desire to truly act with love and sacrifice in order to promote a peaceful community, just like Christ did. As Milbank exhorts, 'to act charitably we must break through the existing representation of what is our duty towards our neighbour and towards God', and 'break through the bounds of duty which "technically" pre-defines its prescribed performance'.[121] This initially involves understanding the Parable of the Good Samaritan in its theological context.

The superficial content of the parable is straightforward. A man was travelling from Jerusalem to Jericho and was mugged and severely injured, left for dead. A priest and a Levite pass by and avoid the man, but a Samaritan comes and has compassion, tending to his wounds and paying for him to recover at an inn. The full parable is recorded only in Luke's account, though he is probably drawing from an earlier, truncated account in Mark 12:28–31.[122] There are some important differences between the accounts. Mark's account has only the initial conversation, where Jesus is asked about the greatest commandment and responds by saying that the greatest commandment is to love God and love your neighbour. Where Mark has the question raised by a scribe, Luke mentions a lawyer; Luke's concern in the context of the account is eternal life, whereas Mark focuses on the greatest commandment.[123] Finally, Mark has Jesus answer the question regarding the greatest commandment, while in Luke it is the lawyer who answers the parallel question of what one must do to inherit eternal life.

These factors indicate Luke's focus on the inclusivity or universalism of the gospel of Jesus, and particularly how Jesus sought to reconcile Jews, Samaritans and Gentiles; some commentators also argue that this parable foreshadows the later Gentile mission recorded by Luke in Acts.[124] Luke attempts to demonstrate how discriminating categories (such as Jew versus Gentile) are dissolved in Jesus, inaugurating a global harmonious community.[125] Luke's alterations make his account more relevant to his Gentile readers, who would have had little concern for scribes

[121] Milbank, *Word Made Strange*, above n 20, 134.

[122] W Baird, 'The Gospel According to Luke' in C Laymon (ed), *Interpreter's Concise Commentary* (Abingdon Press, 1983) 227.

[123] Scribes were originally copyists of Scripture, while lawyers were the experts in Jewish law and legal procedure. The increasing prominence of scribes in the time of Christ resulted in a merging of the roles, which may be why Mark refers to a scribe and Luke refers to a lawyer. See C Blomberg, *Jesus and the Gospels* (B&H Publishing Group, 2009) above n 123, 47.

[124] Blomberg, ibid, 163–64; also see, eg, TJ Lane, *Luke and the Gentile Mission: Gospel Anticipates Acts* (Peter Lang, 1996).

[125] R Gundry, *A Survey of the New Testament* (Zondervan, 1970) 94–95.

and the commandments of the Jewish law.[126] Jews and Samaritans especially had an extremely acrimonious relationship, a deeply entrenched process of negative stereotyping stemming back even to respective accounts of origins of the Samaritans, and a theological dispute over the proper place of worship.[127] Jesus was using this parable as a hyperbole to demonstrate the extent to which one should love your neighbour, regardless of different prejudices, races or legal categories. Samaritans were considered as objects of contempt in first-century Jewish culture, but, by having a Samaritan help a Jew in need, Jesus breaks down the boundary between Jew and Samaritan and claims that whoever responds to human need is the truly loving neighbour.[128]

Furthermore, the term 'half dead' is best understood to mean that he appeared alive, but in a severe condition requiring help. This renders the actions of the priest and the Levite inexcusable for Jesus, since going to the aid of another is not a matter of legal category, but of the heart and compassion (and it was the Samaritan who had compassion).[129] It is also worth remembering that the question asked of Jesus, 'Who is my neighbour?', was asked by a lawyer. In this context, the lawyer is an 'expert in the law', someone 'trained to interpret and teach the law of Jewish tradition'.[130] Jesus does not directly answer the question of who the neighbour is, but rather redirects the focus towards the lawyer (and us as the reader). He effectively changes the question from 'who is my neighbour?' to 'who acted like a neighbour?' and 'to whom can I be a neighbour?', implying that we should not try to avoid the divine demand through formal legalisation, but should instead show love to all who need it without distinction.[131] According to this anthropological reading, Jesus finally emphasises we should 'go, and do likewise'; that is, we should be like the Good Samaritan, loving and showing mercy to any who are in need without seeking to restrict the scope of the command through legal definition or ethnic prejudice.

> The one who asks, 'Who is my neighbour?' thinks of others in the world as classifiable commodities. One can build fences to determine who is in the circle of those to be cared for, and who is not. Then we and all others can 'take care of our own', thinking that our help should be directed to those we are related to by ties of family or friendship—things based on law, rights, bloodlines, culture or tradition. By means of this parable Jesus calls his hearers away from a legalistic or culturally conditioned mind-set to a life of authentic love. One should not seek to define who the neighbour is, but simply be a neighbour to the one in need … the example of the Samaritan, who does good to a person in need without any apparent regard for religion or ethnicity, illustrates how authentic love pays no attention to religious, ethnic, or cultural distinctions.[132]

126 Baird, above n 122, 227.

127 H Williamson, 'Samaritans' in J Douglas (ed), *The Illustrated Bible Dictionary Part 3* (InterVarsity Press, 1980) 1378.

128 A Hultgren, *The Parables of Jesus: A Commentary* (Wm B Eerdmans, 2002) 98.

129 ibid 96.

130 ibid 95.

131 Baird, above n 122, 228; Blomberg, above n 123, 338; Gundry, above n 125, 163.

132 Hultgren, above n 128, 100.

So authentic compassion, a Christian love based on selfless sacrifice, transcends the boundaries and limits violently imposed by law, and instead tends to establish a community life of selfless sacrifice. Indeed, the lawyer's question could be seen as a 'typical' lawyer's question, a 'boundary question of an exclusionary type'—and the common answer, in accordance with the focus of the Mosaic law, was a fellow Israelite, excluding Samaritans and Gentiles and encouraging the engagement of group differentiation and stereotyping.[133] However, 'that a representative of one of the hated outgroups is brought along that road challenges the whole structure of group differentiation which the law functioned to maintain', and the fact that it was this representative who exhibited admirable conduct further disrupts this legally imposed alienation.[134]

The type of compassion envisaged has no limits, as shown by the rich and loving detail Jesus supplies. The force of the parable directs us to conclude that love which transcends legally sanctioned boundaries is a more desirable form of life.[135] And, as with the atonement, this is not intended to be an isolated incident, but a way of life permanently instantiated through human relations. By shifting the focus from neighbour as category to neighbour as proper love-action, and telling his audience to do likewise, Jesus intends to universalise such behaviour and generate a new principle of existence in community.[136]

It is this sublime vision of truly and universally loving one's neighbour, particularly when that neighbour is in dire need, which indicates its theological foundation. In fact, your neighbour extends to your greatest enemy, and to love your neighbour means to show mercy even to your greatest enemy; there are no boundaries to the concept. Here, the Parable of the Good Samaritan can be read not only anthropologically, but also christologically. In this light (that we are the person in need, helpless and dead in our sins, rescued by the sacrifice of the Samaritan, who represents Christ), the logic of the parable 'raises the possibility that we first need to be shown compassion by a neighbour as a condition of becoming neighbours ourselves'—and 'only the divine persons are capable of showing us this kind of compassion', particularly by Christ, who became flesh and gave himself for us—'claiming us … as persons sharing his communion with the Father and the Spirit'.[137]

These observations are important for understanding the source for love of neighbour. We love our neighbour because we have first been loved by God—the modelling of sacrificial love through Christ, who showed love, mercy and forgiveness to all humanity, his former enemies, by willingly dying on the cross in their

[133] P Esler, 'Jesus and the Reduction of Intergroup Conflict: The Parable of the Good Samaritan in Light of Social Identity Theory' (2000) 8 *Biblical Interpretation* 325, 329–37.

[134] ibid 342.

[135] ibid 343.

[136] ibid 350.

[137] I McFarland, 'Who is my Neighbour? The Good Samaritan as a Source for Theological Anthropology' (2001) 17 *Modern Theology* 57, 62–63.

place, enables us to love one another. Those who love another are in turn loved by the other. So Jesus says to love your neighbour means to show similar love, mercy and forgiveness to all individuals without bound, and he commands us to do this in a model after himself. In this sense we are liberated from the letter, legalism and limit of the law, but, as Paul identifies in Galatians 5:13–15, this liberation is for obedience and peace, not selfish striving which leads to destruction:

> For you were called to freedom, brothers. Only do not use your freedom as an opportunity for the flesh, but through love serve one another. For the whole law is fulfilled in one word: 'You shall love your neighbor as yourself.' But if you bite and devour one another, watch out that you are not consumed by one another.

So, through the revelation of Christ, through the law of love, we are liberated from the alienation and antagonism of the secularised (formal, codified, limited) law, so that we may have life and freedom. Paradoxically, we fulfil the law by going beyond it, and establish a truly sacred community of peace.

VI. Fulfilling the Christian Vision of a Peaceful Legal Community

This book has argued that the modern (secular) legal system retains some vestiges of the Christian theology, but these have been distorted and limited, with the result that the secular system of law produces violence. The promotion of the liberal legal subject, with their autonomy and reason, has ultimately failed, for this alienates the members of the universal community in favour of privileging the individual, which leads to violence. However, the alternative vision of the socialist collective alienates the individual in favour of privileging the community, similarly resulting in violence. Consequently, what is required is not simply the positing of a secularised and impotent 'law of love' in the civil legal system, nor merely ad hoc adjustments according to the law of the letter (ie the passing, amending and repealing of legislation or the steady progression of the common law) which are already built on the foundation of the secular, but a complete restoration; a rebuilding on the new foundation of the theological law to love one's neighbour as yourself to reinvigorate the legal system, a law of the spirit which will reconcile the individual and the community, allowing all persons, particular and universal, to exist in a legal ontology of harmony and peace.

This 'new creation' of the law from its very spirit will lead to a peace beyond violence and a law beyond force, for instead the law of love, of selfless sacrifice and the pursuit of peace, will inhere in the interactions of individual persons, constituting a community of peace modelled on the relations between the members of the Tri-Unity, graciously enabled and revealed in Christ. This beautiful relationship of love exchange and receipt between members of a legal community is possible because of the revelation of the Trinity in Christ and his paradoxical work of dying to live—this, in conjunction with the paradoxical need to fulfil law by transcending it in the fashion revealed by Christ, is the move from violence to peace.[138]

However, the aspiration to a fully regenerated legal system in this sense may be too much to ask. After all, there are many questions regarding how we may move from the dominant modern, secular system of law to this kind of community, questions that for now remain unanswered. I am not advocating a Christian theocracy or for a polity governed by something akin to legalistic canon law. Rather, in lieu of a radically regenerated legal community founded upon the law of love, one could settle for an existence within our current legal community which is characterised by the 'fruit of the Spirit': 'love, joy, peace, patience, kindness, goodness, faithfulness, gentleness, self-control'; for 'against such things there is no law'.[139] Perhaps manifesting and displaying this alternative community of love beyond the law, meaning the secular can peacefully coexist, will be enough to persuade people that there is another way to true peace and that it is worth seeking. By revealing this heavenly peace on earth beyond the law, it may be possible to move towards an eschatological, final redemption of law.

Ultimately, it is this vision which Christianity seeks and makes possible—to bring the heavenly peace of community and love to earth in the context of what may effectively become a post-secular system of civil law. This law of love exists in its perfect display within the relations of the Trinity, and is revealed as truth through Christ, who reconciles the eternal and the temporal, rescuing reason from its secular, violent form, and produces an ontology of vertical and horizontal peace between God and humanity. Persuaded by this vision, humanity participates in the glorious divine, implementing the law of the Spirit to love one's neighbour, rather than the law of the letter, thus creating a harmonious community which reflects the heavenly relations.

It is hoped that this indicates that society ought not to yield to an allegedly inevitable ontology of alienation and antagonism, but may instead embrace ontological peace, which loves all individuals in the community and allows the reconciliation of virtue and difference based on the Trinity. It is further hoped that subsequent work will focus on a detailed articulation of redeeming the current secular system of civil law, imbuing it with the law of love as signalled in this chapter. With these developments, the Christian vision of an ontology of peace undergirding human and divine relations can be not only a heavenly vision, but an earthly reality as well.

[138] Milbank, *Being Reconciled*, above n 52, 57.

[139] Galatians 5:22–23.

BIBLIOGRAPHY

A Books/Articles

Agamben, G, *Homo Sacer: Sovereign Power and Bare Life* (Stanford University, 1998).

——, *The Time That Remains: A Commentary on the Letter to the Romans* (Stanford University Press, 2005).

Ahdar, R, 'The Inevitability of Law and Religion: An Introduction' in R Ahdar (ed), *Law and Religion* (Ashgate, 2000).

Alston, W, 'A Realist Conception of Truth' in M Lynch (ed), *The Nature of Truth: Classic and Contemporary Perspectives* (MIT Press, 2001).

Althaus, P, *The Theology of Martin Luther* (Fortress Press, 1966).

Anidjar, G, 'Secularism' (2006) 33 *Critical Inquiry* 52.

Anselm, 'Proslogion' in P Helm (ed), *Faith and Reason* (Oxford University Press, 1999).

Anton-Hermann, C, 'The Fundamental Ideas in St Augustine's Philosophy of Law' (1973) 18 *American Journal of Jurisprudence* 57.

Aquinas, T, 'Summa Contra Gentiles' in P Helm (ed), *Faith and Reason* (Oxford University Press, 1999).

——, *Summa Theologica* (William Benton, 1952) vol 1.

——, *Summa Theologica* (William Benton, 1952) vol 2.

——, 'Commentary on De Hebdomadibus', cited in J Wippel, *The Metaphysical Thought of Thomas Aquinas: From Finite Being to Uncreated Being* (Catholic University of America Press, 2000).

Armstrong, D, *Truth and Truthmakers* (Cambridge University Press, 2004).

Asad, T, *Formations of the Secular: Christianity, Islam, Modernity* (Stanford University Press, 2003).

Augustine, *Concerning the City of God Against the Pagans* (Penguin, 2008).

Austin, J, *The Province of Jurisprudence Determined* (Ashgate, 1998).

Avis, J, 'A Radical Phenomenology of Love: Divine Love as Understood by the Radically Orthodox John Milbank' (MA Thesis, Liberty University, 2009).

Babie, P, 'Breaking the Silence: Law, Theology and Religion in Australia' (2007) 33 *Melbourne University Law Review* 296.

Badiou, A, *St Paul: The Foundation of Universalism* (Stanford University Press, 2003).

Baird, W, 'The Gospel According to Luke' in C Laymon (ed), *Interpreter's Concise Commentary* (Abingdon Press, 1983).

Bankowski, Z and C Davis, 'Living In and Out of the Law' in P Oliver et al (eds), *Faith in Law: Essays in Legal Theory* (Hart, 2000).

Barker, P, 'The Role of Religion in the Lutheran Response to Copernicus' in M Osler (ed), *Rethinking the Scientific Revolution* (Cambridge University Press, 2000).

Barrett, M, *The Politics of Truth: From Marx to Foucault* (Polity Press, 1991).

Barth, K, *Dogmatics in Outline* (SCM Press, 1966).

Bass, A, 'Translator's Introduction' in J Derrida, *Writing and Difference* (Routledge, 1978).

Benjamin, W, 'Critique of Violence' in M Steger and N Lind (eds), *Violence and its Alternatives: An Interdisciplinary Reader* (St Martin's Press, 1999).
Berkhof, H, *Christian Faith* (William Eerdmans Publishing Company, 1985).
Berman, H, *Law and Revolution: The Formation of the Western Legal Tradition* (Harvard, 1983).
The Bible, English Standard Version (Crossway, 2007).
Bix, B, 'Natural Law Theory' in D Patterson (ed), *A Companion to Philosophy of Law and Legal Theory* (Blackwell Publishing, 1999).
——, *Jurisprudence: Theory and Context* (Carolina Academic Press, 2006).
Black, D, *Learn to Read New Testament Greek* (Broadman and Holman Publishers, 1994).
Blackman, EC, 'The Letter of Paul to the Romans' in C Laymon (ed), *The Interpreter's Concise Commentary on Acts and Paul's Letters* (Abingdon, 1983).
Blackwell, R, 'Introduction' in T Campanella, *A Defense of Galileo* (University of Notre Dame Press, 1994).
Bloechl, J, 'Between Law and Love: Paul and Philosophy', paper presented at the Annual Simone Weil Lecture on Human Value, Australian Catholic University (June 2013).
Blomberg, C, *Jesus and the Gospels* (B&H Publishing Group, 2009).
Boyle, J, 'Thomas Hobbes and the Invented Tradition of Positivism: Reflections on Language, Power and Essentialism' (1986) 135 *University of Pennsylvania Law Review* 383.
Brooks, R, 'Introduction' in R Brooks (ed), *Cicero and Modern Law* (Ashgate, 2009).
——, 'Violence, Norms and the "Rule of Law"' (2003) 101 *Michigan Law Review* 2275.
Brown, R, *The Gospel According to John* (Geoffrey Chapman, 1984).
Bruce, F, *The Letter of Paul to the Romans: An Introduction and Commentary* (InterVarsity Press, 1985).
Buchanan, S, *So Reason Can Rule: Reflections on Law and Politics* (Farrar, Straus, and Giroux, 1982).
Buonamano, R, 'The Economy of Violence: Derrida on Law and Justice' in P Legrand (ed), *Derrida and Law* (Ashgate, 2009).
Butt, P, *Concise Australian Legal Dictionary* (LexisNexis, 2004).
Cahoone, L (ed), *From Modernism to Postmodernism: An Anthology* (Blackwell Publishing, 2003).
Calvin, J, 'The Sensus Divinitatis' in P Helm, *Faith and Reason* (Oxford University Press, 1999).
——, *Institutes of the Christian Religion* (Hendrickson Publishers, 2008).
Campanella, T, *A Defense of Galileo* (University of Notre Dame Press, 1994).
Caputo, J and L Alcoff (eds), *St Paul among the Philosophers* (Indiana University Press, 2009).
——, *The Prayers and Tears of Jacques Derrida: Religion without Religion* (Indiana University Press, 1997).
——, 'Adieu-sans Dieu: Derrida and Levinas' in J Bloechl (ed), *The Face of the Other and the Trace of God: Essays on the Philosophy of Emmanuel Levinas* (Fordham University Press, 2000).
Casey, E and J Woody, 'Hegel, Heidegger, Lacan: The Dialectic of Desire' in S Žižek (ed), *Jacques Lacan: Critical Evaluations in Cultural Theory* (Routledge, 2003).
Chase, E, 'Law and Theology' in D Patterson (ed), *A Companion to Philosophy of Law and Legal Theory* (Blackwell Publishing, 1999).
Clemen, C, *Primitive Christianity and its Non-Jewish Sources* (T & T Clark, 1912).

Coakley, S, 'Why Gift? Gift, gender and Trinitarian relations in Milbank and Tanner' (2008) 61 *Scottish Journal of Theology* 224.

Collins, J, *Jewish Cult and Hellenistic Culture: Essays on the Jewish Encounter with Hellenism and Roman Rule* (Brill, 2005).

Collins, R, *Introduction to the New Testament* (Doubleday and Company, 1983).

Cornell, D, 'Violence of the Masquerade: Law Dressed up as Justice' (1989) 11 *Cardozo Law Review* 1047.

Cotterrell, R, *The Politics of Jurisprudence: A Critical Introduction to Legal Philosophy* (Butterworths, 1989).

Cover, R, 'Nomos and Narrative' (1983) 97(4) *Harvard Law Review* 4.

——, 'Violence and the Word' (1986) 95 *Yale Law Journal* 1601.

Craig, WL and JP Moreland, *Philosophical Foundations for a Christian Worldview* (InterVarsity Press, 2003).

Critchley, S, *The Ethics of Deconstruction* (Blackwell, 1992).

Crowe, J, 'Natural Law Beyond Finnis' (2011) 2(2) *Jurisprudence* 293.

Crowe, M, *The Changing Profile of the Natural Law* (Martinus Nijhoff, 1977).

Culler, J, *On Deconstruction: Theory and Criticism After Structuralism* (Routledge, 1983).

Cushman, R, 'Faith and Reason in the Thought of St Augustine' (1950) 19 *Church History: Studies in Christianity and Culture* 271.

Davies, M, *Delimiting the Law: Postmodernism and the Politics of Law* (Pluto Press, 1996).

——, *Asking the Law Question: The Dissolution of Legal Theory* (Law Book Company, 2002).

Davis, C, 'Introduction' in C Davis (ed), The Monstrosity of Christ: Paradox or Dialectic? (MIT Press, 2009).

Davison, A (ed), Imaginative Apologetics: Theology, Philosophy and the Catholic Tradition (SCM, 2011).

Deagon, A, 'Rendering to Caesar and God: St Paul, the Natural Law Tradition, and the Authority of Law', *Law, Culture, and the Humanities*, first published on 10 March 2014 as DOI: 10.1177/1743872114524324.

Dean, J, 'Žižek on Law' (2004) 15 *Law and Critique* 1.

Derrida, J, *Of Grammatology* (Johns Hopkins University Press, 1976).

——, *Writing and Difference* (Routledge, 1978).

——, *Dissemination* (University of Chicago Press, 1981).

——, *Positions* (University of Chicago Press, 1981).

——, *Margins of Philosophy* (University of Chicago Press, 1982).

——, 'Force of Law: 'The Mystical Foundation of Authority', paper presented on Deconstruction and the Possibility of Justice, Cardozo Law School (1989).

——, *Acts of Literature* (Routledge, 1992).

——, 'Force of Law: The Mystical Foundation of Authority' in M Davies, *Asking the Law Question: The Dissolution of Legal Theory* (Law Book Company, 2002).

——, 'Difference' in L Cahoone (ed), *From Modernism to Postmodernism: An Anthology* (Blackwell Publishing, 2003).

Devereux, D, 'Particular and Universal in Aristotle's Conception of Practical Knowledge' (1986) 39 *The Review of Metaphysics* 483.

Dostoevsky, F, *The Brothers Karamazov* (Vintage, 2004).

Douzinas, C, 'Law and Justice in Postmodernity' in S Connor (ed), *The Cambridge Companion to Postmodernism* (Cambridge University Press, 2004).

Dumitrescu, M, 'Derrida vs Saussere: Two Ways of Looking at the Linguistic Sign' (2007) 3 *Cultural and Literary Studies* 118.
Duns Scotus, J, cited in A Wolter, 'Introduction' in *Duns Scotus on the Will and Morality* (Catholic University of America, 1997).
——, *Philosophical Writings: A Selection* (Hackett, 1997).
Ellis, E, *Principles and Practice of Law* (Lawbook Co, 2005).
Elshtain, J, *Sovereignty: God, State, Self* (Basic Books, 2008).
Esler, P, 'Jesus and the Reduction of Intergroup Conflict: The Parable of the Good Samaritan in Light of Social Identity Theory' (2000) 8 *Biblical Interpretation* 325.
Evans, G, *Law and Theology in the Middle Ages* (Routledge, 2002).
Fallers-Sullivan, W, Yelle, R and Taussig-Rubbo, M, 'Introduction' in W Fallers-Sullivan, R Yelle and M Taussig-Rubbo (eds), *After Secular Law* (Stanford University Press, 2011).
Ferguson, E, *Backgrounds of Early Christianity* (Wm B Eerdmans, 2003).
Ferris, P, 'Background to the Old Testament' in D Horton (ed), *The Portable Seminary* (Bethany House, 2006).
Findlen, P, 'The Janus Faces of Science in the Seventeenth Century: Athanasius Kircher and Isaac Newton' in M Osler (ed), *Rethinking the Scientific Revolution* (Cambridge University Press, 2000).
Finnis, J, *Natural Law and Natural Rights* (Oxford University Press, 1980).
——, *Natural Law and Natural Rights*, 2nd edn (Oxford University Press, 2011).
Firestone, C, 'Rational Religious Faith and Kant's Transcendental Boundaries' in K Vanhoozer and M Warner (eds), *Transcending Boundaries in Philosophy and Theology: Reason, Meaning and Experience* (Ashgate, 2007).
Fitzpatrick, P, *The Mythology of Modern Law* (Routledge, 1992).
Force, J, 'The Nature of Newton's "Holy Alliance" between Science and Religion: From the Scientific Revolution to Newton (and Back Again)' in M Osler (ed), *Rethinking the Scientific Revolution* (Cambridge University Press, 2000).
Foucault, M, *Discipline and Punish: The Birth of the Prison* (Pantheon, 1977).
——, *Power/Knowledge* (Harvester Press, 1980).
——, 'Truth and Power' in P Rabinow (ed), *The Foucault Reader* (Penguin, 1984).
——, 'Nietzsche, Genealogy, History' in L Cahoone (ed), *From Modernism to Postmodernism: An Anthology* (Blackwell Publishing, 2003).
——, 'Truth and Power' in L Cahoone (ed), *From Modernism to Postmodernism: An Anthology* (Blackwell Publishing, 2003).
——, 'The Discourse on Language' in J Medina and D Wood (eds), *Truth: Engagements across Philosophical Traditions* (Blackwell Publishing, 2005).
——, 'Truth and Power' in J Medina, and D Wood (eds), *Truth: Engagements across Philosophical Traditions* (Blackwell Publishing, 2005).
Freeman, M, *Lloyd's Introduction to Jurisprudence*, 8th edn (Thomson Reuters, 2008).
Fulkerson, M and S Dunlap, 'Michel Foucault: Introduction' in G Ward (ed), *The Postmodern God: A Theological Reader* (Blackwell Publishers, 1997).
Furnish, VP, 'The Letter of Paul to the Colossians' in C Laymon (ed), *The Interpreter's Concise Commentary on Acts and Paul's Letters* (Abingdon, 1983).
——, 'The Letter of Paul to the Ephesians' in C Laymon (ed), *The Interpreter's Concise Commentary on Acts and Paul's Letters* (Abingdon, 1983).
——, 'The Letter of Paul to the Galatians' in C Laymon (ed), *The Interpreter's Concise Commentary on Acts and Paul's Letters* (Abingdon, 1983).

Galileo, cited in WL Wisan, 'Galileo and God's Creation' (1986) 77 *The History of Science Society* 473.
Garver, N, 'Preface' in J Derrida, *Speech and Phenomenon* (Northwestern University Press, 1973).
George, R, 'Natural Law' (2008) 31 *Harvard Journal of Law and Public Policy* 171.
Grisez, G, 'Natural Law, God, Religion and Human Fulfilment' (2001) 46 *American Journal of Jurisprudence* 3.
——, *God? Philosophical Preface to Faith* (St Augustine's Press, 2004).
——, Boyle, J and Finnis, J, 'Practical Principles, Moral Truth, and Ultimate Ends' (1987) 32 *American Journal of Jurisprudence* 99.
Green, M, 'Hans Kelsen and the Logic of Legal Systems' (2003) 54 *Alabama Law Review* 388.
Griffin, D, 'Introduction: The Reenchantment of Science' in D Griffin (ed), *The Reenchantment of Science: Postmodern Proposals* (State University of New York Press, 1988).
Griffiths, P, 'The Cross as the Fulcrum of Politics: Expropriating Agamben on Paul' in D Harink (ed), *Paul, Philosophy, and the Theopolitical Vision* (Cascade Books, Eugene, 2010).
Gundry, R, *A Survey of the New Testament* (Zondervan, 1970).
Gunton, C, *The One, the Three and the Many* (Cambridge University Press, 1992).
——, *The Triune Creator: A Historical and Systematic Study* (Wm B Eerdmans, 1998).
Habermas, J, *Truth and Justification* (MIT Press, 2003).
Hankey, W, 'Theoria versus Poesis: Neoplatonism and Trinitarian Difference in Aquinas, John Milbank, Jean-Luc Marion and John Zizioulas' (1999) 15 *Modern Theology* 387.
Hankey, W and Hedley, D (eds), *Deconstructing Radical Orthodoxy: Postmodern Theology, Rhetoric and Truth* (Ashgate, 2005).
Hannam, J, *God's Philosophers: How the Medieval World Laid the Foundations of Modern Science* (Icon Books, 2009).
Hart, H, *The Concept of Law* (Oxford University Press, 1994).
Hart, K, 'Jacques Derrida' in G Ward (ed), *The Postmodern God: A Theological Reader* (Blackwell Publishers, 1997).
Hendrickson, W, *Exposition of the Gospel According to John* (Baker, 2004).
Hendrix, S, 'Luther' in D Bagchi and D Steinmetz (eds), *The Cambridge Companion to Reformation Theology* (Cambridge University Press, 2004).
Heraclitus, cited in G Jantzen, *Foundations of Violence* (Routledge, 2004).
Hillerbrand, H, *The Protestant Reformation* (Walker and Company, 1968).
Hirvonen, A, 'Promising Justice: Derrida with Jewish Jurisprudence' (2001) 12 *Law and Critique* 159.
Hobbes, T, *Leviathan* (Longman, 2008).
Holsclaw, D, 'Subjects Between Death and Resurrection: Badiou, Žižek and St Paul' in D Harink (ed), *Paul, Philosophy, and the Theopolitical Vision* (Cascade Books, 2010).
Horwich, P, *Truth, Meaning, Reality* (Oxford University Press, 2010).
Hull, D, 'Charles Darwin and Nineteenth Century Philosophies of Science' in R Giere and R Westfall (eds), *Foundations of the Scientific Method: The Nineteenth Century* (Indiana University Press, 1973).
Hultgren, A, *The Parables of Jesus: A Commentary* (Wm B Eerdmans, 2002).
Hurtado, L, 'First-Century Jewish Monotheism' (1999) 21 *Journal for the Study of the New Testament* 3.

Jacobs, J, 'Introduction' in J Jacobs (ed), *Reason, Religion, and Natural Law: From Plato to Spinoza* (Oxford University Press, 2012).
Jaconelli, J, 'What is a Trial?' in M Mulholland and B Pullan (eds), *The Trial in History: Volume 1* (Manchester University Press, 2003).
Jameson, F, 'Imaginary and Symbolic in Lacan: Marxism, Psychoanalytic Criticism, and the Problem of the Subject' (1977) 55 *Yale French Studies* 338.
Jantzen, G, *Foundations of Violence* (Routledge, 2004).
Johnson, B, 'Translator's Introduction' in J Derrida, *Dissemination* (University of Chicago Press, 1981).
Johnson, L, *Reading Romans* (Smyth and Helways, 2001).
Kant, I, *Critique of Pure Reason* (Cambridge University Press, 1998).
Kaplan, R, 'Cultural Thought Patterns in Inter-Cultural Education' (2006) 16 *Language Learning* 1.
Kautzsch, E (ed), *Gesenius' Hebrew Grammar* (Clarendon Press, 1898).
Kee, HC, 'The Gospel According to Matthew' in C Laymon (ed), *Interpreter's Concise Commentary* (Abingdon Press, 1983).
Kelsen, H, *Pure Theory of Law* (University of California Press, 1967).
Kepler, J, *The Harmony of the World* (American Philosophical Society, 1997).
Kirkham, R, *Theories of Truth: A Critical Introduction* (MIT Press, 1992).
Kostenberger, A, *Exegetical Commentary on John* (Baker, 2004).
Kroger, J, 'The Philosophical Foundations of Roman Law: Aristotle, the Stoics and Roman Theories of Natural Law' [2004] *Wisconsin Law Review* 905.
Lacan, J, *The Triumph of Religion Preceded by Discourse to Catholics* (Polity, 2013).
LaCapra, D, 'Violence, Justice and the Force of Law' (1989) 11 *Cardozo Law Review* 1065.
LaCugna, C, *God for Us: The Trinity and Christian Life* (HarperCollins, 1991).
Lane, TJ, *Luke and the Gentile Mission: Gospel Anticipates Acts* (Peter Lang, 1996).
Laplace, P, cited in G Stent, 'Epistemic Dualism of Mind and Body' (1998) 142 *Proceedings of the American Philosophical Society* 578.
Laymon, C (ed), *The Interpreter's One-Volume Commentary on the Bible* (Abingdon Press, 1971).
Legrand, P, 'Introduction (of Derrida's Law)' in P Legrand (ed), *Derrida and Law* (Ashgate, 2009).
Leithart, P, *Against Christianity* (Canon Press, 2002).
Leon-Dufour, X, *Dictionary of the New Testament* (Harper and Row, 1980).
Linder, A, 'The Legal Status of the Jews in the Roman Empire' in S Katz et al (eds), *The Cambridge History of Judaism. Volume 4. The Late Roman-Rabbinic Period* (Cambridge University Press, 2006).
Litowitz, D, *Postmodern Philosophy and Law* (University Press of Kansas, 1997).
Lloyd, V, 'On the Use of Gillian Rose' (2007) 48 *The Heythrop Journal* 697.
——, 'The Secular Faith of Gillian Rose' (2008) 36 *Journal of Religious Ethics* 683.
——, 'Complex Space or Broken Middle? Milbank, Rose, and the Sharia Controversy' (2009) 10(2) *Political Theology* 1.
Lochman, J, *The Faith We Confess* (Fortress Press, 1984).
Locke, J, *Two Treatises of Government* (Cambridge University Press, 1967).
Luther, M, 'Commentary on St Paul's Epistle to the Galatians' in H Hillerbrand, *The Protestant Reformation* (Walker and Company, 1968).
——, 'The Bondage of the Will' in P Helm (ed), *Faith and Reason* (Oxford University Press, 1999).

Lynch, M, 'Deflationary Views and their Critics: Introduction' in M Lynch (ed), *The Nature of Truth: Classic and Contemporary Perspectives* (MIT Press, 2001).
——, 'Realism and the Correspondence Theory' in M Lynch (ed), *The Nature of Truth: Classic and Contemporary Perspectives* (MIT Press, 2001).
MacCormick, N, *Practical Reason in Law and Morality* (Oxford University Press, 2008).
MacCullough, D, *Reformation* (Penguin, 2003).
Machiavelli, N, *The Discourses* (Penguin, 1970).
——, *The Prince* (Chicago University Press, 1985).
——, *The Prince* (Yale University, 1997).
——, *Discourses on Livy* (Federalist Papers, 2013).
MacNeil, W, *Lex Populi* (Stanford University Press, 2007).
Manderson, D, *Proximity, Levinas and the Soul of the Law* (McGill-Queens, 2006).
Marshall, B, '"We Shall Bear the Image of the Man of Heaven": Theology and the Concept of Truth' in L Jones and S Fowl (eds), *Rethinking Metaphysics* (Blackwell, 1995).
——, *Trinity and Truth* (Cambridge University Press, 2000).
Mascall, E, 'Faith and Reason: Anselm and Aquinas's (1963) 14 *Journal of Theological Studies* 67.
Mattei, U and Nader, L, *Plunder: When the Rule of Law is Illegal* (Blackwell, 2008).
McFarland, I, 'Who is my Neighbour? The Good Samaritan as a Source for Theological Anthropology' (2001) 17 *Modern Theology* 57.
McGrath, A, *Christian Theology* (Blackwell, 2011).
McGushin, E, *Foucault's Askesis: An Introduction to the Philosophical Life* (Northwestern University, 2007).
Medina, J and D Wood, 'General Introduction' in J Medina and D Wood (eds), *Truth: Engagements across Philosophical Traditions* (Blackwell Publishing, 2005).
Medley, M, 'God for Us and with Us: The Contributions of Catherine LaCugna's Trinitarian Theology' (2001) 35 *Lexington Theological Quarterly* 219.
Meyer, S, 'The Return of the God Hypothesis' (1999) 11 *Journal of Interdisciplinary Studies* 1.
Milbank, J, *Theology and Social Theory: Beyond Secular Reason* (Blackwell Publishing, 1990).
——, 'A Response' in R Gill (ed), *Theology and Sociology: A Reader* (Cassell, 1996).
——, 'Postmodern Critical Augustinianism: A Short Summa in Forty-Two Responses to Unasked Questions' in G Ward (ed), *The Postmodern God: A Theological Reader* (Blackwell Publishers, 1997).
——, *The Word Made Strange: Theology, Language, Culture* (Blackwell, 1997).
——, 'Knowledge: The Theological Critique of Philosophy in Hamann and Jacobi' in J Milbank et al (eds), *Radical Orthodoxy: A New Theology* (Routledge, 1999).
——, Being Reconciled: Ontology and Pardon (Routledge, 2003).
——, 'Sublimity: The Modern Transcendent' in R Schwartz (ed), *Transcendence: Philosophy, Literature and Theology Approach the Beyond* (Routledge, 2004).
——, *Theology and Social Theory: Beyond Secular Reason*, 2nd edn (Blackwell, 2006).
——, 'The Thomistic Telescope: Truth and Identity' (2006) 80 *American Catholic Philosophical Quarterly* 193.
——, 'A Closer Walk on the Wild Side: Some Comments on Charles Taylor's A Secular Age' (2009) 22 *Studies in Christian Ethics* 89.
——, 'The Double Glory, or Paradox versus Dialectics: On Not Quite Agreeing with Slavoj Žižek' in C Davis (ed), *The Monstrosity of Christ: Paradox or Dialectic?* (MIT Press, 2009).

——, *The Future of Love: Essays in Political Theology* (Cascade Books, 2009).
——, 'The Gift of Ruling' in J Milbank and S Oliver (eds), *The Radical Orthodoxy Reader* (Routledge, 2009).
——, 'The Grandeur of Reason and the Perversity of Rationalism: Radical Orthodoxy's First Decade' in J Milbank and S Oliver (eds), *The Radical Orthodoxy Reader* (Routledge, 2009).
——, 'Paul Against Biopolitics' in J Milbank et al (eds), *Paul's New Moment: Continental Philosophy and the Future of Christian Theology* (Brazos Press, 2010).
——, 'The Return of Mediation' in J Milbank et al (eds), *Paul's New Moment: Continental Philosophy and the Future of Christian Theology* (Brazos Press, 2010).
——, 'Hume vs Kant: Faith, Reason and Feeling' (2011) 27 *Modern Theology* 276.
——, 'The Thomistic Telescope: Truth and Identity' (25 February 2013), available at www.scribd.com/doc/19773690/John-Milbank-The-Thomistic-Telescope-Truth-and-Identity.
Milbank, J and Pickstock, C, *Truth in Aquinas* (Routledge, 2001).
Milbank, J et al, 'Introduction' in J Milbank et al (eds), *Radical Orthodoxy: A New Theology* (Routledge, 1999).
Milbank, J et al (eds), *Radical Orthodoxy: A New Theology* (Routledge, 1999).
Milbank, J et al, 'Introduction' in J Milbank et al (eds), *Paul's New Moment: Continental Philosophy and the Future of Christian Theology* (Brazos Press, 2010).
Minow, M, *Making All the Difference: Inclusion, Exclusion and American Law* (Cornell University, 1990).
Moore, M, 'Good without God' in R George (ed), *Natural Law, Liberalism, and Morality* (Clarendon Press, 1996).
Morrison, W, *Jurisprudence: From the Greeks to Post-modernism* (Cavendish Publishing, 1997).
Mulcahy, B, *Aquinas's Notion of Pure Nature and the Christian Integralism of Henri de Lubac: Not Everything is Grace* (Peter Lang, 2011).
Mulholland, M, 'Introduction' in M Mulholland and B Pullan (eds), *The Trial in History: Volume 1* (Manchester University Press, 2003).
Murphy, M, *Natural Law in Jurisprudence and Politics* (Cambridge University Press, 2006).
Murray, J, *The Epistle to the Romans: The English Text with Introduction, Exposition and Notes* (Wm B Eerdmans, 1997).
Neagoe, A, *Trial of the Gospels* (Cambridge University Press, 2002).
Newton, I, cited in E Strong, 'Newton and God' (1952) 13 *Journal of the History of Ideas* 147.
Nicolson, D, 'Truth, Reason and Justice: Epistemology and Politics in Evidence Discourse' (1994) 57 *Modern Law Review* 726.
Nietzsche, F, *Beyond Good and Evil* (Vintage, 1966).
——, *A Genealogy of Morals* (Vintage, 1967).
——, 'On Truth and Lies in a Nonmoral Sense' in D Breazeale (ed), *Philosophy and Truth: Friedrich Nietzsche* (Humanities Press International, 1979).
——, 'The Will to Power' in J Medina and D Wood (eds), *Truth: Engagements across Philosophical Traditions* (Blackwell Publishing, 2005).
Novakovic, L, 'Background to the New Testament' in D Horton (ed), *The Portable Seminary* (Bethany House, 2006).
Ofrat, G, *The Jewish Derrida* (Syracuse University Press, 2001).
Oliver, P et al, 'Introduction' in P Oliver et al (eds), *Faith in Law: Essays in Legal Theory* (Hart, 2000).

Oliver, S, 'Introducing Radical Orthodoxy: From Participation to Late Modernity' in J Milbank and S Oliver (eds), *The Radical Orthodoxy Reader* (Routledge, 2009).

——, 'Introduction' in J Milbank and S Oliver (eds), *The Radical Orthodoxy Reader* (Routledge, 2009).

Orr, J (ed), Entry for Truth (17 February 2012) International Standard Bible Encyclopedia, available at www.studylight.org/enc/isb/view.cgi?number=T8929.

Painter, J, 'John the Evangelist as Theologian' in D Peterson and J Pryor (eds), *In the Fullness of Time* (Anzea, 1992).

Pascal, B, cited in J Cargile, 'Pascal's Wager' (1966) 41 *Philosophy* 250.

Patterson, D, *Law and Truth* (Oxford University Press, 1999).

Pearson, K and D Large, 'Introduction' in K Pearson and D Large (eds), *The Nietzsche Reader* (Blackwell Publishing, 2006).

Pfeiffer, R, *Introduction to the Old Testament* (Adam and Charles Black, 1966).

Pherigo, L, 'The Gospel According to Mark' in C Laymon (ed), *The Interpreter's Concise Commentary on the Gospels* (Abingdon Press, 1983).

Plantinga, A, *Warranted Christian Belief* (Oxford University Press, 2000).

Porter, J, *Nature as Reason: A Thomistic Theory of Natural Law* (Wm B Eerdmans, 2005).

Price, J, 'The First Letter of Paul to the Corinthians' in C Laymon (ed), *The Interpreter's Concise Commentary on Acts and Paul's Letters* (Abingdon Press, 1983).

——, 'The Second Letter of Paul to the Corinthians' in C Laymon (ed), *The Interpreter's Concise Commentary on Acts and Paul's Letters* (Abingdon, 1983).

Prokopczyk, C, *Truth and Reality in Marx and Hegel: A Reassessment* (University of Massachusetts Press, 1980).

Pugliese, M, *One, the Many, and the Trinity: Joseph A Bracken and the Challenge of Process Metaphysics* (Catholic University of America Press, 2011).

Rawls, J, *A Theory of Justice* (Oxford University Press, 1972).

Raz, J, *Practical Reason and Norms* (Oxford University Press, 1999).

Reardon, B, *Religious Thought in the Reformation* (Longman, 1981).

Rescher, N, *The Coherence Theory of Truth* (Oxford University Press, 1973).

Rhonheimer, M, 'Practical Reason, Human Nature, and the Epistemology of Ethics: John Finnis's Contribution to the Rediscovery of Aristotelian Ethical Methodology in Aquinas's Moral Philosophy: A Personal Account' (2012) 57 *Villanova Law Review* 873.

Riley-Smith, J, *The Crusades, Christianity and Islam* (Columbia University Press, 2008).

Rist, J, 'Faith and Reason' in E Stump and N Kretzmann (eds), *The Cambridge Companion to Augustine* (Cambridge University Press, 2001).

Rockmore, T et al (eds), *Marxism and Alternatives* (D Reidel Publishing Company, 1981).

Rose, G, *Dialectic of Nihilism: Post-Structuralism and Law* (Blackwell, 1984).

——, *The Broken Middle: Out of Our Ancient Society* (Blackwell, 1992).

Ross, A, *Introducing Biblical Hebrew* (Baker, 2001).

Rouse, J, 'Power/Knowledge' in G Gutting (ed), *The Cambridge Companion to Foucault* (Cambridge University Press, 2003).

Sanders, EP, *Paul, The Law, and the Jewish People* (Fortress Press, 1983).

Sarat, A, Douglas, L and Umphrey, MM (eds), *Law and the Sacred* (Stanford University Press, 2007).

Saussure, F, 'Course in General Linguistics' in L Cahoone (ed), *From Modernism to Postmodernism: An Anthology* (Blackwell Publishing, 2003).

Schmitt, C, *Political Theology: Four Chapters on the Concept of Sovereignty* (University of Chicago Press, 2005).

Sheehan, P, 'Postmodernism and Philosophy' in S Connor (ed), *The Cambridge Companion to Postmodernism* (Cambridge University Press, 2004).
Shelley, B, *Church History in Plain Language* (Thomas Nelson, 2008).
Shepherd, M, 'The Gospel According to John' in C Laymon (ed), *Interpreter's Concise Commentary* (Abingdon Press, 1983).
Sherwin-White, A, *Roman Society and Roman Law in the New Testament* (Oxford University Press, 1963).
Sizgorich, T, *Violence and Belief in Late Antiquity* (University of Pennsylvania Press, 2009).
Smith, J, *Introducing Radical Orthodoxy: Mapping a Post-Secular Theology* (Baker, 2004).
Smith, P (ed), *The Nature and Process of Law: Introduction to Legal Philosophy* (Oxford University Press, 1993).
Sokolowski, R, *The God of Faith and Reason: Foundations of Christian Theology* (Catholic University of America Press, 1982).
Spivak, G, 'Translator's Preface' in J Derrida, *Of Grammatology* (Johns Hopkins University Press, 1976).
Stringfellow, W, *Instead of Death* (Wipf and Stock, 1963).
Taubes, J, *The Political Theology of Paul* (Stanford University Press, 2004).
Taylor, C, *A Secular Age* (Harvard University Press, 2007).
Thacker, J, *Postmodernism and the Ethics of Theological Knowledge* (Ashgate, 2007).
Thayer and Smith, Greek Lexicon Entry for Aletheia (15 February 2012) *The New Testament Greek Lexicon*, available at www.studylight.org/lex/grk/view.cgi?number=225.
Thayer and Smith, Greek Lexicon Entry for Pistis (19 June 2014) *The New Testament Greek Lexicon*, available at www.studylight.org/desk/interlinear.cgi?q1=Ephesians+2%3A8&x=20&y=17.
Thompson, J, 'Sanhedrin' in J Douglas (ed), *The Illustrated Bible Dictionary Part 3* (InterVarsity Press, 1980).
Thuren, L, *Derhetorising Paul: A Dynamic Perspective on Pauline Theology and the Law* (Mohr Siebeck, 2000).
Todd Billings, J, 'John Milbank's Theology of the "Gift" and Calvin's Theology of Grace: A Critical Comparison' (2005) 21 *Modern Theology* 87.
Volf, M, '"The Trinity is our Social Program": The Doctrine of the Trinity and the Shape of Social Engagement' (1998) 14 *Modern Theology* 403.
Wacks, R, *Law: A Very Short Introduction* (Oxford University Press, 2008).
Walker, L, 'Biblical Languages' in D Horton (ed), *The Portable Seminary* (Bethany House, 2006).
Warrington, R et al, *Postmodern Jurisprudence: The Law of Texts in the Texts of Law* (Routledge, 1991).
Weinreb, L, *Natural Law and Justice* (Harvard University Press, 1987).
Wheaton, D, 'Pilate' in J Douglas (ed), *The Illustrated Bible Dictionary Part 3* (InterVarsity Press, 1980).
Willemson, J and P Verhaeghe, 'When Psychoanalysis Meets Law and Evil: Perversion and Psychopathy in the Forensic Clinic' in A Hirvonen and J Porttikivi (eds), *Law and Evil: Philosophy, Politics, Psychoanalysis* (Routledge, 2010).
Williams, B, *Truth and Truthfulness* (Princeton University Press, 2002).
Williams, L, 'Kant, Naturophilosophie and Scientific Method' in R Giere and R Westfall (eds), *Foundations of the Scientific Method: The Nineteenth Century* (Indiana University Press, 1973).
Williams, M, 'Meaning and Deflationary Truth' (1999) 96 *Journal of Philosophy* 545.

Williamson, H, 'Samaritans' in J Douglas (ed), *The Illustrated Bible Dictionary Part 3* (InterVarsity Press, 1980).
Winter, P, *Studia Judaica: On the Trial of Jesus* (Walter de Gruyter, 2010).
Wippel, J, *The Metaphysical Thought of Thomas Aquinas: From Finite Being to Uncreated Being* (Catholic University of America Press, 2000).
Witte, J, 'Law and Religion: The Challenges of Christian Jurisprudence' (2004) *University of St Thomas Law Journal* 439.
Wojcik, J, 'Pursuing Knowledge: Robert Boyle and Isaac Newton' in M Osler (ed), *Rethinking the Scientific Revolution* (Cambridge University Press, 2000).
Wright, A, *The Counter-Reformation* (Weidenfeld and Nicolson, 1982).
Young, R, *Analytical Concordance to the Bible* (Wm B Eerdmans, 1977).
Žižek, S, *The Sublime Object of Ideology* (Verso, 1989).
——, *The Fragile Absolute: Or, Why is the Christian Legacy Worth Fighting For?* (Verso, 2000) 2.
——, *The Puppet and the Dwarf* (MIT Press, 2003).
——, 'The Thrilling Romance of Orthodoxy' in C Davis et al (eds), *Theology and the Political: The New Debate* (Duke University Press, 2005).
——, 'Dialectical Clarity Versus the Misty Conceit of Paradox' in C Davis (ed), *The Monstrosity of Christ: Paradox or Dialectic* (MIT Press, 2009).
——, 'The Fear of Four Words: A Modest Plea for a Hegelian Reading of Christianity' in C Davis (ed), *The Monstrosity of Christ: Paradox or Dialectic* (MIT Press, 2009).
——, 'Is it Still Possible to be a Hegelian Today?' in L Bryant et al (eds), *The Speculative Turn: Continental Materialism and Realism* (RE Press, 2011).
Zizioulas, J, *Being as Communion* (RSM Press, 1985).
——, *Communion and Otherness* (T and T Clark, 2006).

B Cases

Donoghue v Stevenson [1932] AC 562.
Hargrave v Goldman (1963) 110 CLR 40.
Home Office v Dorset Yacht Co Ltd [1970] 2 All ER 294.

INDEX

aletheia, 7, 13, 121–22, 134–37, 140, 142, 145, 171
alienation, *see* antagonism and alienation
antagonism and alienation, 1, 14, 22, 83, 109, 144, 160, 163, 165, 182
  alienation, 2–3, 6
  antagonism, 2–3
    Hobbes, 97
  revelation and, 193
Aquinas, T, 1, 12
  being and essence, 29–30, 98
    univocity of being compared, 91–92
  divine simplicity doctrine, 20–21
  human rationality as participation in the divine reason, 38, 167
  natural law, 85–87
  new interpretation:
    uniting faith and reason, 58–60
  participation, 28–29, 49
  thought and being, 29
  truth, faith and reason, 36–37, 43–44, 49–51, 57–60
  truth as correspondence, 30
  types of truth:
    accessible by human reason, 50
    above reason, 50–51
Augustine (Saint):
  City of God, 7–8, 181
  eternal law, 86–87, 181–82
  heavenly peace, 173–75
  natural law, 86–87
  pagan violence, 4–5, 6–7, 10, 33–34, 109, 173–75
  truth, faith and reason, 35–36, 37
Austin, 1, 13
  authority of law, 150
  coercion by God, 100–02
  command theory, 100–02
  God as the ultimate sovereign, 100

Barth, K:
  community, 108
  faith, 37
being and participation:
  correspondence theory of truth, 28–31
Benjamin, W, 13
  contemporary law as violence, 105–07
  divine violence, 69, 81
    mythical violence distinguished, 106
  forgiveness, 186
  non-violent regulation of humanity, 107
    peaceableness and trust, 107–08
  notion of fate, 106–07
  relation of violence to law and justice, 105–06
Big Other, *see* symbolic law
blind faith, 44, 57–58, 105, 131, 154–55, 166–67, 169
boundaries between people, 3, 6, 39, 75, 177–78, 192
Boyle, R, 47–48

Calvin, J, 53
  authority of Scripture, 54
  faith, 37, 54
    human reason distinguished, 55
Christian theology:
  'absolute truth', 26
  faith and reason:
    historical Catholic perspective, 35–37
    Protestant perspective, 37–38
  relevance to a secular audience, 13–14, 41–42, 147–48, 163–64, 193–94
Cicero:
  natural law, 87
coercion, 1, 12, 90, 166, 172, 176
  coercion by God, 100–01
  control and coercion, 11
    positivists, 100–02
  love and, 185–86
coherence theory, 30
common law, 2–3, 113, 188, 193
communities of differences, 7–8, 170
  see also communities of peace; legal communities
communities of peace, 180–81
  harmony between individuals and society, 144, 170
    developing a Christian theology, 78–82
    loving neighbour as self, 7–9
    law of love, 7–9
    mutual trust and dependence, 140–42
    secular reason, 9–11
    unity and diversity, 7–9
  see also legal communities

correspondence theory of truth, 15, 26–27
  being and participation, 28–31
  coherence theory, 30
  meaning, 27–28
  revelation and persuasion, 31–33
Counter-Reformation, 55–57
Cover, R:
  violence, 102–03, 108
crucifixion, 19, 26, 38, 109, 111, 118, 129–30, 131, 133, 152, 163, 167, 184
  Christ's refusal of violence, 149–50
  conflation with resurrection, 155, 158
  law of love, 8, 14, 142–43, 149–50, 160–61, 172–73
  see also trial of Christ

decisions:
  violent drive for:
    avoiding, 138–39
    pursuit of certainty, 137–38
deconstruction as justice, 12, 69–70
Derrida, J, 12–13, 63–64
  atheism, 67–68
  authority of law, 150
  Christian theology, 70–71
    differance and difference, 72–73
  contemporary law as violence:
    blind faith, 105
    'enforcing' law, 104
    law, 103–04
    secularisation of law, 104–05
  context and background, 64
    Saussurean linguistics, 64
    deconstruction concept, 65
  differance and difference, 72–73
    criticisms of, 79
  Judaism, 68–69
  justice, 161–62
    deconstruction as, 12, 69–70
  paganism, 67–68
    differance, 73–77
  radical orthodoxy, 18
differance and difference, 72–73
  pagan differance, 73–77
divine simplicity doctrine, 20–21, 66
Duns Scotus, J, 1, 13, 49–50, 56–57
  knowledge of God by pure reason, 92–94
  univocity of being, 90–91
  see also voluntarism

Epistle to the Romans, 115–16
  law of sin and law of the spirit contrasted, 116
  obedience and the spirit of trust, 119–20
eternal law, 140
  Aquinas, 85–86
  Augustine, 87
  Finnis, 88–89
  Stoics, 87
  see also natural law

faith and reason, 1
  faith:
    faith in law, 11
    mutual interdependence of truth, reason and faith, 42
    persuasion, faith as, 14, 31–33
    truth, reason and, 42
  natural law:
    Aquinas, 85–86
    Augustine, 86–87
    Cicero, 87
    eternal law and, 85–89
  reason:
    knowledge of God by pure reason, 92–94
  reconciliation of reason and faith, 168–70
    incarnational paradox, 158–60, 169
    paradox of relational reconciliation, 159–60
  see also separation of faith from reason
Finnis, J:
  natural law, 87–89
forgiveness, 81, 143, 151, 160, 171, 174–75, 192–93
  harmony and mutual trust, 165, 186
  law of love, 7
    gift of forgiveness, 184–85
  legal communities, 165
  Reformation theology, 53
Foucault, M, 21–22, 177
  power, 23–25
  radical orthodoxy, 18

Galileo, G, 43
  unity of truth, 45–46
God's will
  Hobbes:
    arbitrary and material power, 99
    clash of wills, 97–98
  see also voluntarism
Gospels:
  trial of Christ, 13, 113–15

Habermas, J
  discursive theory of truth, 31–32
Hart, HLA, 13
  criticisms of Austin, 101–02
  rules and obligations, 101
    rule of recognition, 101–02
heaven, 6–8, 34, 46–47, 72–73, 158, 177–78
heavenly peace, 4, 19, 26, 145, 173, 179, 181–82, 194
Hobbes, T, 1
  antagonism, 97
  contractual relationships between God and humanity, 97–98

God's will:
arbitrary and material power, 99
clash of wills, 97–98
natural law, 108–09
pure sovereign power, 97

incarnation, 8, 171
incarnational reason, 39–42
law of love revealed, 160–61
peace and Trinitarian relations, 171
reconciliation of reason and faith, 158–60
transcendent truth, 173
trust and reason, 39
see also sublime
incarnational paradox:
reconciliation of reason and faith, 158–60

Jantzen, G, 4, 11, 74
justice, 2–3, 24, 67, 75, 90, 104–06, 109, 113, 124–25, 127–28, 137, 160–62, 174–75
deconstruction as justice, 12, 65, 69–70

Kant, I, 22
true reason:
Kantian antinomies, 168
reason and reality, 168
unity with faith, 169
violence and, 169
Kelsen, H:
law of love as *grundnorm*, 186–88
Kepler, J, 43, 51
precision of God's decree, 46–47

Laplace, P, 43, 51–52
law of love, 139–40
communities of differences, 7–8
crucifixion, 8
grundnorm, as, 186–88
heaven, 7–8
incarnation, 8, 160–61
law of sin contrasted, 111, 116
life, death and resurrection of Christ, 119
mutual trust and dependence, 140–42
pagan mythos compared, 8
participation through faith in the resurrection, 161–62
Trinitarian relations, 7
unity and diversity, 7–9
law of sin, 117–18
law of love contrasted, 111, 116
law of the spirit, *see* law of love
legal communities, 145, 193–94
developing a Christian theology, 81–82
Augustine, 181–82
Hobbes, contrast, 182–83
law of love, 183–85
non-violent means of developing, 105–06
incarnational paradox, 162–63
law of love, 163–64
gift and law contrasted, 183–84
gift of forgiveness, 184–85
grundnorm, as, 186–88
see also harmony between individuals and society
Letter to the Galatians:
law as a curse, 118
law of sin, 117–18
law of the spirit, 118
reliance on the law, 117–18
Lloyd, V:
violence in law, 179
loving neighbour as self, 1, 7–9
legal interpretation, 188–89
theological interpretation, 189–93
unity and diversity, 7–9
see also law of love

Machiavelli, N:
control, 95
development of secular, violent political systems, 95–97
power, 95
promotion of greatness, 95–96
war, 95
MacNeil, W:
Austinian positivism, 101–02
criticisms of Hart, 101–02
materialism:
atheistic Christian materialism, 148–49
definition, 149
faith and, 153–56
necessity of Christianity, 149–50
Milbank, J, 4
alienation, 6
context:
doctrine of the Trinity, 20–21
postmodern critical Augustinianism, 16–17
radical orthodoxy, 17–20
Machiavellian moment, 94–95
natural law, 90
persuasion to the ultimate truth, 31
postmodern critical Augustinianism, 6–7, 11–12, 16–17
radical orthodoxy, 17–20
violence of the secular and violence allowed by faithful Christianity, 177–78
see also radical orthodoxy

natural law, 13
Aquinas, 85–86
Augustine, 86–87
Cicero, 87
Finnis, 88–89
Hobbes, 108–09
Milbank, 90

Porter, 88–89
Weinreb, 88
negligence law:
Donoghue v Stevenson, 188–89
Hargrave v Goldman, 189
law of love, 188–89
duty of care, 189
legal interpretation, 188–89
loving neighbour as self, 188
Parable of the Good Samaritan, 14
legal interpretation, 188–89
neighbour principle, 142, 165
theological interpretation, 189–93
theological interpretation
loving neighbour as self, 189–93
New Testament:
linguistic analysis
truth and revelation, 121–23
Newton, I, 43
God as sovereign architect, 47–48
Nietzsche, 77–78
power, 23–26
radical orthodoxy, 18
truth and, 21–23
nihilism, 9, 15, 16–17, 25–26, 40, 131, 158
faith and, 20
pagan post-modernism, 66–67, 77–81
post-structuralist nihilism, 176–77
reason and, 31, 33–34, 63, 65, 166–67

Old Testament:
emuth, 124
language, 123–24
relationship between law and truth, 124–25

pagan communities:
law of love compared, 8
pagan violence, 3–5, 174–75
Augustinian response, 5
secular reason, 9–11
Parable of the Good Samaritan, *see* negligence law
Paul (Saint), *see* Epistle to the Romans; letter to the Galatians; *Torah*
persuasion, 31–33
see also faith
Pickstock, C, 29–30
Porter, J:
natural law 88–89
positivism, 1, 13, 100–02
Austinian positivism, 101–02
postmodern critical Augustinianism and, 84
secular positivism, 100–02
see also Austin, J; Hart, HLA
postmodern critical Augustinianism, 6–7, 16
law and:
natural law, 84
positivism, 84
social significance of law, 84–85
nihilism, 16–17

radical orthodoxy, 15, 17–18
key aspects, 18
Milbank's critique, 19–20
peace and violence, 18–19
reason, *see* faith and reason; true reason
Reformation:
separation of faith from reason, 52–53
Calvinism, 54–55
Lutheranism, 53–54
resurrection, 13–14, 115, 145, 151–52
crucifixion and, 149–50
divine forgiveness, 53, 109, 136
faith, 154–56, 158–60, 172–73
heavenly peace, 26, 136, 143–44
hope, 152–53
law of love, 112, 119–20, 147–48, 160–62, 184
legal communities, 145, 179
sublime materialism, 157–58
see also incarnation; sublime
revelation, 14, 30–31, 120–21, 132–33
aletheia, 121–22, 134–37
attestation and, 139
correspondence through, 171
law of love, 7–8
persuasion and, 31–33
Protestantism, 37–38
rhetoric and, 171–72
science and reason:
Galileo, 45–46
Kepler, 46–47
Newton, 47–48
see also science; trial of Christ; truth
Rose, G, 177–78
love and violence, 176–79
post-structuralist nihilism, 176
violence and peace, 178–79

science, 12
revelation and reason, 43–44
Galileo, 45–46
Kepler, 46–47
Newton, 47–48
secularisation of, 43–44, 51–52
faith and reason, 48–51
Galileo, 45–46
Kepler, 46–47
Newton, 47–48
uniting faith and reason, 58–61
secular foundations of modern jurisprudence, 1
control and coercion, 11
positivists, 100–02
emergence of governing violence:
dominance, 94–97

rule by force and clash of wills, 97–99
secular positivism, 100–02
natural law, 85–90
pagan communities distinguished, 9–11
voluntarism, 90–94
secularisation of reason, 12–13
limits of secular reason, 38–39
rejection of, 33–34
see also separation of faith from reason
separation of faith from reason, 13
Counter-Reformation, 55–57
historical Catholic perspective, 35–37
nihilism, 16–17, 33
Protestant perspective, 37–38
Reformation, 52–53
Lutheranism, 53–54
Calvinism, 54–55
see also secularisation of reason; uniting faith and reason
sovereign power, 170, 183
arbitrary sovereign power, 132, 139, 143
pure sovereign power, 97, 108–09
secularised sovereign power, 143
sublime, 156
defeating death, 156–58
Kant, 156
paradoxical nature, 156–57
reconciliation of reason and faith, 158–62
resurrection, 157–58
Žižek, 156–58
symbolic law, 149, 150–51, 161

Torah:
law of the Spirit distinguished, 111
Paul, 116–17
law of sin, 117
Trinitarian doctrine, 1, 6–7, 61, 72, 90–91, 145, 159–60, 163, 167, 171–72, 175, 180
faith, 20
law of love, 7–9
postmodern critical Augustinianism, 20–21
radical orthodoxy, 20–21
truth, 12, 26–27
see also correspondence of truth
trial of Christ, 13
analysis of Gospel accounts, 114–15
context:
Jewish context, 123–25
Old Testament context, 123–25
Roman context, 125–27
court procedure, 127
John's account, 114
Luke's account, 113–14
Mark's account, 113
Matthew's account, 113
Pilate, 129–32
Sanhedrin:
political machinations, 127–28
universality of court proceedings, 112
see also revelation
true reason:
Kantian antinomies, 168
reason and reality, 168
unity with faith, 169
violence and, 169
truth:
faith, reason and:
mutual interdependence, 42
revelation, as, 14, 30–31
linguistic analysis of New Testament, 121–22
types of truth:
accessible by human reason, 50
above reason, 50–51
see also aletheia; correspondence theory of truth

uniting faith and reason:
participation model, 58–60
reinterpreting Aquinas, 58–60
unity and diversity:
law of love, 7–9
see also communities of peace; differance and difference

violence (legal):
alienation, 2–3
antagonism, 2–3
atomistic individualism, 2
Christianity, 176
Lloyd, 179
Milbank, 177–78
Rose, 177–78
violence of the secular and violence allowed by faithful Christianity, 176–79
contemporary law as:
Cover, 102–03
Benjamin, 105–07
Derrida, 103–05
governing violence:
pagan violence, 3–5
Machiavelli, 94–97
Hobbes, 97–99
legal formalism, 137, 139–40
legal violence, 2–3
mythical violence and divine violence distinguished, 106
pagan violence, 3–5, 174–75
Augustinian response, 5
relation of violence to law and justice, 105–06
secular positivism, 100–02

voluntarism, 13, 44–45
  Duns Scotus:
    univocity of being, 90–91
  Galileo:
    unity of truth, 45–46
  Kepler:
    precision of God's decree, 46–47
  Newton:
    God as sovereign architect, 47–48
  separation of faith from reason, 13, 167
    Calvinism, 54–55
    Counter-Reformation, 55–57
    Lutheranism, 53–54
    Reformation, 52–55

Weinreb, L:
  natural law, 88

Žižek, S, 147–48
  atheistic Christian materialism, 148–50
  authority of law, 150
  Christ's death as sacrifice, 152
    refusal of violence, 152–53
  death of hope, 152
  dialectical nature of Christianity, 151
  materialism, 150–51
    atheistic Christian materialism, 148–50
  resurrection, 151–52
    hope, 152–53

www.ingramcontent.com/pod-product-compliance
Ingram Content Group UK Ltd.
Pitfield, Milton Keynes, MK11 3LW, UK
UKHW021907150926
475560UK00003B/235

9 781509 912902